HAMPTON COURT

By the same author:

HAMPTON COURT

R. J. Minney

CASSELL · LONDON

CASSELL & COMPANY LTD
35 Red Lion Square, London WC1
Sydney, Auckland, Toronto, Johannesburg

First published 1972

I.S.B.N. 0 304 93841 6

Printed in Great Britain by
Cox & Wyman Ltd,
London, Fakenham and Reading
F.871

For Penny and Judith

The annals of Hampton Court, which is half as old as the Tower of London, cover its entire span of four and a half centuries. Records preserved at the Public Record Office and the British Museum provide a wealth of information about the construction of the buildings, the extensions and alterations, supplying in many instances the names of the masons, carpenters, numerous artisans, sculptors and gardeners, together with the costs incurred.

The letters of foreign ambassadors, the diaries and memoirs of those who visited or stayed at Hampton Court abundantly supplement these factual details with lively gossip and at times scandal.

I have drawn on all these sources and also on the report of the Royal Commission on Historical Monuments (Middlesex) published by H.M. Stationery Office; nor has Ernest Law's carefully compiled three-volume history of Hampton Court, which he wrote while in residence in a 'grace and favour' apartment there, been neglected.

A deep debt of gratitude is due individually to the Inspectors of Ancient Monuments, Messrs John Charlton and P. E. Curnow, to Mr A. M. Cook of the Ancient Monuments section, Mr E. Robinson, Superintendent of Works at Hampton Court, and all at the Public Record Office, the British Museum and the London Library who have advised and helped me; and to Miss Jean Mauldon at the Tunbridge Wells Public Library.

For her assistance with illustration research my thanks are due to Mrs M. E. Harper, Photographic Librarian at the Ministry of Environment. All the Ministry's photographs reproduced in this book are British Crown Copyright.

CONTENTS

Contents

after page 42

Aerial view of Hampton Court with its parks and gardens
(*Aerofilms Ltd*)

Plan of ground floor, showing rooms open to the public

The layout of the Palace, with Henry VIII's Great Hall between
Wolsey's Tudor buildings on the left and Wren's vast Renaissance
structure (*Aerofilms Ltd*)

after page 74

The Great Gatehouse, the main entrance to Hampton Court, built
by Cardinal Wolsey (*A. F. Kersting*)

The bizarre but attractive Tudor chimneys*

Plan of first floor

Cardinal Wolsey. By an unknown artist (*National Portrait Gallery*)

The famous astronomical clock, made for Henry VIII in 1540*

after page 106

Henry VIII. After Holbein (*Mansell – Alinari*)

Anne Boleyn. A Holbein drawing (*Reproduced by gracious permission of
H.M. the Queen*)

Jane Seymour. A Holbein drawing (*Reproduced by gracious permission
of H.M. the Queen*)

Antonius van den Wyngaerde's panoramic sketch of Hampton
Court made in 1558 (*Ashmolean Museum*)

Queen Elizabeth I as a young girl (*Reproduced by gracious permission of
H.M. the Queen*)

The attractive Fish Court (*National Monuments Record*)

Illustrations

after page 138

The Great Hall with its magnificent hammer-beam roof (*Reproduced by gracious permission of H.M. the Queen*)

Wolsey's Closet*

The Great Kitchen, built in Henry VIII's time*

The Chapel Royal, with its ornate vaulted timber ceiling and carved and gilded pendants, was built for Wolsey and lavishly redecorated for Henry VIII*

The family of Henry VIII. The King, with Jane Seymour, Prince Edward and the Princesses Mary and Elizabeth (*Reproduced by gracious permission of H.M. the Queen*)

Charles I and Henrietta Maria leaving for the chase. From a painting by Daniel Mytens (*Reproduced by gracious permission of H.M. the Queen*)

Jeffery Hudson, the dwarf, only 18 in. tall when he was given to Charles I and Henrietta Maria by the Duchess of Buckingham (*Reproduced by gracious permission of H.M. the Queen*)

after page 170

Charles II's lovely young sister Minette. A portrait by Claude Mellan (*Nationalmuseum, Stockholm*)

Etching by Dirk Stoop showing the arrival at Hampton Court of King Charles II and his bride, Catherine of Braganza (*British Museum*)

William III when Prince of Orange (*Reproduced by gracious permission of H.M. the Queen*)

Wren's South Front. The King's State Rooms are on the first floor*

Mary II when Princess of Orange (*Reproduced by gracious permission of H.M. the Queen*)

Wren's East Front with the Queen's State Rooms*

Sir Christopher Wren. From a portrait by Sir Godfrey Kneller (*National Portrait Gallery*)

The King's Staircase, Wren's grand approach to the State Rooms*

x

after page 202

The Great Fountain Garden, laid out for Charles II and developed by William III*

A Victorian view showing the two great parks of Hampton Court—Bushey Park and the Home Park

William III's bedroom has a fine cornice and Verrio's richly decorated ceiling (*Reproduced by gracious permission of H.M. the Queen*)

Wood carving by Grinling Gibbons in the Chapel Royal (*Warburg Institute*)

An attractive fireback in the King's Dressing-room (*Warburg Institute*)

The locks made in 1699 by Josiah Key for the State Apartments (*Q. Lloyd*)

Wren's Fountain Court*

The Dutch Garden and the Banqueting House overlooking the river*

One of the magnificent wrought-iron panels designed by Jean Tijou for the Palace gardens*

* *Crown Copyright*

Hampton Court, begun more than a century before the first château at Versailles, has been called the loveliest palace in Europe. It was not founded by a king or a queen, but by the son of a prosperous Ipswich butcher. The butcher's son entertained Henry VIII there with unsurpassed lavishness, providing banquets, masked balls, mummeries, music and song, pretty women, love, and laughter. The King so relished this joyous palace that eventually he took it away from the man who built it and arrested him—but Cardinal Wolsey, who had served the King as Lord Chancellor with devotion and unrivalled brilliance, died while being taken to the Tower of London, charged with high treason and facing execution.

All of Henry's six wives spent some time at Hampton Court. So did his three children, Edward VI, Mary I, and Elizabeth I, and their successors to the throne; even Oliver Cromwell, who ruled without being king. It was the private residence of rulers for more than two centuries. You see them here in their more intimate moments. Flirtations were numerous. Illicit love affairs flourished. Queen Elizabeth's lover, the Earl of Leicester, had a room near hers, and yet, for reasons of State, she offered him to Mary Queen of Scots as a possible husband.

There were fierce quarrels during some of the honeymoons spent here—Charles I quarrelled with his bride Henrietta Maria, their son Charles II with Catherine of Braganza. Some kings moved mistresses into Hampton Court; some queens objected with anger, fainting, and tears, others were philosophical. James I had his boy friends here, and so did William III. There were marriages, one a forced marriage despite the bride's resistance; there were births, and one birth celebrated that never happened; and there were deaths.

Elizabeth was imprisoned by her sister Mary in the Water Gallery, built by their father, and Charles I was held prisoner too at Hampton Court until he managed to escape, hoping to cross to France.

Most far-reaching of the decisions made at Hampton Court

occurred during a heated discussion between Anglican bishops and Puritans, when James I rose and announced that there should be a new translation of the Bible. Its outcome, the Authorised Version, was to be used in every English-speaking country.

Much of Wolsey's late-medieval structure, altered and expanded by Henry VIII, still stands. When William and Mary brought in Sir Christopher Wren towards the end of the following century, it was decided to tear down the old palace and build a new one in the Renaissance idiom of Versailles. A beginning was made, but lack of money and the deaths of Mary and then of William curtailed the scheme. So the massive Tudor gateways remain, the towers and turrets, the tall twisted chimneys (however much renewed) and above all, Henry's impressive Great Hall, where Shakespeare's plays were performed and Shakespeare himself, as a member of the company of players, must have been present and possibly was one of the cast.

Now the beautiful ancient tapestries, priceless paintings, attractive old furniture, the gardens and ornamental waters imaginatively and lovingly laid out, help to complete the incomparable glory of Hampton Court. Here, where kings and queens walked, the public has been welcome since the beginning of Victoria's reign: at first only on certain days of the week in certain months of the year, now on every day except Christmas Day, Boxing Day, and Good Friday. The State Apartments, Great Hall, Great Kitchen, Cellars, Lower Orangery and the Vine are open from May to September on weekdays from 9.30 a.m. to 6 p.m. and on Sundays from 11 a.m. to 6 p.m.; in October, March and April on weekdays from 9.30 a.m. to 5 p.m. and on Sundays from 2 p.m. to 5 p.m.; and from November to February on weekdays from 9.30 a.m. to 4 p.m. and on Sundays from 2 to 4 p.m. The Tennis Court and the Banqueting House are open daily during the summer months.

Before the Norman Conquest, more than nine hundred years ago, when Edward the Confessor was King of England and engaged upon his great building enterprise at Westminster Abbey, there stood on the graceful sweeping curve of the River Thames where Hampton Court now stands, a small manor belonging to the Saxon lord, Earl Algar. Within a year of King Edward's death in 1066 it was given by William the Conqueror to one of his Norman knights, Walter de St Valeri. The value of the land and its fisheries was at that time £40.

St Valeri's descendants held the land and the house for a hundred and fifty years. In 1218 Thomas de St Valeri gave it to Henry de St Albans, who sold it twenty years later to the Prior of the Hospital of St John of Jerusalem for a thousand marks—£555 13s. 4d. This Order, formed during the First Crusade after the capture of Jerusalem from the Infidel as a military order for the protection and care of Christian pilgrims, ran hospitals for the ill and infirm. Their activities spread in time all over Europe and even to England where land as well as money was given to them to carry on their work; their black bell-like cloaks with a white eight-pointed cross on the breast were seen in the outskirts of London (St John's Wood derives its name from them) and already in 1180 they had a preceptory, or communal house, near Hampton Court.

When some years later they bought the manor from Henry de St Albans the land consisted of two thousand acres (Domesday Book gives the measure '18 hides in demesne') and was used for grazing two thousand sheep. There was a garden attached to the house, a dovecote, and a chapel; and the Knights Hospitallers, as they were called, added a preceptory for sisters of the Order. The annual income of the manor from rents and farming was £83 13s. 10d. in 1338.

Towards the end of the following century Henry Earl of Richmond, after his victory at Bosworth in 1485, ascended the English throne as King Henry VII. This marked the end of thirty devastating years of the Wars of the Roses and the beginning of the Tudor monarchy which brought stability to the country. Henry was only twenty-nine, long-faced, big-nosed, tight-lipped, with dark, lashless eyes. He had to adopt tough measures to enforce law and order and revive the prosperity of the country which had suffered acutely. He planned carefully and worked unremittingly, and to find rest from his strenuous labours he built a palace at Richmond, about four miles from Hampton Court manor-house. Being of a religious disposition, he arranged with the Knights Hospitallers to spend some of his time there and to use their chapel.

During the quarter-century of his reign, from 1485 to 1509, he went to Hampton Court, accompanied sometimes by his wife, the beautiful, fair-haired Elizabeth of York, who by this marriage had united the two rival factions of Lancaster and York. In January 1503 she went to the Hampton Court manor-house to pray in the chapel for the safe delivery of her fifth child and then went on to the Tower of London, where a few weeks later in the royal apartments in the White Tower, her daughter Katherine was born. Nine days later the Queen died at the age of thirty-seven. It was in the Tower that her two young brothers, known as 'The Princes in the Tower', had been murdered.

Two years later the manor was leased by the Knights at a rent of £50 a year to Henry VII's Chamberlain, Lord Daubeney. One wonders if the King, who was much attracted to the place, was using his Chamberlain to acquire it for him. One rumour of Henry's intentions has cropped up since, as follows.

In the eighteenth century, Sir Hans Sloane, the distinguished physician, plant collector, and President of the Royal Society whose name is attached to a street and a square in Chelsea, is said to have asserted that Bartholomew Columbus, the brother of Christopher Columbus, came to England to see King Henry and ask for financial assistance for his brother's voyage across the Atlantic in quest of a new route to the East Indies. Henry, who was well on the way to becoming the wealthiest monarch in Europe, is said to have listened patiently to the plan. Parsimonious by disposition yet eager always to increase his fortune, Henry turned it over in his mind, and deciding that it was a gamble unlikely to yield him any advantage, pleaded his inability to assist and is believed to have said that the money was needed for 'the purchase of a suite of fine tapestry hangings, brought from Antwerp and afterwards to be used for the decoration of Hampton Court'.

Sloane was not a contemporary of Henry VII but chief physician to King George II. It is impossible to tell if there is any truth in the statement attributed to him. Had Henry financed Columbus, the vast wealth that soon began to flow across the Atlantic would have filled the English royal coffers. Henry was certainly covetous of that fortune, brought in ship-loads to Ferdinand and Isabella of Spain, who did back Columbus. Thereafter it was Henry's main purpose to see that some of it came into his family circle. He pulled every diplomatic string to get his heir Arthur married to the Spanish Infanta Catherine of Aragon; and when Arthur died he saw to it that his second son Henry should take Arthur's place as her husband.

The Hospitallers' manor at Hampton remained in their hands for a little while longer.

Henry VII did not take over Hampton Court, but five years after his death a priest named Thomas Wolsey, who had served him well on diplomatic missions and various administrative tasks and was by now on the Council of the new King, Henry VIII, rented the manor from the Knights Hospitallers for £50 a year. His tenancy began on 24 June 1514. A few weeks later he was appointed Archbishop of York and in the following year he became Lord Chancellor and was made a Cardinal by the Pope.

Wolsey's lease, a contemporary copy of which can still be seen in the British Museum, was granted to him by the Prior, Sir Thomas Docwra. It was set out in an indenture executed (with the usual legal delay) on 11 January 1515, and was to run for a period of ninety-nine years and could be renewed at the same rent for a further period of ninety-nine years; it would have kept Hampton Court in the Wolsey family until the eve of Queen Anne's death in the early eighteenth century. A clause provided him and his successors with the right to obtain from St John's Wood, now part of London and at the time owned by the Knights of St John of Jerusalem, four loads of wood and timber yearly for use as piles for the repair of the weir and the maintenance of Hampton Court. At the end of his term as tenant Wolsey was required to provide 'a thousand couple of conies (rabbits) in the warren or pay in compensation fourpence for each couple'.

When building began in 1515, Wolsey was about forty, portly, with brown eyes and drooping lids, a small wart under his right eye. His manner could be gay and charming, or stern and severe. Wolsey's biographer, George Cavendish, his gentleman-usher, called him the son of a Suffolk butcher; although later inquiry into his antecedents has shown that Wolsey's father, whatever his origins, became a prosperous member of the new middle class. The young King, handsome, interested in women, dancing, and hunting, was twenty-four in 1515 and left his Lord Chancellor to rule the country. Wolsey ruled it well. His energy was astounding. He handled the entire direction of home and foreign affairs and had in addition numerous ecclesiastical responsibilities.

It is interesting to note that on 20 March 1514, three months before Wolsey's tenancy began, the young King and Queen Catherine visited the small manor-house at Hampton Court. Was it to inspect the place after Wolsey had talked of it or did Henry VIII think of acquiring it himself because of his parents' link with it? It is possible that Henry VIII found the place much too small for his purpose and left it to Wolsey to rent it.

What had caused Wolsey to select this particular site? One obvious advantage was its nearness to London: it was only thirteen miles away and could easily be reached, for though the roads were often fraught with danger, the river offered a safe and convenient highway.

Wolsey was not blessed with good health. For many years he suffered from the stone, which no doctor was then able to cure, but could only provide some relief. He also had dropsy and was a victim of quinsy, colic, and the ague. Hampton Court was found to be free from damp due to its gravelly soil. Yet another advantage was that Hampton Court provided an escape from London's smoke and fog: the air there was pure and clean; its extraordinary salubrity was vouched for by the most eminent physicians in England and from Padua, who had been instructed to find the most healthy spot within twenty miles of London.

The ancient manor-house was demolished and work was begun on a palace of vast size, beauty, and magnificence that was without parallel in England or for that matter in all Europe at that time.

Wolsey denied himself nothing. He insisted on the provision of a most elaborate system of drainage. Brick sewers were constructed three feet wide and five feet high to carry refuse to the Thames. Lavatories were provided in various parts of the building and quite a number of baths were also installed. His drinking water was brought from the springs at Coombe Hill, three miles away, by means of a double set of strong leaden pipes from Coombe to Kingston—where the remains of conduit-houses still exist—then taken under the Hogsmill river, which is a tributary of the Thames, and under the Thames itself, across what is now the Home Park to the grounds of Hampton Court where it was divided in several conduits and piped to the house. Each pipe was two and a half inches in diameter and the total amount of lead used was about two hundred and fifty tons: the cost of this together with the cost of labour for laying the pipes is said to have been about £50,000. Despite these precautions, in the summer of 1517, within two years of embarking on the construction of Hampton Court, his health caused considerable anxiety and he received an affectionate note from the King advising him to take exercise and enjoy the country air of Hampton to improve the condition of his stomach.

Wolsey's income from his numerous bishoprics and high offices was enormous. He was Bishop of Lincoln, Durham (which he later exchanged for Winchester), Bath, Worcester and Hereford, also of Tournai in France, Abbot of St Albans as well as Archbishop of York, Grand Almoner, and Lord Chancellor of England. Not all these made calls upon his time. The demands of only three of his main activities were exacting and doubtless exhausting. As Lord Chancellor he had to conduct the government of the country and attend to duties later assigned to the Foreign Secretary—receive foreign ambassadors, read despatches from the English ambassadors in foreign capitals, and send them his instructions; he also had to administer justice in Westminster Hall each day until noon. The other two were his ecclesiastical offices as Cardinal and Archbishop. Moreover he had embarked on three further building projects— Cardinal College at Oxford (now Christ Church); the school at his birthplace Ipswich; and York Place (named for his archbishopric) in London which he converted into yet another impressive palace, later part of the Palace of Whitehall.

The two thousand acres of land around the small manor-house at Hampton Court were divided into two parks (Bushey Park and the Home Park); he had them enclosed partly by high, well-buttressed red-brick walls, most of which still stand. The bricks, like those used for the building of the palace, were a deep crimson in colour and patterned at intervals with chequered lines of brick that had been burnt black, set to form the shape of the Calvary cross.

Wolsey's garden was laid out to the south between the palace and the river. His head gardener was John Chapman of Kingston, with four under-gardeners whose names are in the entries at the Public Record Office. Long lists of garden implements and seeds are also given: 3 spades—4*s*; 2 iron rakes—12*d*; 2 lines—10*d*; 4 dibbles (for making holes)—7*d*; 1 wheelbarrow—10*d*; for mending the key to the park gate—1*d*; for carrying 2 loads of pots for herbs—16*d*; 2 lb. of leek seed; 2 lb. of parsley seed; 3 lb. of aniseed, as well as carrot, caraway, thyme, coriander, cucumber, and melon. Baskets for strawberries cost 3*s*. 6*d*; for primroses 2*s*. 4*d*; and so on.

The weeding was done chiefly by women (although fourpence a day was paid to either sex), the worst weed being known as 'tare', which we call vetch. Hedges were used to keep the orchards from 'beastes'. The deer in the parks could be kept away, it was thought, by anointing the fruit trees with the 'pisse of a deer'; it was also believed that if one put spittle on the sprouts it would keep off the hares.

Wolsey started the Knot Garden—of which the present one is a revival—in intricate patterns made with low close-growing shrubs, with flowers planted in the interstices. The flowers included roses, lilies, sunflowers, violets, poppies, daffodils, and hyacinths.

The house Wolsey built marks the passing of the feudal era. After the Wars of the Roses, castles were no longer functionally necessary for the monarch or his more powerful subjects to live in. At peace at last, they needed not fortress-houses but residences in which they could live in comfort or even luxury instead of suffering the severe austerity of high-walled, heavily guarded structures surrounded by wide moats crossed by drawbridges. Wolsey's solitary gesture to the past was the inclusion of the moat, which went right round the house and gardens, said to have been the last domestic moat built in England. Was this prompted by sentiment or did it provide a flourish of grandeur?

The 'architect' who designed and drew up the plans for Wolsey's great palace, admired by the King and all who saw it then and in the succeeding centuries, is unknown—unless Lawrence Stubbs, Wolsey's almoner who appears in some records as his 'surveyor of . . . buildings', was the man. The overall plan was undoubtedly Wolsey's; and the work was carried out by a master mason, a master carpenter, and numerous others including the best craftsmen for ornamental details and embellishments. No limit seems to have been set on the cost.

Grandeur was not the only aim of the Cardinal: he insisted that his palace should provide both space and luxury, neither normally a feature of older houses.

Apart from the great west gatehouse (a more massive and a loftier structure then than now), the building consisted of a series of two-storeyed structures around two main courts and a number of smaller ones with cloisters, all spread out over approximately eight acres, a spacious site for much later demolition and alteration. There were in all a thousand rooms, a Great Hall, at least one chapel and numerous kitchens, sculleries, butteries, sauceries, and bakehouses. In addition to reception rooms, audience chambers, more than one banqueting hall, and an elaborate suite for the King, there were two hundred and eighty bedrooms for guests who were chiefly ambassadors and distinguished visitors, all of whom brought their own retinues of secretaries, aides, gentlemen, and ladies. Wolsey himself had a retinue of five hundred.

The deep red of the brick used for these buildings was at times more of a rich plum in colour. The doorways, windows, and parapets had stone dressings and there was varied elaboration on the gables and elsewhere of pinnacles, gargoyles, and heraldic beasts.

The first section to be built was the west front, with its Great Gatehouse and huge oriel window. Flanking the Gatehouse and running eastwards to form the first courtyard, called the Base Court, the whole layout measured about four hundred feet from north to south; it was strikingly beautiful with its cloisters, mullioned windows, embrasured parapets, gables with gargoyles, brave turrets, and gilded pinnacles, and its carved and twisted brick chimneys of various shapes, grouped in pleasing clusters and rising above the battlements.

And this was not all. Wolsey commissioned the Italian sculptor, Giovanni da Maiano, to make terracotta medallion busts of the Roman Emperors for the turrets on each side of the gateways to the courts, thus adding a touch of Renaissance to the Gothic: six years after delivering the medallions Maiano sent a pitiful letter begging for payment, for not a penny had been paid him. He was paid £2 6s. each in 1521.

The guest rooms surrounded the Base Court. The second gateway leading to the Inner Court, later called the Clock Court, displayed the Cardinal's arms with a cross above it, supported by two cherubim and surmounted by the Cardinal's hat. This was set in a pilastered framework, classical in design, and topped by a pediment which carried a monogram of his initials 'T.W.' entwined with a cordon and bearing the date 1525 with the motto *Dominus michi adivtor* (The Lord My Helper) on a pedestal below the feet of the cherubim.

The rooms had decorated ceilings, friezes abounded, rich in colour and often very beautiful without being gaudy. Wolsey's artistic sensibility and taste may still be admired in surviving rooms on the upper floor on the south side of the Clock Court, and now reached from Wren's King's Guard Chamber. These rooms overlooked the Cardinal's garden and the river. The first room is called Wolsey's Antechamber. Exquisitely panelled in oak, it has a rare pattern of linenfold and a mullioned window, which originally overlooked the

9

courtyard. The next room, thought to have been Wolsey's Privy Chamber, has a plain Tudor panelling, the original stone fireplace with a herring-bone brick backing, and an oriel window. The decorated frieze is no longer there, but the ceiling remains and one can admire its panels of various shapes with small wooden bosses at the intersection of the ribs and plaques between the ribs—with traces of the original colours and gilt which made the ceiling so beautiful. Next to it, the largest room of the three is too much altered for us to visualise Wolsey seated in it: even the old mullioned bay window has gone. Only a bit of the ceiling remains, similar to the one in the adjoining room, but with a different pattern and plaques displaying Wolsey's badge of cross-keys and pillars. Adjoining these are two other rooms that Wolsey used, the walls covered with linenfold oak panelling.

Detached from these, off Wren's so-called Communication Gallery, is Wolsey's Closet, now reduced in size but with its ceiling and frieze in perfect condition: we get from it an excellent impression of the beauty of a Tudor room. The abundant plasterwork is picked out in gold on a blue field. If the ceiling is Wolsey's, then the emblems in the large panels must have been added later by Henry VIII, for they display the Tudor Rose and the Prince of Wales's feathers, possibly added after the birth of Henry's son Edward.

The frieze is decorated with little scenes in low relief, and running below them is Wolsey's motto *Dominus michi adivtor* (old lettering for *adjutor*) repeated again and again. The upper parts of the walls are hung with painted panels of the Passion of Our Lord, thought to have been there since Wolsey's time; recent restoration work shows that these panels originally bore older paintings. There is a contemporary fireplace with a Tudor cast-iron fireback (the oldest in Hampton Court) and a large mullioned window looking eastward.

The Venetian ambassador Giustiniani, who often stayed with Wolsey at Hampton Court, wrote: 'One has to traverse eight rooms before one reaches his audience chamber, and they are all hung with tapestry, which is changed every week.' Another visitor, Du Bellay, Bishop of Bayonne, reported: 'The very bed-chambers had hangings of wonderful value, and every place did glitter with innumerable vessels of gold and silver. There were two hundred and four score beds, the furniture to most of them being silk, and all for the entertainment of strangers only.'

The garden overlooked by the south-facing rooms was Wolsey's Knot Garden, which Cavendish describes:

> My gardens sweet, enclosed with walles strong
> Embanked with benches to sytt and take my rest,
> The Knots so enknotted, it cannot be exprest;
> With arbors and ayles so pleasant and so dulce,
> The pestylent airs with flavours to repulse.

There were dovecotes in it and the extent of the garden may still be seen, but now it has enclosed parterres that were laid out by Henry VIII.

Along the north side of the present Clock Court was Wolsey's (demolished) Great Hall, where minstrels played in the gallery while guests dined and supped, danced and joined in the mummery. To the north of it were the kitchens (they are still there), so placed that both ends of the Hall could be served at the same time. To the east was the Chapel, altered by Henry VIII and in Queen Anne's time, but still in the same place.

Throughout the palace, in the numerous reception rooms, bedrooms, dressing-rooms, even closets, the pictures, the hangings, the carpets, the beds, the mattresses, the pillows and counterpanes, all the furniture—tables, chairs, and mirrors—were superb and fabulously expensive. Emissaries from the courts of France, Italy, Spain, and Germany gasped and declared that they had never seen anything so magnificent before. Wolsey sent agents all over the Continent to buy the finest articles they could find regardless of cost. His letters to Sir Richard Gresham, father of Sir Thomas Gresham, the founder of the Royal Exchange in London, instructed him to measure the eighteen principal chambers at Hampton Court and buy Arras tapestry wholesale. From another trip abroad Gresham returned with one hundred and thirty-two pieces of tapestry for the rooms in the Great Gatehouse: the subjects were scriptural—'Six pieces of the Story of Esther' for the large room, 'six pieces of the Story of Samuel' for another.

But Wolsey's tastes were not confined to the sacred. He bought a great many sets of fine tapestries influenced by the Italian Renaissance, depicting triumphal cars drawn by elephants, or bulls, or unicorns, with Julius Caesar and Pompey or Venus driven by naked cupids. There were stories of Jupiter and Ceres, Hercules and Jason,

Priamus, the 'Romance of the Rose', and Hannibal; others with birds and beasts and flowers; many about hunting and shooting; one of a lady putting a black shoe on a man's foot; and a series of Flemish tapestries depicting the Triumph of Death, Time, and Renown, which may still be seen in Henry VIII's Great Watching Chamber. Many of the richest tapestries were hung in the guest bedrooms.

In his own rooms Wolsey had cloth-of-gold hangings. When he dined he sat under canopies of cloth of gold at a table covered with cloth of gold. For his rooms, he told Giustiniani, he wanted nothing but the choicest carpets from the East and asked him to procure some through Venetian merchants.

Most of these costly purchases Wolsey paid for, but occasionally he accepted gifts that were sent him. Giustiniani told the Doge of Venice: 'Cardinal Wolsey is very anxious for the Signory to send him a hundred damascene carpets for which he has asked several times and expected to receive them by the last galleys.' The ambassador urged the Senate to make a present of the carpets 'as this might easily settle the affair of the wines of Candia' or 'might make him pass a decree in our favour; and, at any rate, it would render the Cardinal friendly to our nation in other matters'. Sixty carpets were sent.

An inventory of the furniture, which is still in existence, gives details that make one gasp—beds of red, green, and russet velvet, satin and silk, with rich curtains and fringes of the same materials. Hundreds of counterpanes were bought for the beds. Some were of 'tawny damask lined with blue buckram'; others of 'blue damask with flowers of gold'; one of 'red satin with a great rose in the midst wrought with needlework'; and one of 'blue sarcenet with a tree in the midst and beastes with scriptures all wrought with needlework'.

Wolsey's own pillow-cases are described as 'seamed with black silk and *fleur-de-lys* of gold' and with 'white silk and *fleur-de-lys* of red silk'. His bed was possibly the 'greate riche bedstede, having four gilte postes and four boulles with Cardinall hattes gilte'; and the bed's ceiling of red satin 'wrought with a great rose of needlework embossed with garters and portcullis, with a valance and fringe of white, green, yellow, tawny and blue silk'. Or he may occasionally have slept in the 'trussing bedstede of alabaster with my Lordes arms and flowers gilt upon the sides'.

There were five Chairs of State for Wolsey and his principal guests

—one covered with 'cloth of tissue' fringed with gold of Venice; another with blue cloth of gold fringed with blue silk and gold of Venice, red with red silk, and so on. Some of the chairs in the palace had high backs, others were low-backed, all were covered with red, blue, or black velvet, fringed with gold and silks of a matching colour. Many cushions were of cloth of gold; the napery was of the finest damask with 'flowers, paned losinge-wise'.

Some of the andirons (firedogs) displayed mermaids, dragons, and lions, angels, or roses, others were topped with the Cardinal's hat and Wolsey's coat-of-arms. There were images in the chapel, clothed in saint's apparel which was changed from time to time: the Virgin Mary had two coats, one of crimson velvet and cloth of gold decorated with pearls, the other of black damask and cloth of gold. The gold and silver plate, which included censers, chalices, monstrances, paxes, crosses, and other sacred vessels, was estimated by the Venetian ambassador to be worth 300,000 golden ducats, equal at that time to about £150,000 and equivalent today to at least ten times that sum, namely one and a half million pounds sterling. Wolsey had no personal need for jewels, but he had an enormous collection of rings, signets, aiglets, girdles, and chains to give away as presents, mostly to the ladies.

All this, however much it may have pandered to his vanity, had for Wolsey one overriding purpose: he wanted the world, which at that time meant Europe, to recognise that England was not a country in irredeemable decline from the glory it had enjoyed when Henry II had almost all France in his grasp, when after the Battle of Agincourt Henry V held even Paris and his son was crowned King of France as well as King of England. Much had been lost and the Wars of the Roses had severely affected the economy and the life of the English, but—and it was this that was important to Wolsey—Henry VII had achieved a worth-while recovery and since then Wolsey had forced all Europe to recognise that England was great again and able to play a vital role in Europe. To his astonishing new palace they sent their ambassadors to discuss policies and treaties: and these in turn, wide-eyed with admiration, sent long, glowing despatches of the power and glory of the island country's greatest minister.

In less than two years the old manor-house had been replaced by the splendour of Hampton Court: the new building had been completed, decorated, and richly furnished, the parks and gardens had been laid out with arresting and inviting taste; and in 1517 the palace was ready to receive its first guests—the young King Henry VIII and his wife Catherine of Aragon, daughter of the fabulously wealthy Ferdinand and Isabella of Spain and bringer of 200,000 crowns as marriage dowry: she was six years older than her husband, blonde, squat, with prominent, rather watery blue eyes, and was deeply religious.

An enormous staff, housed in quarters on the north side, was required to run Hampton Court. In addition to his five hundred retainers Wolsey had also a great many lords and other members of the most noble families in England in constant attendance: they went everywhere with him and resided in Hampton Court when he was there. Sixteen priests presided over the services in the main Chapel; for religious festivals their numbers were swollen to sixty: dressed in copes, they walked in procession round the cloisters of Hampton Court, led by the Dean, with the sub-Dean walking behind him, followed by a Gospeller with two priests singing the gospel, a Pisteller singing the epistle of the day, and a choir of twelve singing children, sixteen singing laymen, and twelve singing priests.

He had a full complement of staff for his kitchens, one of which was his privy kitchen where dishes to suit his personal taste and to meet the requirements of his diet were prepared under the supervision of his master chef, dressed in velvet and satin with a gold chain round his neck. The servitors in the kitchens numbered eighty and ranged from cooks and assistant cooks to pastry-cooks, bakers, and scullery maids; there were in addition cellarers, butlers, and table servants. In the Great Hall, where meals were served, three officers presided—a priest who acted as steward, a treasurer who was a knight, and a comptroller. Under them were a 'cofferer' who was a doctor, marshals, yeomen, ushers, grooms, and almoners. Numerous valets looked after Wolsey's wardrobe and his guests' wardrobes, and there was an enormous laundry with nearly a hundred washerwomen.

Beyond the walls of the palace on the other side of the Green were the stables, built round a large courtyard approached through an archway. Parts of Wolsey's stables are probably still there, as enlarged by Henry. Above the stalls and coach-houses, the grooms and other stable workers such as saddlers, farriers, muleteers, charioteers, and carters lived. There was in addition a stud. In control Wolsey had his Master of the Horse.

As befitted his exalted station, Wolsey also had his own High Chamberlain and a Vice-Chamberlain with twenty gentlemen ushers, forty gentlemen cup-bearers, forty-six yeomen of his chamber 'daily to attend upon his person', four counsellers 'learned in the law', sixteen doctors and a host of secretaries, clerks, and 'running footmen'.

Such magnificence and splendour evoked not only the admiration of his guests but roused the scorn of critics, some of whom, like John Skelton, a priest turned poet, and the Franciscan friar Roy, poured out their disgust in satirical verse. Skelton wrote:

> Some say 'Yes' and some
> Sit still as they were dumb.
> Thus thwarting over them
> He ruleth all the roast
> With bragging and with boast,
> Borne up on every side
> With pomp and with pride.

Wolsey laughed at their jibes and was equally indifferent to the contemptuous asides of the aristocracy who looked on him as an upstart usurping an eminence greater even than the King's. Giustiniani, the Venetian ambassador, described him as 'Omnipotent. All the power of the State is centred in him. He is, in fact, *Ipse rex*, and no one in this realm dare attempt aught in opposition to his interests', adding that he was 'seven times greater than the Pope himself'.

Dr Barnes, one of the earliest Puritans, on reproaching Wolsey for his ostentation, received this answer: 'How think ye? Were it better for me, being in the honour and dignity that I am, to coin my pillars and pole-axes and give the money to five or six beggars? Do you not reckon the commonwealth better than five or six beggars?' Barnes replied that it would be more to the honour of God and to the salvation of his soul and also to the comfort of his poorer brethren that this silver were coined and given in alms. But Wolsey could point with satisfaction to the 'twins of learning' he had established— his School at Ipswich and Cardinal College at Oxford. His red hat now rests in the library of that college.

Was it the Cardinal's hat that had turned Wolsey's head? That, at any rate, was beyond the reach of the King. William Tyndale, translator of the Bible, asserts that when the hat arrived from Rome, it 'was set on a cupboard and tapers about, so that the greatest Duke in the land must make curtesie thereto'. There were occasions when even the saintly upholder of papal power, Sir Thomas More, could not resist being sarcastic about it.

Wolsey regarded Hampton Court as a place of rest. Not that he got much rest there. When not entertaining his exalted visitors—and the King came many times, often unexpectedly, occasionally masked (as a private person on pleasure bent) but always with a considerable entourage—Wolsey found no solitude. He would rise early and after celebrating Mass in his private chapel, would have breakfast and then emerge wearing his Cardinal's robes and give audience to a succession of important visitors. After that he signed documents, wrote numerous letters to English ambassadors abroad, and sent a lengthy despatch to the King on the affairs of the country. The afternoon was spent in taking some form of mild exercise: he walked in the gardens and the parks if the weather was fine, when it rained his walk was confined to the galleries and cloisters.

Though a Cardinal, Wolsey had mistresses. The most notable of them was 'the daughter of one Lark', who is thought to have been Peter Lark, an innkeeper of Thetford in Norfolk. He was faithful to her for some years and it used to be said that the Cardinal had 'uncanonically married' her. There were children, and she and the children were often in residence at Hampton Court, as were also her three brothers, one of whom, Thomas Lark, was Wolsey's confessor as well as chaplain to the King.

On tiring of her Wolsey passed her on, with a substantial dowry by way of encouragement, to a man named Lee in Cheshire, from whom the famous American general Robert E. Lee was possibly descended. Wolsey was not very interested in his own two brothers and saw little of either, nor were they helped to make a fortune or attain positions of importance in the Church.

King Henry VIII had relied on Wolsey ever since becoming King at the age of eighteen; the King's manner revealed how he admired him and had an unbounded affection for him. Arriving unexpectedly at Hampton Court with a group of friends, His Majesty would slip his arm through the Cardinal's and walk with him in the garden, talking, laughing, and occasionally hugging him. Wolsey's gentle-man-usher George Cavendish has given us a vivid record of the King's visits.

Banquets were set forth, masks and mummeries, in so gorgeous a sort and costly manner that it was heaven to behold. There wanted no dames, nor damsels, meet or apt to dance with the maskers. . . . Then was there all kinds of music and harmony set forth, with excellent fine voices both of men and children. I have seen the King come suddenly thither in a mask, with a dozen maskers, all in garments like shepherds, made of fine cloth of gold and fine crimson satin paned [with strips of different coloured cloth] and caps of the same, with visors of good proportion and physiognomy; their hairs and beards either of fine gold wire or of silver, or else of good black silk; having sixteen torch-bearers, besides three drums, and other persons attending them, with visors, clothed all in satin of the same colour.

And before his entering into the hall, ye shall understand, that he came by water to the watergate without noise; where were laid divers chambers, and guns charged with shot, and at his landing they were shot off, which made such a rumble in the air that it was like thunder. It made all the noblemen, gentlemen, ladies, and gentlewomen to muse what it should mean coming so suddenly, they sitting quiet at a solemn banquet; under this sort. First, ye shall perceive that the tables were set in the chamber of presence, banquet-wise covered, and my Lord Cardinal sitting under the cloth of estate, there having all his service alone; and then was there set a lady and a nobleman, or a gentleman or gentlewoman, throughout all the tables in the chamber on the one side, which were made adjoining as it were but one table. All which order and devise was done and devised by the Lord Sandes, then Lord Chamberlain to the King; and by Sir Henry Guildford, Comptroller of the King's Majesty's house.

Then immediately after this great shot of guns, the Cardinal desired the said Lord Chamberlain and the said Comptroller to look what it should mean, as though he knew nothing of the matter. They, looking out of the windows into the Thames, returned again and showed him that it seemed they were noblemen and strangers arrived at his bridge, coming as ambassadors from some foreign prince. With that quoth the Cardinal 'I shall desire you, because you can speak French, to take the pains to go into the hall there to receive them according to their estates and to conduct them into this chamber where they shall see us, and all these noble personages being merry at our banquet, desiring them to sit down with us and to take part of our fare.'

Thus the charade went on. The Lord Chamberlain and the Comptroller escorted the masked visitors in to the accompaniment of fifes and drums. They entered two by two, went up to Wolsey and saluted him very reverently. The Lord Chamberlain spoke for them. 'Sir, for as much as they be strangers and cannot speak English, they have desired me to declare unto you that they, having understanding of this triumphant banquet, where was assembled such a number of excellent fair dames, could do no less, under the supportation of your Grace, but to repair hither to view as well their incomparable beauty, as for to accompany them at mumchance and then after to dance with them and to have their acquaintance.' Wolsey said he would be happy if they did so. Cavendish continues:

Then went the maskers, and first saluted all the dames, and then returned to the most worthiest and there opened their great cup of gold, filled with crowns and other pieces of gold, to whom they set certain pieces of the gold to cast at [a game apparently combining 'drawing lots' and 'catch-as-catch-can']. Thus pursuing all the ladies and gentlewomen, to some they lost and of some they won. And pursuing after this manner all the ladies, they returned to the Cardinal with great reverence, pouring down all the gold left in the cup, which was above two hundred crowns.

a

Wolsey then cast the dice and won, 'whereat was made great noise and joy'. After a time Wolsey told the Lord Chamberlain that he felt there was a noble among them 'more meet to occupy this seat and place than I, to whom I would gladly surrender the same according to my duty if I knew him'. He was informed that there was such a personage and that if Wolsey could pick him out from the rest, he would be content to disclose himself and take the seat of honour.

'Me seemeth,' said Wolsey eventually, 'the gentleman with the black beard should be even he,' and rose from his chair and went up to the man cap in hand. But he was wrong. The man proved to be Sir Edward Neville, 'a comely Knight of a personage that much more resembled the King than any other. The King, hearing and perceiving the Cardinal so deceived in his estimation and choice, could not forbear laughing; but pulled down his visor and Master Neville's also, and dashed out such a pleasant countenance and cheer that all noble estates there assembled, perceiving the King to be there amongst them, rejoiced very much.'

The King withdrew 'to shift his apparel', as His Majesty phrased it, and walked straight into Wolsey's bedchamber, 'where was a great fire prepared for him; and there new apparelled him with rich and princely garments. And in the time of the King's absence the dishes of the banquet were clean taken up and the table spread again with new and sweet perfumed cloths; every man sitting still until the King's Majesty, with all his maskers, came in among them again, every man new apparelled. Then the King took his seat under the cloth of estate.'

A fresh banquet then began 'wherein', says Cavendish, 'I suppose, were served two hundred divers dishes of wondrous costly devices and subtleties. Thus passed they forth the night with banqueting, dancing and other triumphant devices to the great comfort of the King and pleasant regard of the nobility there assembled.'

When the King came more formally, he and Queen Catherine occupied rooms that had been permanently set aside for their use. The entrance to Catherine's rooms, which were on the east side of the present Clock Court, may still be seen. Later, even before his marriage to Anne Boleyn, special apartments were provided for Anne at Hampton Court.

Wolsey rarely went hunting. Sometimes, at the King's persuasion, he would set out with His Majesty; at others it would be with the

Earl of Southampton, who pressed him to come over from Hampton Court to Chertsey so that 'he could kill a stag with his bow and another with his greyhound'.

He had little time to spare for such day-long diversions. The weeks at Hampton Court passed only too rapidly and unrestfully; and suddenly the beginning of the legal term would be upon him and he would have to set out for Westminster Hall. His progress to London was attended by the utmost pomp and ceremony. While the participants in the procession assembled in the long wide drive from the Great Gatehouse to the outer gates and the street, Wolsey, with numerous dressers in attendance, was meticulously and obsequiously got ready in his Privy Chamber, from which he would presently emerge 'apparelled all in red' as a Cardinal. In the Presence Chamber 'noblemen and very worthy gentlemen' waited for his entrance, preceded by his pursuivant-at-arms with a great mace of silver gilt and by his gentlemen ushers crying: 'On, my lords and masters! Make way for my Lord's grace!'

Outside the Great Gatehouse waited a long line of men on horseback. At the head of the procession were Wolsey's attendants in livery of crimson velvet and gold chains. Next were the lesser officers in coats of scarlet bordered with black velvet. Then two gentlemen, one bearing his Cardinal's hat, the other his Seal of State. Behind them were two priests carrying silver pillars, called 'poleaxes', followed by 'two great crosses of silver, whereof one of them was for his Archbishopric, the other for his legacy'—Wolsey was the Papal legate—'borne always before him whithersoever he went, or rode, by two of the most tallest and comeliest priests that he could get within all this realm'.

For Wolsey not a horse but a mule waited, sumptuously caparisoned with crimson velvet and stirrups of copper gilt. Behind him four footmen on horseback carried gilt pole-axes; and behind them were Wolsey's yeomen dressed in tawny French liveries with the letters T and C embroidered on the breasts and back.

Not all Wolsey's journeys to London were made by road. Sometimes he went by boat, travelling in a magnificent state barge with 'yeomen standing on the sails and crowded with his gentlemen within and without'.

Despite the endless poetic effusions against Wolsey by Skelton and the other satirists, despite the contempt of the aristocracy for the 'haughty upstart' and the whispered sneers of courtiers and politicians, the King was still, in 1525, deeply attached to his Lord Chancellor. Since the King's accession in 1509, Wolsey had given him sixteen years of service. The raising of England's status from a third-rate power to a basis of equality with the two great European powers, France and the Holy Roman Empire, was due, Henry realised, solely to Wolsey's shrewdness and skill. A letter from French emissaries reporting to François Ier indicates what they thought of Wolsey: 'We have to do,' they wrote, 'with the most rascally beggar in the world, and one who is wholly devoted to his master's interest—a man as difficult to manage as can be.' Henry was only too well aware that his own importance had benefited. A change was wrought even in the mode of address to the King. Hitherto the monarch had always been referred to as 'His Grace'; Wolsey spoke of Henry as 'His Majesty' and to him as 'Your Majesty'.

It may be wondered why then in June 1525 Henry should have asked Wolsey why he had built for himself so magnificent a palace as Hampton Court. Wolsey is said to have replied: 'To show how noble a palace a subject may offer to his sovereign.'

Possibly by the words 'to offer' Wolsey meant that his palace had been built for His Majesty's entertainment. But the King took it literally and the lease was accordingly transferred to him together with all the furniture, the costly tapestries and hangings, the pictures and the plate. But Wolsey continued to live there. For some years before this Wolsey had been heading his letters to the King with the words 'From Your Manor'—one of them is dated as early as 7 March 1521. To other correspondents, even after all of it was transferred to the King, his letters began 'From my manor at Hampton Court'.

In 1526 and 1527 important missions from various European

countries arrived at Hampton Court. The first of these was headed by the French ambassador. Discussions went on for some days and resulted in a treaty whereby England and France agreed that neither country should assist Charles V, Emperor of the Holy Roman Empire (who happened to be a nephew of Catherine of Aragon) against the other. Later that summer there were visits from the Papal Nuncio and the Venetian ambassador.

In March 1527, while Henry VIII and Catherine of Aragon were staying with Wolsey at Hampton Court, a treaty was drawn up for the marriage of their only surviving child, Princess Mary, then ten years old, to the thirty-three-year-old, debauched king, François Ier of France. With a view to cementing a closer alliance between the two countries, its ratification later that year was marked by the greatest and most magnificent of all Wolsey's receptions. It was his last important reception at Hampton Court.

The Constable of France, the Duc Anne de Montmorency, arrived with a retinue of 'the noblest gentlemen in all France' comprising a hundred persons with captains of the guard and their followers, numbering as many as six hundred horse.

Cavendish tells us of the elaborate preparations in the Palace for the guests:

> My Lord Cardinal called before him his principal officers—his steward, treasurer, comptroller, and the clerks of his kitchen . . . whom he commanded neither to spare for any costs, expenses or travail to make them such a triumphant banquet as they may not only wonder at here but also make a glorious report thereof in their country to the great honour of the King and his realm. . . . They sent forth all the caterers, purveyors, and divers persons to prepare of the finest viands that they could get either for money or friendship among my Lord's friends. Also they sent for all the expertest cooks and cunning persons in the art of cookery which were within London or elsewhere that might be gotten to beautify this noble feast. . . . The cooks wrought both night and day in subtleties and many crafty devices; where lacked neither gold, silver, nor any costly thing meet for the purpose.

For days various activities went on all over the palace. To see that all the rooms were 'nobly garnished' carpenters, joiners, and masons were brought in. 'The yeomen and grooms of the wardrobes were busied hanging of the chambers with costly hangings, and furnishing the same with beds of silk and other furniture for the same in every degree. . . . Our pains were not small or light, travelling daily up and down from chamber to chamber.'

The distinguished French visitors arrived 'before the hour of their appointment'. Nobody was perturbed: they were taken off for a hunt at Hanworth, about three miles from Hampton Court, returning when darkness fell, and were then escorted to their various chambers where enormous fires had been lit and wine had been placed for their refreshment until supper was served. 'The chambers where they supped and banqueted were ordered in due form. First the great waiting-chamber was hanged with rich arras [tapestry made at Arras] as all others were, one better than another and furnished with tall yeomen. There was set tables round about the chambers banquet-wise, all covered with fine cloths of diaper.'

Adjoining was the Chamber of Presence with very rich arras, 'wherein was a gorgeous and precious cloth of estate hanged up replenished with many goodly gentlemen ready to serve'. The high table was in the centre of the room under the cloth of state and the damask table cloths were perfumed. In this, as in the other rooms, were enormous candlesticks of silver, or gilt, with giant wax candles as big as torches and large silver and gilt plates hung on the walls behind them to reflect the light. In the fireplaces there were great fires of wood and coal.

The guests were summoned by trumpets, and the more exalted were escorted from their chambers to their tables by the Cardinal's lordly retainers. The music was supplied by divers instruments which 'rapt the Frenchmen into a heavenly paradise'.

Not till the first course had been eaten did Wolsey himself appear, booted and spurred. The entire assembly rose and remained standing until he sat down, clad as he was in his riding apparel, 'laughing and being as merry as ever I saw in my life'. Then the second course was brought in 'with so many dishes, subtleties, and curious devices, which were above a hundred in number, of so goodly proportion and costly that I suppose the Frenchmen never saw the like. . . . There were castles with images in the same; Paul's church and steeple'—this, of course, the old St Paul's—'counterfeited as the painter should have painted it upon a cloth or wall. There were beasts, birds, fowls of divers kinds, and personages, most lively made and counterfeit in dishes; some fighting, as it were, with swords, some with guns and crossbows; some vaulting and leaping; some dancing with ladies, some on horses in complete harness, jousting with long and sharp spears and with many more devices.' One dish represented a chessboard with men. Wolsey presented this to a gentleman of France who was skilled at playing chess, and ordered that a case should be made for it to preserve the food from perishing during the voyage to France.

'Then took my Lord a bowl of gold which was esteemed of the value of five hundred marks, filled with hypocras [hippocras, a spiced wine] whereof there was plenty, and putting off his cap, said: "I drink to the King my Sovereign Lord, and next unto the King your master", and therewith drank a good draught.' He then asked the Duc de Montmorency 'to pledge him, cup and all, the which cup he gave him; and so caused all the other lords and gentlemen in other cups to pledge these two royal princes'.

By the end of the meal the Frenchmen had drunk so much wine that they had to be assisted to their beds. In every bedroom there was a basin and an ewer, some of silver, others gilt, a pot of wine, another with beer, and silver candlesticks with white and yellow candles and a loaf of bread.

Wolsey did not eat much while with them, but had a special, modest meal served later in his private quarters. The next day there was more hunting and then Wolsey took his guests on a tour of Windsor Castle, including St George's Chapel, only finished after Henry came to the throne, with its splendid stalls for the Order of the Garter, and Eton College.

The following year, during July and August 1528, as many as forty thousand people in London were affected by an outbreak of sweating sickness, and two thousand of them died. Wolsey withdrew to Hampton Court and spent three months there. Henry VIII, who had also moved out of London, sent Wolsey many affectionate letters, urging him to take great care of himself, to 'keep out of the air, to have only a small and clean company about, not to eat too much supper, or drink too much wine', and sending some pills Henry had had prepared for him. In January 1529, when the danger of infection had passed, Henry and Catherine came to stay with Wolsey at Hampton Court. It must have been a visit charged with undercurrents of anxiety.

Divorce proceedings against Catherine of Aragon had been begun by Henry eighteen months before they came as man and wife to stay with Wolsey at Hampton Court early in 1529. Henry had been talking of divorcing her in 1516. He wanted an heir; there had been too many miscarriages and still-born children. When at last Catherine gave birth in 1516 to Princess Mary, Henry's hopes rose: 'We are both young; if it was a daughter this time, by the grace of God sons will follow.' He wanted a son. No woman had ruled England in her own right. In 1525 when Catherine reached the age of forty all hope of having another child began to vanish and Henry talked of the urgency of a divorce. Two years later Wolsey was entrusted with the task of obtaining it. It would be wrong to assume that Henry was tired of Catherine. Their eighteen years together reveal how much they had in common. She shared his great love for music, attended the masques, however bawdy, and took a keen interest in gardening: a Spanish gardener was brought over to plant various vegetables for salads and reintroduce cherry, peach, and plum trees, which had once been known in England. She shut her eyes to the succession of mistresses, one of whom, a lady at Court, Elizabeth Blount, had presented him with a son named Henry Fitzroy, Duke of Richmond.

Anne Boleyn had not yet come into Henry's life. Her elder sister Mary had been his mistress. Attracted by Anne's youth (she was not yet twenty), by her soft black eyes and long raven hair which she wore loose, Henry tried to take her to his bed, but she refused. She had no wish to be discarded like her sister. Only when he obtained his divorce from Catherine would the way be opened for marriage. The Pope's sanction was necessary and Henry was confident that Wolsey could obtain it. His plea was based on the 'sinfulness' of his marriage to his brother's widow. Pope Clement VII was persuaded to accept this reasoning despite the dispensation granted by an earlier Pope at the time of Henry's marriage.

Machinery for the divorce started well. But war broke out between François Ier and the Emperor Charles V and, although England was not involved at first, when Wolsey learned of the French troops' sweeping advance through Italy, he decided to support France. At first this helped. As the French neared Naples, one of the Emperor's kingdoms, the Pope hurriedly despatched Cardinal Campeggio to England with full powers to grant Henry a divorce. But some months later, in August 1529, on France being defeated, all these arrangements were cancelled. The Pope was by now a prisoner of the Emperor and it was obvious that Charles would never agree to allowing the divorce of his aunt Catherine of Aragon. Hurriedly Pope Clement sent messages for the immediate return of Campeggio and firmly refused to grant a divorce.

That Wolsey could not be blamed for this was obvious; and it was equally obvious to Henry that he no longer needed him. Wolsey's enemies, who had been waiting for this moment, were joined now by jealous churchmen, for Wolsey had already set in motion the suppression of monasteries.

The King, frustrated and angry, felt that Wolsey had been anxious to become Pope himself and had betrayed him. He decided to take over the running of the country and asked Wolsey to surrender the Great Seal of the Lord Chancellor and all his other offices except the Archbishopric of York. Wolsey was also ordered to leave Hampton Court and move to Esher, a few miles away. Informed that he was to be tried for numerous acts of high-handedness, for his defiance of the law, and for appropriating colossal sums of money for his own use (much of which was spent on the construction of Hampton Court), the fallen Chancellor sent a most pitiable appeal to the King for mercy. He even begged the French Ambassador, Cardinal du Bellay, with tears streaming down his cheeks, to plead with the French king to persuade Henry not to be too harsh. Though his lands and his goods were confiscated, he was allowed a pension of one thousand marks a year from one of his bishoprics, Winchester; and in addition he was given by the King a sum in cash and plate, which in present-day currency would be equal to nearly £100,000.

Without waiting for the divorce Henry moved into Hampton Court with Anne Boleyn in 1530. He sent a ring to Wolsey as a token of goodwill, and almost daily messages to give him comfort and hope; he even induced Anne, who loathed Wolsey, to send him 'with very gentle and comfortable words' a tablet of gold which she used to wear at her girdle.

Wolsey left for York in August 1530 and the rumour began to

circulate that he was contemplating flight. Slowly he made his way northward to fulfil his duties as Archbishop on 7 November. His entry into York with an escort of eight hundred horse enraged not only his successors in the various high offices he had vacated, but also the King, who had learned that a Papal bull had been issued forbidding his marriage with Anne and that he was about to be excommunicated.

Believing that Wolsey was responsible for this too, Henry decided to act swiftly. A Groom of the King's Chamber was sent north with guards to arrest Wolsey. They arrived while the Cardinal was having his dinner and set out with their prisoner by easy stages for London. On 22 November, while Wolsey was staying with the Earl of Shrewsbury at Sheffield, the Constable of the Tower of London arrived with a guard of twenty-four men to conduct him to the cell in the Tower that had been prepared for him. The charge was high treason, which meant execution. Abandoning all hope, Wolsey, whose health had been failing, was helped on to a horse and rode with difficulty to Leicester. There he died in the Abbey on the morning of 29 November 1530. He was fifty-five years old.

Before moving in with Anne Boleyn, the King had paid one more nostalgic visit with Catherine of Aragon to Hampton Court and stayed there for a few days with her. A letter to the Duke of Milan tells us that they 'paid each other reciprocally the greatest possible attention, or compliments in the Spanish fashion, with the utmost mental tranquility, as if there had never been any dispute whatever between them'.

But Henry was in fact busy all the time trying to get his divorce. He was in touch with divines and doctors of civil law in all the universities of Europe for their opinion that the King's marriage with his deceased brother's wife was contrary to divine and natural law and so should be declared null and void. Catherine, aware of this, was herself trying to get support for the sanctity of their marriage, yet, prompted by her devotion to him, kept insisting that Henry was only doing it 'for conscience's sake and not from any wanton appetite'.

Shortly after she had left, the King moved into Hampton Court with Anne Boleyn. Delighted though both were with their magnificent new country home, they began at once, while Wolsey was a few miles away at Esher, to make considerable structural alterations.

To begin with, Henry wanted to make it clear that this was now the King's Palace. So Wolsey's arms were taken down and the King's arms and badges were affixed all over the various buildings. On the gateways of the west front and the first or Base Court vast stone tablets were put up, elaborately carved with his arms. For three of these Edmund More of Kingston was paid £34 4s. 10d. Heraldic beasts began to appear everywhere. On every pinnacle and coping, on gables and battlements one now saw lions, dragons, leopards, hinds, harts, greyhounds and antelopes carrying gilded vanes, bearing the crown, rose, fleur-de-lys, and portcullis. Henry then bought the freehold of the house and land from the Knights of St John of Jerusalem.

Wolsey's main Chapel was most lavishly redecorated. A lovely ceiling was put in, made of wood painted blue and sprinkled with stars, and gorgeous with great carved and gilded pendants with little boys trumpeting from each pendant. The entrance to the Chapel is from the cloisters, but Henry VIII's Royal Closet is only accessible from the long gallery on the upper floor, known as the Haunted Gallery.

The house itself was enlarged. New rooms were built as well as new kitchens together with the 'offices appertaining to the same', such as pantries, butteries, spiceries, larders, dry-fish rooms and cellars. Work on all this was begun before Wolsey's death.

A new library, a new study and a number of smaller rooms were erected at about the same time. The King also put in an 'upmost gallery', the roof of which was of fine work, gilded and richly decorated with carved badges, leaves, balls, and angels with the King's mottoes on scrolls, and with most attractive cornices and casements. Wolsey had already provided a number of galleries, both at Hampton Court and at York House in London, which Henry had also now taken from him and was to convert into Whitehall Palace. These galleries were regarded with wonder and admiration by foreign visitors. A Venetian visitor Mario Savorgnano described the Hampton Court galleries as 'long porticoes or halls, without chambers, with windows on each side, looking on gardens or the river, the ceilings being marvellously wrought in stone with gold, and the wainscot of carved wood representing a thousand beautiful figures'.

In this late phase of Tudor Gothic architecture, influenced though it was by the Renaissance, the strict mathematical balance of windows and chimneys had not yet come into vogue; and so we see the battlements at different levels, and turrets placed here and there according to the position of the staircase, often with one higher than another, single windows, others in pairs or in threes, and some even grouped in fours and eights. They were put in where they were needed—that was what the master-builder took as his guide. They are delightfully attractive and have a natural charm that is lacking in the symmetrical arrangements one sees in Wren's later additions and alterations.

The entire interior of the building, Wolsey's section as well as the King's, was redecorated at enormous expense; so great indeed was the cost that the comparatively meek Thomas Cromwell, who eventually became Henry's Chief Minister, nervously cautious after what had happened to Wolsey, patiently watched the drain on the royal funds for three years and then timidly advised the King to hold up all further alterations at Hampton Court for a brief span of just one year, pointing out 'how profitable' that would be to His Majesty.

The details of the costs survive in twelve large folio volumes of about a thousand pages each, giving the name of every mason, brick-layer, carpenter, joiner, painter, carver, glazier, gilder, tiler, and even of the daily labourers together with the sum of money paid to each one. The cost of the material is also given and details of the work which help us to identify every moulding and carving, their colouring and gilding. A few foreign artists were employed by Henry, including Holbein, the painter, Toto del Nunziato (called Anthony Tote) and Lucca Penni (known as Bartholomew Penne): for example, the records state 'To Anthony Tote for the painting of 5 tables standing in the King's library—first one table of Joachin and St. Anne, another of Adam driven out of Paradise, another of the burying of Our Blessed Lady . . . £6 13s. 4d'.

The location of all Henry's structural changes cannot always be identified. We can recognise his kitchens and the butteries and sauceries he built round them. At the cloister end of the cellar a flight of stone steps leads up to the 'Drynkynge House', which is on the site of Wolsey's parlour 'next the cellar barre', but much larger.

The Chapel was partly rebuilt, though on the same plan. Around Clock Court Henry remodelled the west side and also made certain alterations to the east side: it was often referred to as 'The Inner Court where the fountain standeth'—a fountain, decorated with many heraldic beasts, was put in by Henry VIII. The whole of Wolsey's Watching Chamber block was demolished and rebuilt on a more extensive scale.

The King added a new quadrangle, called Cloister Green Court, to the east of Wolsey's buildings, where Wren's Fountain Court is now: this section was assigned to the royal apartments. At the west gatehouse a stone bridge was erected across the moat to replace Wolsey's wooden bridge.

Henry's most impressive alteration was the demolition of Wolsey's Great Hall and the erection of a far grander structure. So eager was the King to get the work done rapidly that tallow candles were used by the workmen at night so that darkness should not cause inter-ruption. For this night work His Majesty agreed to pay overtime rates. The bricks were brought from Taplow in Buckinghamshire, the stone from Reigate in Surrey and from the Cotswolds, and the firmer white stone from Caen in Normandy—as William the Conqueror had once had Caen stone brought for the White Tower of the Tower of London. The timber, chiefly oak, was brought from Dorking and Banstead in Surrey, as well as from St John's Wood, then north-west of London.

The Great Hall is one hundred and six feet in length, or ninety-seven excluding the dais, by forty feet in width, and sixty feet in height to the spectacular roof. The original heraldic coloured glass in the windows was made by Galyon Hone, the 'Kynges Glasier' in 1534, but the glass here now is all Victorian. The great east window shows the descent of Henry VIII from Edward III and also the union of the Houses of York and Lancaster by the marriage of Henry's father and mother. In the two upper lights are the arms of the Kingdom of France, the Kingdom of England, the Lordship of Ireland, and the Principality of Wales. In the upper spaces of the great west window are displayed the arms, badges, and cyphers of Henry VIII, with a representation of himself in the centre light and, on the two flanks, the arms and badges of his six wives and his three children. No less than forty-eight lights were fitted to the great bay window which rises from the floor to the ceiling and illumines the dais on which the King dined. At the lower end is a screen of deep-toned oak with a minstrel gallery above; behind this are the main entrances to the Hall—the one on the south side leads down a flight of stone steps to the so-called Anne Boleyn Gateway built by Wolsey and embellished by Henry.

The roof of great hammer beams, one of the finest in the country, is abundantly ornate and contains features that no other Gothic roof has. The large, beautifully carved pendants from the hammer beams, Italian Renaissance in style, were carved by Richard Rydge of London. Henry had a partiality for gold leaf and used it both inside and outside the house. All the timbers of the Great Hall roof were picked out in gold. The centre of the roof, immediately above the open fireplace on the Hall floor, was fitted with an elaborate vent or louvre for the escape of smoke from the large logs burning below. The louvre, now gone, was made of wood and consisted of three tiers, diminishing in size with open-work at the sides and leaden roofs. The walls of the Hall were covered with rich tapestries, eight of them representing incidents in the life of Abraham, and their overall length extending to eight hundred and twenty-six yards. These appear to have been acquired by Henry, not Wolsey. Under the Hall are the vast wine cellars.

The Great Hall was used for such state functions as banquets and receptions. Jane Seymour and in her turn Catherine Howard sat with the King at the high table on the dais, and it was in this Hall that Catherine Parr, Henry's sixth and last wife, was proclaimed Queen on 12 July 1543. In this Hall too Henry had his numerous masques; and on the stage, at the screen end of the Hall, to entertain the King and his guests, the players of the Royal Theatre performed.

Henry's Great Watching Chamber, which adjoins the Great Hall, was used as the guard-room. It is sixty-two feet long, twenty-nine feet in width and twenty-nine and a half feet in height. The ceiling is flat, with moulded oak ribs, and enriched with panels ornamented with medallions displaying the arms and badges of Henry VIII, with a few of Jane Seymour. They are rich and strikingly attractive.

On the walls hang the most beautiful tapestries in the Palace, some of which belonged to Wolsey and adorned his rooms when he lived there. The most interesting, belonging to the finest period of Flemish art, illustrate Petrarch's 'Triumphs of Love' and tell the story of 'The Seven Deadly Sins'.

One other imposing room built by Henry was the Presence Chamber, which adjoined the Watching Chamber; it had two bay windows overlooking the Inner or Clock Court: not much more is known of it, for unfortunately it was destroyed in the course of alterations made two centuries later.

For outdoor sports Henry had an inexhaustible enthusiasm. Nine acres of land, on the left as one enters the Palace grounds through the outer gates, were made into the Tilt Yard for the staging of mock-military contests on horseback. Here richly decorated lists, or palisades, were set up and five towers erected, displaying arms and banners, for guests to watch the numerous jousts, fought by two men, and the tournaments by two teams. The jousts lasted several hours, the tournaments went on for two or three days. Henry, a superb horseman, took part in both. His agility as a young man was astonishing. Clad in full armour, he was able to jump with great dexterity on and off his horses, 'making them', as Giustiniani exclaimed, 'fly rather than leap, to the delight and ecstasy of all'.

The tournaments were even more exciting. The spectators, clad in satin and velvet of many colours, sat on stages all round the Tilt Yard. As the teams rode into the lists, gorgeously equipped, attended by squires and pages, heralds and trumpeters, all in glittering array, the audience of dazzlingly dressed women, already excited about one or other of the teams, became even more excited. Soon the trumpets sounded, there was a clash of steel and the tournament had begun.

When the King took part in the contest he was preceded into the lists by the Marshal dressed in cloth of gold and thirty footmen in livery of yellow and blue. Then came drummers and trumpeters, all in white damask; then forty knights and lords in splendid attire, riding in pairs. Even the horses 'had silver chainwork and a number of pendant bells'. At the end of this long procession came the King, wearing a surcoat of silver cloth, accompanied by thirty gentlemen on foot dressed in velvet and white satin. Twice round the lists the procession circled before the tournament began. Henry's own armour, showing his great size as he grew older, can now be seen in the Tower of London.

Archery was another of his diversions. He used the famous Welsh long-bow introduced into the English army by his ancestor Edward I:

Anne Boleyn and her brother Lord Rochford were equally enthusiastic and often shot at the butts with him. Henry was engaged in archery practice when Wolsey's gentleman-usher George Cavendish arrived at Hampton Court to tell him that the Cardinal was dead. Cavendish's account in its original spelling ran thus:

> And perceyvyng hyme occupied in shotying, I thought it not my dewtie to troble him; but leaned to a tree entendying to stand there, so to attend hys gracious pleasyr. Beying in a great study, at last the Kyng came sodynly behynd me where I stode, and clappt his hand uppon my sholder; and whan I percyved hyme, I fyll uppon my knee; to whome he sayd, callying me by name, I woll, quod he, make an end of my game and then woll I talke with you, and so departed to his marke, whereat the game was endyd. Then the Kyng delyvered hys bowe to the yoman of hys bows, and went his way inward to the palace, whom I followed.

He waited while the King changed his clothes and put on a night-gown of velvet furred with sable. Cavendish knelt again and remained on his knees throughout the interview which lasted an hour. Memories of Wolsey's friendship and long years of service affected the King, who said: 'I would rather than twenty thousand pounds that he had lived', ignoring the fact that Wolsey had been on his way to die in the Tower.

Henry laid out two bowling alleys at Hampton Court, one of which was two hundred and seventy feet long: neither of these alleys has survived. But more than bowling he loved tennis. He played it often and was considered extremely good at the game. The covered tennis court that Henry built at Hampton Court is the oldest in England (its present windows are later). Quite different from lawn tennis, 'real' tennis as it is now called is still played regularly there and in similar courts elsewhere in England. The records tell of the games Henry VIII played on this court. One entry states that on 15 December 1531 five shillings was paid 'to one that served on the King's side at tennis', other items note the bets he lost to his opponents and to the spectators: there were always large numbers of them in the gallery under the penthouse when the King played. 'It is the prettiest thing in the world,' wrote Giustiniani, the Venetian ambassador, 'to see him play, his fair skin glowing through a shirt of the finest texture.' Special tennis shoes and drawers were made for him and after the game he put on a tennis coat of blue and black velvet. Round the tennis court dressing-rooms had been built, as well as lodgings for the Master of the Court, markers, and servers.

Fishing was also one of his delights, Not only did he fish in the Thames while at Hampton Court, but he also had all the garden ponds well stocked for his own and his courtiers' diversion.

His great love was for music. There were virginals, clavichords, portable organs, viols, flutes, lutes, and recorders in Hampton Court and in all his other palaces. A number of these instruments he could play well, especially the organ, the harpsichord and the lute. His singing was highly praised—his fine powerful voice, it has been said, could be heard echoing in the courts and cloisters of Hampton Court. It is well known that he composed poetry, some of it in French. Many of his lyrics became very popular during his lifetime. His favourite composition was 'Pastime in Good Company' in which he tells of his delight in hunting, dancing and love, insisting that youth 'must have some dalliance'. In others he tries to justify his constancy, saying

> As the holly groweth green and never changeth hue,
> So I am—ever have been unto my lady true.

He was fond of books and moved all Wolsey's books from York Place, when he took it over, to Hampton Court. Skilful in theological subtleties, he contributed a preface to a religious treatise published in 1543 and known as 'the King's book'. Apart from French, he could also speak Spanish, Italian, and Latin. His other indoor diversions were such games as backgammon, dicing, and shovel-board. Often he gambled for money, obsessively as time went on, losing as much as £3,500 in a year.

Though Henry moved into Hampton Court with Anne Boleyn early in 1530, he did not marry her until three years later.

Divorce from Catherine still eluded him. On 11 August 1530 Henry called a meeting of the clergy at Hampton Court with William Warham, Archbishop of Canterbury, at their head, and lawyers led by Sir Thomas More, Wolsey's successor as Lord Chancellor. They were told 'to ascertain whether, in virtue of the privilege possessed by this kingdom, Parliament could and would enact that, notwithstanding the Pope's prohibition, this cause of the divorce should be decided by the Archbishop of Canterbury'.

The discussions were prolonged but nothing was achieved. Henry then tried to influence the Pope by threatening to set aside his authority in England if the divorce were not granted. The Papal Nuncio was invited to Hampton Court and was told by the King that he was set on having the divorce.

If his Holiness would not show him in future more consideration than at present, the King would take up his pen and let the world know that the Pope possessed no greater authority than that held by Moses, which was only grounded on the declaration and interpretation of the Holy Scripture, everything beyond that being mere usurpation and tyranny; and that, should he be driven to take such a step, the damage and injury thereby inflicted on the Apostolic See would be irreparable and far more fatal than that caused by all the writings of others, for with his learning and rank, Kings, Princes and all others would side with him.

Soon the verdict sought from the divines and doctors of the universities of Europe was made known. Naples, Charles V's kingdom, was against the divorce; so understandably was Spain; but Padua and Bologna were for the divorce. The opinions from Germany were divided. The Universities of Oxford and Cambridge supported the King. Parliament was summoned, but their deliberations went on unendingly. In the end, the House of Commons, the majority of whom disliked the Catholic clergy and wanted to get rid of the Pope, gave the King the verdict he wanted.

The marriage with Catherine was not annulled until 23 May 1533. In the preceding winter Anne Boleyn was found to be pregnant and Henry married her in January 1533, four months before he was legally free to do so.

Meanwhile Anne and the King had continued to live at Hampton Court. Special lodgings were being built for Anne by Wolsey, but he left before their completion. A completely new range of State Apartments for her was now being constructed by Henry, on a scale that dwarfed the former Queen's lodgings and surpassed it in splendour. They were being erected in a new quadrangle to the east of Clock Court where Wolsey had his Privy Garden. Anne never lived in them. She was sent to the Tower while the builders were still at work.

Nothing was denied her by the King. The gifts came in an unending stream. Spending Christmas at Hampton Court in 1530, he gave her £100 and followed it up with another £180 and then £40. In addition he bought her furs, crimson cloth of gold, crimson satin, and purple velvet; a costume to wear for archery and shooting gloves, a number of bows and arrows. A lovely nightgown of black satin edged with black velvet and lined with black fur cost the King £101 15s. 8d.—in all he spent on her clothes £500 in three years, the equivalent of a very princely sum in our money.

Waiting for his divorce, Henry moved restlessly from one palace to another, staying at Greenwich, Richmond, Windsor, or Hunsdon in Hertfordshire, or Whitehall, or his Palace in the Tower of London. The Imperial Ambassador Chapuys reported in his despatch to Vienna: 'I sent one of my men to Hampton Court to ask for an audience from the King, but he was already gone to Windsor and other places to amuse himself and pass away the time, accompanied only by the Lady, Anne Boleyn, who in these excursions rode behind him on his pillion. . . . For the last fortnight he has done little else but go from place to place. . . .'

Even when not in residence the King kept a vast number of retainers at Hampton Court—gentlemen-ushers, grooms-in-waiting, yeomen, waiters, cup-bearers, and hordes of other servants. When His Majesty was there his Ministers, Privy Councillors and other high officers of State, all of whom brought their own retainers as well as servants, swelled the total to well over a thousand. Spread out over the many buildings and lodgings of the Palace most of the servants were never seen and discipline was impossible to enforce, as Wolsey had found, for he had kept issuing directives for 'the establishment of good order and the reformation of sundry errors and misuses'.

Things were far worse for the King with the greatly increased number of motley hirelings. Locks were being wrenched off doors. Thefts occurred all the time. Even large pieces of furniture such as tables and chairs and at times also cupboards were stolen. Often many of the rooms and public galleries were left unswept. The King insisted that all the galleries, courts and other parts of the Palace must be swept and cleaned twice a day by the scullions and that no dishes, saucers, or vessels should be left lying about or remains of food thrown about the place. The penalty was imprisonment. No one was allowed to keep greyhounds, mastiffs, hounds, or other dogs at Hampton Court. A few spaniels belonging to ladies were permitted 'with the King's or Queen's permission'.

Five months after her marriage Anne was crowned Queen at Westminster Abbey with a splendour that had never been equalled. Shortly afterwards the King and the new Queen went to Hampton Court for their honeymoon. There were banquets and masques in the Great Hall. Despite her advanced pregnancy Anne's delight in dancing was indulged to the full; she even joined in most of the outdoor sports—hunting, bowls, and long-bow archery.

Sir Thomas More, who was to find himself in the Tower for refusing to acknowledge Henry's supremacy over the Pope, exclaimed at the new Queen's passion for dancing: 'These dances of hers will prove such dances that she will spurn our heads off like footballs, but it will not be long ere her head will dance the like dance.'

As the time drew near for her confinement, she settled down to her needlework. Some of it was most attractive and was on display at Hampton Court throughout the reign of her daughter Elizabeth. For music she had a modest talent: she was particularly proficient on the virginals and often accompanied the King when he sang. During these months of waiting, Henry treated her with tenderness. He was acutely disappointed when the child born on 7 September 1533 at Greenwich was a girl.

It is inaccurate to assume, as some do, that Henry's love for Anne Boleyn was so all-absorbing that he had no glances to spare for other women at Court and that he remained devoted to her until evidence was brought to him of her unfaithfulness.

As early as their first Christmas together at Hampton Court, when he was heaping gifts and money on her, Henry's roving eye began to linger on a number of very pretty ladies. One could not fail to see signs that he was getting tired of Anne. Her quick temper irritated him. Her rebukes he resented angrily. Unprepared to suffer them, he would turn away abruptly; and before long he was involved in some ardent flirtations, which were not likely to improve his wife's temper. He had himself noticed that she was too free and flirtatious with some of the courtiers. But what disturbed the King most was her inability to provide an heir. The pregnancy which led to her marriage produced only a daughter, the future Queen Elizabeth. In the following year, 1534, she had a miscarriage and in January 1536, a day or so after the death of Catherine of Aragon, Anne had a premature confinement and that child died. This was caused by the shock to Anne of seeing, as she entered one of the rooms (in Hampton Court, it is believed, though there is no certainty of this), a beautiful lady-in-waiting, Jane Seymour, 'seated on Henry's knee, receiving his caresses with every appearance of complacency'.

Understandably, Anne flew into a rage and wept as she protested. 'Be at peace, sweetheart,' Henry warned her, 'and all shall be well with thee.' Her stormy outburst led to the premature birth of the child she was carrying. It was a boy. The King, being told of it, went angrily into her room and blamed her for the loss of his son. She pointed out that it was entirely his fault.

It was then that he decided to seek a fresh consort. Events provided him with the means to get rid of Anne very quickly. Evidence was found to convict her of adultery with two courtiers named Sir Henry Norris and William Brereton and a Court musician Mark Smeaton, as well as incest with her brother Lord Rochford. She was arrested and sent to the Tower. On the night of her execution some months later, the King had supper with Jane Seymour and ten days later he married her. She was four years younger than Anne, not as attractive, but quiet, reserved, gentle and most considerate; the change from the noisy, eye-rolling vivacity of Anne was to Henry a pleasing contrast.

Work on Anne's apartments, called the Queen's New Lodgings, went on uninterrupted. The largest and most magnificent room was the Queen's Long Gallery, one hundred and eighty feet long and twenty-five feet wide: it had numerous windows, richly emblazoned with heraldic glass displaying arms and badges. Some changes were now necessary and they were speedily carried out. Every badge of Anne's, showing the falcon beside the royal rose or a portcullis and the initials 'A & H' in a true lover's knot, were now removed. Only in the lovely groined ceiling of the Clock Tower arch was her initial overlooked. Even the figure of St Anne in stained glass in the east window of the Chapel was taken down. Everywhere new initials were displayed, a 'J' joined the 'H' now in true lover's knots.

But Jane did not move into Hampton Court at once: it was well over a year later, on 16 September 1537, that she took up her residence there with Henry awaiting the birth of her expected baby. It is thought that she occupied the Queen's New Lodgings. On Friday, October 12, St Edward's day, in the King's presence at Hampton Court, she presented him with the heir he had so long wanted. The baby was named Edward and, though weak and ailing, he seemed likely to live and in fact survived to succeed Henry.

Not the King alone, but the entire nation rejoiced when the joyous news was announced. Bells were rung in almost every town in England. *Te Deums* were sung in the churches. Bonfires were lit all over the country. The child was christened three days later in the Chapel at Hampton Court, freshly decorated for the purpose, with new stained-glass windows and a new organ in a newly built organ-house with an attractive arched roof and great pendants of angels holding escutcheons bearing the arms of the King and Queen.

A great procession was formed to escort the young heir from his nursery, to the north of the Chapel, by a long circuitous route to the Chapel. They assembled in Chapel Court, eighty knights, gentlemen and squires, walking two by two and carrying unlit torches, to be lighted after the christening. Behind them came the singers, mostly children, and the dean and chaplains in their copes and surplices. The King's Council followed; then foreign ambassadors with their suites. After them came two lords bearing 'a pair of covered basins, and a towel upon that and a cup of assay' for the wine. 'Next after, a taper of virgin wax borne by the Earl of Wiltshire'—Anne Boleyn's father—'with a towel about his neck'; then 'a salt of gold, richly garnished with pearl and stone', was borne by the Earl of Essex, with a towel about his neck. The chrisom, the white robe for the child to wear, was placed in the tiny hands of the King's daughter, the Lady Elizabeth, who, being only four years old, was carried by two lords. Behind Elizabeth was the royal baby, borne on cushions by the Marchioness of Exeter assisted by the Duke of Suffolk and the Marquess of Exeter. The train of the child's robe was held by the Earl of Arundel, behind whom were the midwife and a nurse. Four gentlemen of the King's Privy Chamber held a large canopy over the child as they walked, with four others holding torches. Princess Mary, Henry's elder daughter, for whom Jane Seymour had a deep affection, was godmother. Twenty-one years old now, she walked behind the canopy escorted by 'ladies of honour and gentlewomen in order after their degrees'.

The procession went through the Council Chamber, then along the gallery (now known as the Haunted Gallery) to the Watching Chamber beside the Great Hall, then through the Hall itself, under the screens, down the Great Stairs, through Anne Boleyn's Gateway (the inner gate tower in Base Court, which Henry had embellished and named after her) into the next court, the Clock Court, which was strewn with fresh rushes from the river and lined by men-at-arms carrying their halberds; then through the Cloister to the Chapel door.

There was a hush as the procession entered the Chapel, freshly hung with tapestries. On the altar were gold cups and plates and a gold crucifix. The font, of solid silver gilt, was 'set upon a mount or stage made of four degrees in height and eight square in compass, enclosed with double barriers of timber' hung with cloth of gold, with a rich canopy over the font. A pan of hot coals kept the Chapel warm. Behind a screen the nurse prepared the young prince for his christening, while the choir sang the *Te Deum*. After the ceremony the heir was brought to his parents: the King did not walk in the procession but stayed with Queen Jane in her bedchamber.

Jane Seymour did not live long after the boy's birth, a difficult

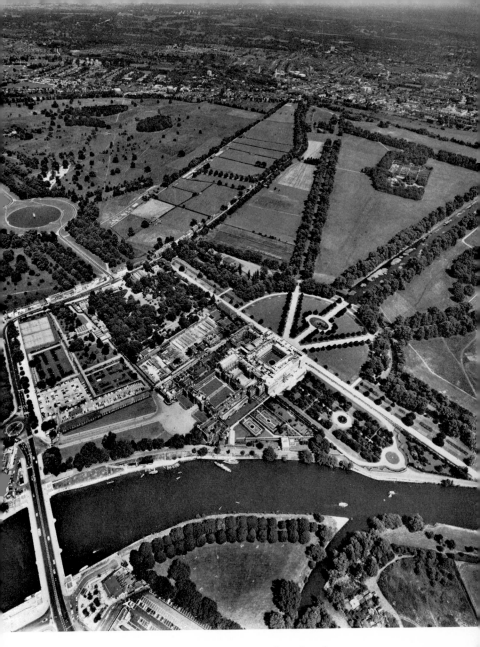

Aerial view of Hampton Court with its parks and gardens

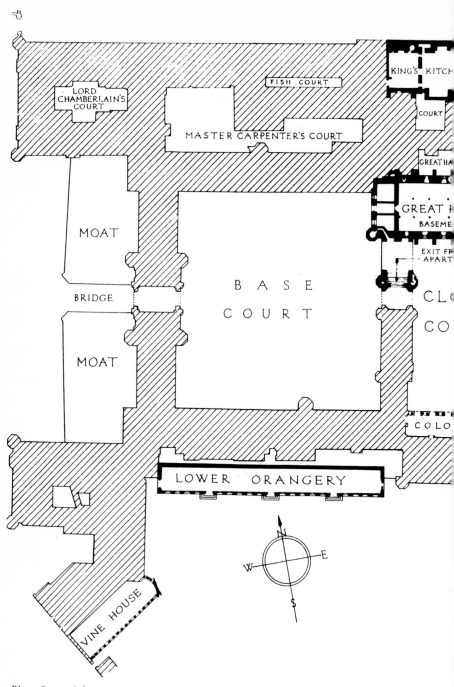

Plan of ground floor, showing rooms open to the public

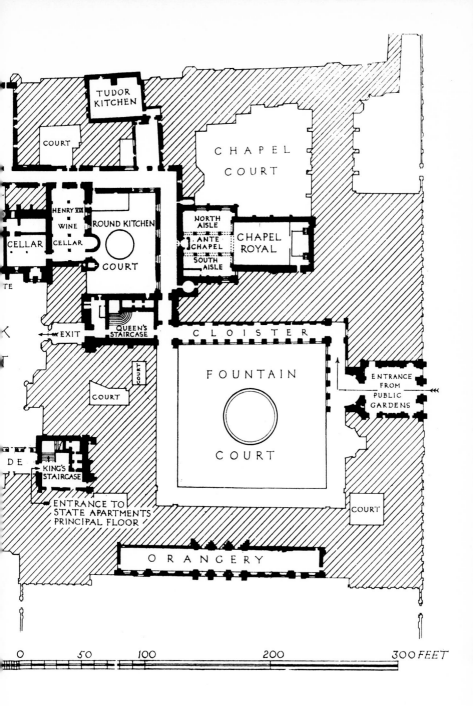

TUDOR KITCHEN

COURT

CHAPEL COURT

HENRY VIII WINE CELLAR

ROUND KITCHEN COURT

CELLAR

TE

NORTH AISLE

ANTE CHAPEL

SOUTH AISLE

CHAPEL ROYAL

EXIT

QUEEN'S STAIRCASE

CLOISTER

FOUNTAIN COURT

ENTRANCE FROM PUBLIC GARDENS

COURT

COURT

K

DE

KING'S STAIRCASE

ENTRANCE TO STATE APARTMENTS PRINCIPAL FLOOR

COURT

ORANGERY

0   50   100   200   300 FEET

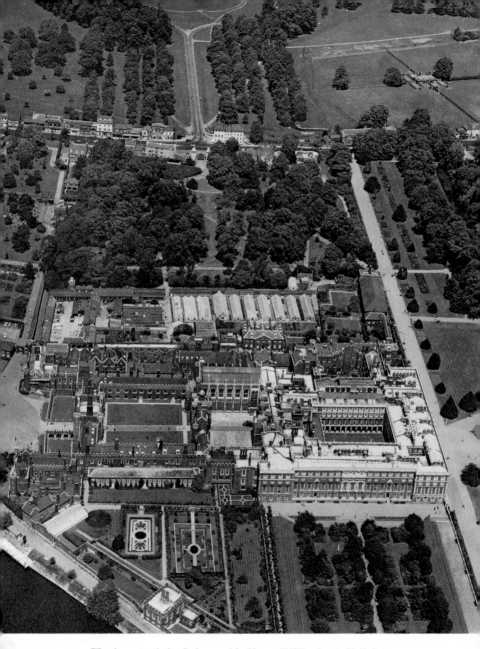

The lay-out of the Palace, with Henry VIII's Great Hall between Wolsey's Tudor buildings on the left and Wren's vast Renaissance structure

confinement; it is believed that a Caesarian operation was necessary. It is said that the King, being asked by Dr Owen, who performed the operation, whether he wished the boy or his wife to be saved, replied: 'The child by all means; other wives can easily be found.'

She died twelve days after the child's birth at eight o'clock in the morning of Wednesday, October 24. Thomas Cromwell, the Lord Privy Seal, who had taken part in the christening procession with the Duke of Norfolk, the Lord Chancellor, and the Archbishop of Canterbury, wrote that Jane's death was caused by 'the fault of them that were about her. which suffered her to take great cold and to eat things that her fantasy in sickness called for'.

Henry, deeply stricken by grief, left Hampton Court for Windsor to avoid seeing the embalming of his wife's body. She lay in state in the Presence Chamber, alongside the Great Watching Chamber. Twenty-four tall tapers were lighted around her and the walls were draped with black. An altar was set up, masses were said, and dirges sung night and day for a whole week. Princess Mary and the ladies of the Court, dressed in deep mourning with white kerchiefs over their heads and shoulders, knelt and kept constant watch round her.

At the end of the week, after it had been sprinkled with holy water and blessed, the Queen's body was moved to the Chapel, from where the coffin was later taken to Clock Court and placed on a funeral car drawn by four horses draped in black velvet, with escutcheons of the King's and Queen's arms beaten in fine gold, and the same arms on each horse's forehead. On the bier was a life-sized wax representation of the Queen, with a crown of gold upon its head, the fair hair loose, a sceptre of gold in the right hand, finger-rings set with precious stones and necklaces adorned with gold and stones. The head rested on a cloth-of-gold pillow, the shoes were of cloth of gold too. Princess Mary, who was the chief mourner, rode with the ladies of the Court on horses caparisoned in black velvet. As the funeral entourage made its way to St George's Chapel at Windsor for Jane's burial, Princess Mary distributed alms to the poor. It was believed then, and is still believed, that Jane, clothed in white, haunted the Queen's apartments, emerging from a doorway with a lighted taper in her hand, proceeding up the stairs to the Silver-Stick Gallery.

At the King's wish the young Prince Edward continued to reside in the Royal Nursery at Hampton Court with a vast household of stewards and nurses under the supervision of a chamberlain, a vice-chamberlain, and a dean. Orders were issued as to the food to be served him and the water he drank, all of it tested beforehand by a reliable staff. The King did not return to Hampton Court until November of the following year; the records do not make clear whether His Majesty visited his heir during that time. Princess Mary, who lived in the nearby palace of Richmond, came often on horseback.

Building operations continued after Jane's death. The next section to be completed was the King's New Lodgings, which formed the southern side of Henry's new quadrangle, the Queen's New Lodgings forming the eastern side. When completed the quadrangle was known as Cloister Green Court.

Henry's additions and alterations to Wolsey's Hampton Court went on for years. At the entrance to the Palace he built two projecting wings, one on each side of the Great Gatehouse, cutting right across the moat. To the south, between the Palace and the river, a great many towers and turrets were erected, connected by galleries which formed an irregular line from the south-east corner of Inner Court to the river, where yet another tower was put up flanked with turrets and stairs leading down to a water-gate, which the King used when he came to Hampton Court by barge. Connected with it was the Water Gallery and, on adjoining ground raised on 250,000 bricks and known as the Mount, he built a three-storeyed summer-house called the Great Round Arbour, which was composed almost entirely of windows. The path spiralling up 'like the turns in a cockleshell' was lined by the King's heraldic beasts on bases painted with white and green stripes: figures of lions, greyhounds, dragons, panthers, hinds, bulls, harts, leopards, and antelopes. Behind these two structures was 'The King's Long Gallery' which ran eastward into the Park with a beautifully furnished room called Paradise, the tapestries on the walls, we are told, being covered with pearls; foreign visitors were enchanted by this room: one called it 'the most eminent room of all—it captivates the eye'.

The gardens and parks were also given Henry's fullest attention. Three new gardens were laid out. One of these, the Mount garden, was made round the summerhouse by the river. Another was the Privy Garden, with parterres, separated by low walls and pebbled paths forming a variety of designs. In the flowerbeds all the plants were English—violets, roses, gillyflowers, and so on. Rosemary, 'for remembrance', and for its scent, was the most treasured of evergreen plants. There were grass plots and flowery bowers for the summer, dry walks and sheltered alleys for wintry and wet weather. Then there was the Pond Garden with its numerous ponds. Sundials and heraldic beasts on pedestals with shields displaying the King's arms abounded. Henry also had kitchen gardens and two orchards to the north of the Palace. The head gardener was Edmund Griffiths, and under him were hundreds of gardeners, each receiving fourpence a day.

The two parks, Bushey and Home Park, separated from each other by a public road running from Hampton to Kingston, were well stocked with game; but as Henry grew older, fatter, and disinclined to go far afield for his sport, he began to purchase estates all round Hampton Court: they stretched for miles, taking in Teddington, Hanworth, Walton-on-Thames, Sandown, Byfleet and West Molesey, and Esher.

The residents in those areas complained that their commons and meadows and pastures were being taken to stock with deer. But they complained only to each other: they dared not raise their voices, for they were well aware of Henry's temper.

Henry's fourth marriage did not take place until three years later. The long interval had been caused by the search on which Thomas Cromwell, his chief minister, had embarked for a suitable bride among the many beautiful young women the King was led to believe could be found in Europe. The painter Hans Holbein the younger was sent on a tour of the principalities and dukedoms to paint portraits of the most attractive of the eligible women. Almost two years had passed by the time he returned with a portrait of Anne of Cleves. In order not to strain the King's impatience further, Cromwell led him to believe that Holbein's portrait (now in the Louvre), which was in fact most flattering, did not do justice to Anne's beauty. Henry was quite excited. Redecoration of his palaces and his ships was begun. She left Düsseldorf in October 1539 and crossed from Calais to Deal in a rough sea, accompanied at the command of the King by a convoy of fifty ships.

Henry was flabbergasted when he arrived at Rochester to greet her. 'I like her not! I like her not!' he kept saying; 'I am ashamed that men have praised her as they have done. I love her not.' At thirty-four she would not then have been considered young; moreover she was tall, thin, pockmarked, and completely lacking in charm. Her manner was austere, there was not the merest hint of gaiety in her. Not only was she unable to speak either English or French, the only language in which she could converse was Low German, of which Henry was completely ignorant. Her knowledge of music is said to have been nil. What he was to do with her Henry was at a complete loss to understand. He turned away and returned to the barge which had brought him to Rochester.

It was clear to everyone that Henry was extremely angry. 'If I had known so much before, she had no coming hither,' he stormed at Cromwell, who, he felt, had played a prominent part in his deception. 'What remedy now?' he bellowed.

Cromwell could think of nothing to say. But after a moment, he risked the remark: 'Me thinketh she hath a queenly manner withal.'

It was difficult to find a way out. Henry realised that if he cast her aside now, her humiliation would enrage not only the Protestant princes in Germany to whom she was related, but also the Emperor Charles V. Henry said: 'If it were not that she is come so far into England and for fear of making a ruffle in the world, and driving her brother (the Duke of Cleves) into the Emperor and the French King's hands, I would never have her; but now it is too far gone.'

So he married her not many days later, trying as best he could to hide his disgust. The marriage did not last long: he refused to sleep with her. Within four months he began to prepare for their divorce. He argued that she had been engaged to marry the Duke of Lorraine and had never been released from that contract; and for good measure he added that he found her personally repugnant.

The marriage was ended a few days later. During their brief spell together, it is not surprising that Anne of Cleves saw very little of Hampton Court. She spent a few days there without him while waiting for her divorce, and then moved to the palace at Richmond.

The moment she left, Henry arrived at Hampton Court with Catherine Howard, who was to be his fifth wife. It was here in the gardens that they did their courting. Often at night they were seen walking together by the moat or sitting in one of the arbours. If the weather was bad they sat in a window-seat holding hands and looking into each other's eyes.

Their marriage, it is believed, since there is no record of place or date, took place at Hampton Court some months later, possibly on 8 August 1540, for Catherine was presented on that day as the new Queen in the Chapel.

Like her cousin Anne Boleyn, Catherine Howard had been a Maid of Honour at the Court and it was while she was in attendance on Anne of Cleves that Henry fell in love with her. The King, stout by now, was nearly fifty, the bride about thirty years younger. Small and slight in build, she had roguish hazel eyes and auburn hair and was the prettiest of all his wives. Unlike her cousin Anne Boleyn, who was hard and calculating, Catherine had a gay and pleasing vivacity.

During their honeymoon at Hampton Court the King had the impressive astronomical clock put up on the tower in Clock Court and it can still be seen there. It is said to have been designed by Nicholas Cratzer—a German horologist brought to England by Wolsey and also responsible for a similar clock at Wolsey's college

47

at Oxford—and was constructed by Nicholas Oursian. The dial, set in a stone frame, is about fifteen feet square, with Henry VIII's initials and badges at the four corners. It has three copper discs of different sizes, one set over the other and revolving at different speeds. It tells the hour of the day, the day of the month, the position of the sun, the phases of the moon, the signs of the zodiac, and the time of high water at London Bridge.

Later that year the King and Catherine left Hampton Court, but returned on 19 December and stayed for four or five months, during which the Privy Council met there every day for the transaction of State business. For only a part of the summer of 1541 were the King and Queen away and they returned to Hampton Court on 24 October.

Brought up by her step-grandmother, the Duchess of Norfolk, Catherine had had a lax girlhood, with lovers creeping by night into the dormitory which she shared with other young girls. Of this past nothing was told to the King before the marriage, but by now rumours had begun to circulate.

On All Saints' Day, the King and Queen received the Sacrament in the Chapel at Hampton Court and Henry asked the Bishop of Lincoln to offer up a prayer of thanks to God for the good life he had with his new Queen. As he emerged from the Chapel Cranmer, the Archbishop of Canterbury, handed to the King a document setting out the facts about Catherine's past. At first Henry refused to believe it; nevertheless he ordered four members of the Council to make full inquiries. Catherine was confined to her room and the King left Hampton Court the next morning. He never saw her again.

The inquiries confirmed all that had been said and provided further evidence of her unfaithfulness since her marriage. Confronted with this by the Council, Catherine at first denied it, but eventually she confessed. Cranmer found her in such lamentation 'as I never saw no creature'. Under armed escort she was moved out of Hampton Court and taken to Syon House a few miles down the river. It had been a monastery; it was now furnished modestly for her and she was allowed to take her clothes and a few ladies of the Court, but not the jewels that had been lavished on her by the King. The men involved—one of them was Thomas Culpepper, a gentleman of the King's Privy Chamber—were sent to the Tower of London and executed. On 10 February 1542 she was taken there too. At the scaffold two days later she said: 'I have sinned grievously. If

I had married the man I loved instead of being dazzled by ambition, all would have been well. I die a Queen, but I would rather have died the wife of Culpepper.'

Henry, shocked and deeply grieved, aged suddenly. He gave way to his grief. His heart, we are told, was 'pierced with pensiveness ... and finally, with plenty of tears, which was strange in his courage'.

Nevertheless, less than eighteen months later he married his sixth wife. Catherine Parr, the daughter of Sir Thomas Parr, was thirty-one and had been widowed twice, the first time on the death of her aged husband Lord Borough, when she was only sixteen, and again on the death of Lord Latimer. Both had left her vast estates. She was by now in love with Sir Thomas Seymour, a brother of Henry's third wife, an ambitious, scheming man who had been trying unsuccessfully to marry one of the King's daughters. Nevertheless on 12 July 1543 she was married to Henry in the Holyday Closet adjoining the Chapel at Hampton Court. The ceremony was attended by barely a score of people. They included the King's two daughters, Mary and Elizabeth. The Queen gave Mary £20: we are not told what she gave Elizabeth, who was nine at the time. This honeymoon too was spent at Hampton Court. The Queen was quiet, gentle, kind-hearted. Henry could be sure she would not betray him.

The royal couple returned to Hampton Court for Christmas. The new Queen's two brothers, Lord Parr, now made the Earl of Essex, and Sir William Parr, now Lord Parr of Horton, were among the Yuletide guests. Another was the Earl of Surrey, poet son of the Duke of Norfolk, whose gift to English poetry was the use of blank verse and who was jointly responsible, with the poet Thomas Wyatt, for the introduction of the sonnet. He wrote a number of lyrics about 'Fair Geraldine', whom he had first loved at Hampton Court, as he reveals in the following lines:

> Hunsdon did first present her to mine eyne;
> Bright is her hue, and Geraldine she hight.
> Hampton me taught to wish her first for mine;
> And Windsor, alas! doth chase me from her sight.

Surrey, aged twenty-five, was already married and Fair Geraldine, who has been identified as Lady Elizabeth Fitzgerald, a lady-in-waiting to Princess Mary, was only fourteen. A portrait of Surrey, attributed to Hans Holbein, may still be seen at Hampton Court.

The week after Christmas Henry, an ally now of the Emperor Charles V, received at Hampton Court in great state 'Ferdinando de Gonzaga, Viceroy of Sicily, Prince of Malfeta and Captain-General of the Army of the Emperor Charles', who had come because of the war that had broken out with France, to discuss what arrangements should be made for the invasion of France by the allied forces. The entertainment was lavish. On his departure the Emperor's Captain-General was presented with a gold plate weighing one hundred and fifty-three ounces and a gilt plate weighing four thousand ounces. Henry left Hampton Court later and went to Boulogne to take command of the English army.

During his absence the Queen stayed at the Palace with her three step-children, Mary, Elizabeth, and Edward. On the King's return to England in October he joined them at Hampton Court and spent a great deal of time there. Indeed during the little more than two years that remained to him of life Henry, old now at fifty-three, grossly fat, and suffering acutely from an ulcerated leg, stayed there almost continuously. Strenuous outdoor sports, such as hunting, had to be abandoned, but he was able to play bowls and an occasional game of tennis, which he loved so much. Cards, backgammon, and shovel-board diverted him indoors: he read a great deal and of course he had his music. There is a miniature painting of Henry, old and fat, seated on a low stool playing the lute while his jester Will Somers, not wearing cap-and-bells (jesters very rarely did), sings to his accompaniment.

In the summer of 1546, a few months before he died, Henry gave his last great reception. It was for the French ambassador Claude d'Annebaut, Lord High Admiral of France, who had come to ratify the treaty that ended the war. Riding to Hampton Court, the ambassador was met on the way by Prince Edward, then eight years old, and an escort of five hundred and forty men wearing the Prince's livery of embroidered velvet coats with sleeves of cloth of gold, and eight hundred more attendants 'royally apparelled'. The Prince embraced the ambassador and rode with him to the Palace, where the Lord Chancellor and the King's Council were waiting at the outer gate to receive him.

The King gave him an audience the next morning and accompanied him to the Chapel where the ambassador swore to honour the articles of the treaty. Guest and host solemnly broke the sacred Host together to seal the compact. Six days of banqueting followed with masques and mummeries. When the ambassador left the King presented him with a silver plate valued at £1,200.

Henry left Hampton Court at the end of 1546 and a few weeks later, on 28 January 1547, died in Westminster Palace. His last words were 'All is lost!'

Henry's marriage to Catherine Parr was not altogether happy. They quarrelled and once he came very near to sending her to the Tower. There was talk of Henry marrying for the seventh time; but he was too ill, his ulcerated leg was causing him great pain, and the war with France, his third, had added greatly to his trials. The marriage lasted three and a half years. Catherine Parr, the only wife to survive him, married Sir Thomas Seymour, by now Lord Seymour of Sudeley, secretly three months after the King's death.

All Henry's six wives stayed at Hampton Court and the ghost of Catherine Howard, as well as that of Jane Seymour, is said to linger there. The gallery leading from the King and Queen's private apartments to the Chapel is believed to be Catherine's haunting-territory. Her ghost, some claim, has been seen rushing and shrieking down the long gallery and disappearing through a door at the far end. The legend is that Catherine, on being confined to her room after the King had heard of her early indiscretions and her unfaithfulness, managed to evade the guards and ran screaming along the gallery to have a word with the King, who was at the time hearing Mass in the Holyday Closet by the Chapel. This was first mentioned in the latter part of the nineteenth century by Mrs Cavendish Boyle, who occupied a 'grace and favour' apartment near the Haunted Gallery, and was confirmed later by her friend Lady Eastlake, who often stayed with her.

Six months after his accession to the throne, Henry's only son Edward VI, aged nine, came to stay at Hampton Court, where he had been born and had spent so much of his childhood. The place had many memories, not all of them happy. The shadow of the mother he never knew lurked about the house, though he was doubtless unaware of her ghost. That he was remarkably like his father in appearance is obvious in Holbein's portrait of him. His health was far from robust: there was constant concern about his condition, and how long he might live.

The first six years of his life, as the young King states in his diary, were spent 'among women'; then Richard Cox, the distinguished headmaster of Eton and a strict Protestant, was brought in as tutor. The boy was subjected to a hard and unremitting course of study— Latin, Greek, French, other European languages, theology—but happily he grew to love scholarship and when he was fourteen he wrote an essay, 'Discourse of the Reformation of Abuses in the Church'. He was also taught to dance, to ride and shoot, and to use the bow at the butts.

When he was six, Jane Dormer, the granddaughter of one of his tutors, was often brought round at the King's request. Of the same age, they played card games, danced, and read to each other. Jane records in her *Memoirs*, written when she was the Duchess of Feria, that when Henry died, the boy said: 'Now, Jane, your King is gone. I shall be good enough for you.' Some years later, while driving in the country, Edward pointed to some ruins of monasteries and asked: 'What buildings were these?' Jane said they were religious houses dissolved and demolished by order of his father for abuses. 'Could not my father,' he asked, 'punish the offenders and suffer so goodly buildings to stand, being so great an ornament to this Kingdom; and put better men that might have governed and inhabited them?' The young King was already showing a lively intelligence.

His mother's brother, Edward Seymour, Earl of Hertford, had been appointed a member of the Council of Regency in Henry's will.

But he lost no time in assuming the role of Lord Protector with the title of Duke of Somerset and so took charge of the person of the young King and also of the government. Somerset made the decisions and gave the orders. A vain, ambitious man, he denied Edward many of the privileges of majesty and even interfered with his amusements.

The Protector's brother Thomas, Lord Seymour of Sudeley, Lord Admiral of England and husband of Henry's widow, Catherine Parr, spent much of his time playing the role of the kind and gentle uncle, and by bribing the boy with pocket money, tried to stir him up to rebel against the Protector. A letter from John Fowler, a gentleman of the King's household, to the Protector's brother, describes the young King's state of duress. His majesty, he says, is never left alone for half an hour but such leisure as he has, he uses for scribbling surreptitious notes to his uncle Thomas on little bits of paper. One of these, which Fowler enclosed, was a request for money. It said: 'My Lord, send me as much as ye think good and deliver it to Fowler— Edward.'

Edward stayed at Hampton Court while the Protector was away fighting the Scots. King Henry had thought it wiser to shut his eyes to the independence assumed by Scotland; but Somerset, attempting to imitate Edward I and ignoring the risk of war with the Scots' old allies the French, defiantly marched his army of eighteen thousand men across the northern border. An early victory was turned into a rout on the arrival of French troops, and Somerset returned home with the remnants of his defeated army.

Nor was his administration of England any better. Had he adhered to Henry's wish, as expressed in his will, that the government of the country should be conducted by the Council of Regency, Hampton Court would have been spared the terrifying scenes that ensued. Unemployment was spreading. Prices began to rise. The coinage was debased by increasing their copper content. By the summer of 1549 conditions had become so serious that two rebellions broke out —one in the western counties, the other spreading from Norfolk to Yorkshire and the Midlands. The former was suppressed with the aid of foreign mercenaries; but Somerset failed in his efforts to suppress the other. The members of the Council felt that urgent action was needed. The Protector must be stripped of his usurped authority.

Learning of their intentions, Somerset, who was with the King at

Hampton Court at the time, decided to deal with them as traitors. A paper, describing the Privy Council as 'but late from the dunghill ... more meet to keep swine than to occupy the offices which they do occupy', was printed on his instructions and distributed widely in London; it also charged the Council with 'conspiring to the impoverishing and undoing of all the commons in the realm' and also of plotting to kill the Protector and then the King.

The Protector's son Lord Edward Seymour was sent with letters in the King's name to Lord Russell and Sir William Herbert, who had been dealing with the insurrection in the west of England, urging them to bring their troops to Hampton Court as quickly as possible for the safety of the King. Towns and villages within fifty miles of the Palace were urged to rise and hasten 'with harness and weapons to defend the Crown'. London was asked to send a thousand armed men urgently and the Lieutenant of the Tower was instructed not to admit any member of the Council inside the fortress.

At Hampton Court there was feverish activity to convert the Palace into a fortress. The lovely quiet country residence by the river, which knew more of laughter and revelry, was barricaded. The moat was filled with river-water. Cannon were placed at numerous strategic points, and an armed guard of five hundred men in armour put on duty to resist any attempts by the Council to seize the King and take him away from Somerset's control.

So far the Council had no such intention. They met in London on 5 October 1549 and, being unaware of these military activities, they mounted their horses to go 'in a friendly manner with their ordinary servants' for a talk with the Protector. Just as they were about to set out some of Somerset's men rode up and warned them that if they intended mischief they would be arrested as traitors. The Council explained that no hostility was intended and, after a frank exchange of views, Somerset's men were won over to the side of the Council. The Lord Mayor was then approached and was persuaded not to send any troops to the Protector at Hampton Court. Even the Lieutenant of the Tower readily opened the gates for the Council.

Meanwhile at Hampton Court men kept pouring in from all parts in response to the Protector's appeal. The motley throng gathered beyond the barred Palace gates. In the evening, alarmed by news of what had happened in London, Somerset decided to bring the King out to talk to the crowd. Edward, in bed suffering from a heavy cold, was made to get up and dress. Pale, walking feebly, he went with his uncle into the foremost Base Court, with the heralds sounding their trumpets and attendants carrying torches. Arriving at the gate, the King said: 'Good people, I pray you be good to us and to our uncle.'

Somerset then addressed them. His voice was hysterical. 'I shall not fall alone. If I am destroyed, the King will be destroyed—the Kingdom, the Commonwealth, all will perish together.' The people listened in silence, the fervour of his appeal evoking not the slightest response.

It was now obvious to Somerset that it would be dangerous to remain at Hampton Court. So, as darkness deepened, he made preparations to move the King to Windsor Castle, which could, he felt, be defended. Edward had by now a hacking cough. But there was no alternative. Bustle and confusion was everywhere. Servants came scurrying with torches. Horses were brought out of the stables. There was the noisy clanking of heavy armour. The Duchess of Somerset collected some of her clothes and all her jewels and dashed across the gardens to the river where a waiting barge took her downstream to Kew.

The King and the Lord Protector accompanied by Cranmer, the Archbishop of Canterbury, who had been staying at Hampton Court and insisted on being with the King, set out on horseback through the chilly October night and reached Windsor a little before dawn. The effect of the breathless scurry and the night air brought on a deterioration of King Edward's health, but they were now in a safer stronghold.

The Council, hearing of their move, immediately sent supplies of food and some furniture to Windsor, together with a message to Edward expressing their absolute loyalty to him; but in a private message to the Archbishop they pointed out the dangerous consequences of Somerset's ill-advised action. They also despatched the Yeomen of the Guard to Windsor for the protection of the King.

The possibility of civil war could not be ruled out. The army, hurrying from the west of England, was prepared to stand by the King, but the Council appealed to them to help by preventing a general rising of the people. A few days later Somerset, after the interchange of further messages with the Council and aware that his position was hopeless, agreed to resign his office as Lord Protector provided his life was spared. To this the Council agreed. Somerset then surrendered and was sent to the Tower.

55

King Edward did not stay on at Windsor (he did not like it: 'Here be no galleries or gardens to walk in', he wrote in his diary), but returned to Hampton Court and as his first act appointed the Earl of Warwick, the outstanding figure in the Council and Somerset's principal enemy, as the new Protector but without that title.

Warwick's father, a tax-collector in the service of King Henry VII, was executed by Henry VIII; nevertheless, without the slightest qualm, he had been driven by his overwhelming ambition to earn the patronage of the man responsible for his father's execution. Now aged fifty, his efficiency as an organiser made him a desirable alternative to Somerset. Realising that the Protestants would be more useful allies than the Catholics, he discarded on taking office Somerset's mild handling of the Catholics. His resolve was to be master, and the failing health of the King made it appear possible that he would achieve it. From the outset he began to gather round him men he could trust and to get the control of military power into his own hands.

Utterly without scruple, he ruled with the utmost ruthlessness. Local rights were tampered with, he even attempted to sway the House of Commons. To stifle criticism he used public whipping and the pillory. In the spring of 1550, needing allies, he courted some of Somerset's followers and before long released Somerset from the Tower. Most of his forfeited lands were restored and the new-found friendship between the two was sealed by the marriage of Warwick's son and heir, John Dudley, to Somerset's daughter Anne.

In July 1551 while the King was at Hampton Court, the Council met there, with Somerset as one of its members—the first return to the Palace of the former Lord Protector since his flight with the King to Windsor. Two years earlier when he was Protector, Somerset, uneasy about the wide range of variety in the church services, had authorised the Book of Common Prayer which provided uniformity and, more important, substituted English for Latin. Now the Council took it further and issued from Hampton Court its famous Proclamation to the bishops, urging them and their congregations 'to resort more diligently to common prayer than they had done, and especially to restrain their greedy appetites from that insatiable serpent, covetousness'; and added the precautionary warning that the sweating sickness—which was then raging in London and had brought the King to Hampton Court—'had been sent as a punishment for their sins'.

That same month the Maréchal de St-André, envoy of the King

of France, arrived at Hampton Court with a retinue of four hundred men. The Duke of Somerset, very much the King's man again, received him at the gates and escorted him to the Palace. After an audience with the King, the guest was taken to his chamber in the Queen's New Lodgings, where, Edward wrote in his diary, it 'was all hung with cloth of arras, and so was the Hall and all my lodging. He dined with me and told me he was come not only for the delivery of the order of St Michael sent to me by his master, but also for to declare the great friendship the King his master bore me, which he desired I would think to be such to me as a father beareth his son, or brother to brother.'

On the next day, in the Chapel, he initiated the King into the Order and invested him in the robes. After communion the Marshal kissed the King on both cheeks, and the entire Court and the visitors then went to the Great Hall for a grand banquet. The possibility of King Edward marrying Princess Elizabeth of France was discussed and the evening, we are told, ended 'with great revelry'.

The next week the Maréchal de St-André came to an 'arraying', described by the King in his diary as a levee held in the State Bedchamber. The rest of the day was devoted to hunting; the Maréchal stayed for dinner and heard the King play on the lute. At their farewell King Edward took off his finger a diamond ring and gave it to the Maréchal as a parting gift.

Meanwhile the moderates, disgusted with Warwick's harsh rule of repression, began to rally round Somerset and were soon intriguing to have him reinstated as Lord Protector. Warwick was determined to prevent this. During the celebration of the festival of Michaelmas at Hampton Court, Somerset, who could not attend because he had been with one of his servants who had died of sweating sickness, was ordered by the Council to 'repair at his conveniente leisure to the Court'. Unsuspecting, he came some days later and, to his surprise, heard the King announce at a meeting of the Council that Warwick had been made the Duke of Northumberland. Somerset was uneasy: he wondered what was to follow, but it was not until nearly a fortnight later that he was arrested in the Council Chamber at Hampton Court and was sent again to the Tower. Accused of conspiring against the Council, he was tried and sentenced to death. The King made this brief, unfeeling entry about his uncle in his diary on 22 January 1552: 'The Duke of Somerset had his head cut off upon Tower Hill between eight and nine o'clock in the morning.'

A few weeks before Somerset's execution the Queen Dowager of Scotland, Mary of Guise, visited Hampton Court. Like so many other distinguished visitors her purpose was to see the famous house. She was met about two miles from the Palace by the Marquess of Northampton who 'brought her to her lodging on the Queen's side, all finely dressed', referring presumably to the lodging. In the evening there was a banquet, followed by music and dancing in the Great Hall. Edward noted in his diary: 'The Dowager perused the house 'Ampton Court, and saw some coursing of dear.' Two days later she left for London, travelling by water with an escort of barges.

King Edward VI visited the palace twice during 1552, in July and in September. He died at Greenwich on 6 July 1553, in his sixteenth year.

14 MARY TUDOR AT HAMPTON COURT

It had been set out in Henry VIII's will that in the event of Edward dying without an heir, he should be succeeded by his half-sister Mary. This Northumberland most cunningly planned to circumvent. Shortly before Edward's death Northumberland had married his youngest son Lord Guildford Dudley to Lady Jane Grey, granddaughter of Henry VIII's sister Mary. Being a Protestant, Jane was thought to be much more acceptable to the people and the natural successor to a Protestant King than the Catholic Princess Mary. Day after day Northumberland had pressed this argument on the desperately ill and dying King; when at last he got Edward to sign the document appointing Jane as his successor, he approached the Council who, being aware of the danger to their lives if they refused, also signed the papers for her succession.

For almost a month Edward's death was kept secret. Fifty pieces of cannon were brought over from Calais and the garrison in the Tower of London was strengthened. Only then was a letter sent to Princess Mary, who was at Hunsdon in Hertfordshire, to say that the King was ill and wished to see her.

Meanwhile the entire Council set out for Syon House, near Hampton Court, to inform Lady Jane Grey that she was now Queen: Northumberland had earlier taken over Syon House as his riverside home and had moved Lady Jane Grey and his son into it. Jane, who was only sixteen, burst into tears, but was in the end persuaded to accept.

Mary, on her way to London, received warning from friends of the dangers that awaited her. She instantly turned back, assembled an army of ten thousand men and set out again for London. To prevent her reaching the capital, Northumberland hurried with a troop of horse and a powerful armed force to waylay her. He was taken prisoner and executed. Lady Jane Grey was also arrested and later executed.

Queen Mary did not come to Hampton Court until the following year. As we have seen, she knew the Palace well: she was there for

Edward's christening and, as his godmother, presented him with a gold cup; she was chief mourner at the funeral of his mother Jane Seymour and rode in the funeral cortège from Hampton Court to Windsor.

Thirty-seven years old now, she was far from pretty, indeed many considered her ugly. She was long-necked and had a deep, gruff voice. Like her brother and her sister Elizabeth, she had been well educated: 'more than moderately read in Latin literature', we are told, 'especially with regard to Holy Writ; and besides her native tongue she speaks Latin, French and Spanish, and understands Italian perfectly, but does not speak it. . . . Takes pleasure in playing the lute and spinet and is a very good performer on both instruments. She seems to delight above all in arraying herself elegantly and magnificently and her garments are of two sorts: one a gown such as men wear but fitting very close, this is her ordinary costume; the other is a gown and bodice with wide hanging sleeves in the French fashion, which she wears on State occasions, and she also wears much embroidery, and gowns and mantles of cloth of gold and cloth of silver, of great value, and changes every day. She also makes great use of jewels.'

Early in 1554, the year following Edward's death, Mary received at Hampton Court the ambassador of the Holy Roman Emperor Charles V, who came to make a formal proposal of marriage on behalf of Charles's son, Philip II of Spain.

Mary appeared to be shy. She looked at the coronation ring on her finger and said that her ministers would have to go into the details of her marriage, but one thing she wanted to make clear— her realm would be her first husband and no other could make her violate her coronation oath. Later that day 'they had great cheer as could be and hunted and killed, tag and rag'. Her bridegroom, the ambassador told her, would be coming to England before Lent, that is to say in a few weeks.

It will be recalled that twenty-seven years earlier, when Mary was only ten years old, Wolsey (whose home it was then) had Henry VIII and Catherine of Aragon as his guests there to discuss with the Duc de Montmorency a treaty for the marriage of Mary to François Ier of France. That marriage did not take place. Mary was not consulted then, but now she was able to make her own choice and had picked Philip despite the strong opposition to the marriage by large numbers of her people, who began demonstrating in London and the provinces the moment they heard of it.

The marriage nevertheless took place that summer and the royal couple came to Hampton Court for their honeymoon. They arrived on 23 August and stayed for five days.

So far as the bridegroom was concerned it was a marriage neither of love nor convenience but of greed—a greed for greater power; he sought to be not Prince Consort but King of England, and Mary would doubtless have granted him this had she been in a position to do so. Her love for him was only too apparent but his attitude to her was one of complete indifference; later he found her repugnant and left her for various mistresses in the Netherlands whom he flaunted quite shamelessly.

A Spaniard discussing the marriage at the time described Mary as 'ugly, small, lean, with a pink and white complexion, no eyebrows, very pious and very badly dressed'. Philip nevertheless behaved in a very correct manner towards her, helping her to mount and dismount, going everywhere with her so that the people might see how happy they were together, and on feast days attending, as a fervent Catholic, all the services in church with her.

Their honeymoon at Hampton Court was spent in quiet retirement. Very few members of the Court were in attendance. There was no display of magnificence and no pageantry. The public soon put their own interpretation on this. They said it was the haughtiness of Philip that kept 'the hall door of the court constantly shut so that no man might enter unless his errand was first known, which seemed strange to Englishmen that had not been used thereto'. There was also comment, put about by the servants at Hampton Court, that the meals served were meagre and niggardly—mostly fish, buttered eggs, and oatmeal—and there were sighs by the household staff for the days of the great Henry, when the tables were heavily laden, the wine flowed carelessly, and the festivities went on for days. Philip's retinue, even his servants, had nothing but contempt for the English, regarding them as heretics and inferiors; they dismissed English women as ugly and ungraceful, ill-dressed in cheap and coarse materials. 'There is not a single Spanish gentleman,' wrote one of Philip's entourage, 'who would give a farthing for any of them and they care equally little for the Spaniards. The English in fact hate us as they do the devil, and in that spirit they treat us.'

On 3 April 1555, Queen Mary, believing she was pregnant, returned to Hampton Court with Philip so that her child should be born there. She withdrew completely from public life; during her

stay in the Palace only two ambassadors were accorded an audience
—the Earl of Courtenay to kiss her hands on the eve of his departure
for the Netherlands, and the Duke of Alva who had come from Spain
to see his sovereign King Philip.

In expectation of the happy event processions went through the
streets of London and other towns, and mass was said in the churches
beseeching the divine blessing 'for King Philip's and Queen Mary's
child, that it might be a male child, well-favoured and witty'.

On 23 April, St George's Day, high mass was celebrated in the
Chapel Royal at Hampton Court, and Philip, who had been made
sovereign of the English Order of the Garter, walked in the procession
round the cloisters and courts of the Palace with the knights, the
Lord Chancellor and other Lords of the Council dressed in their
robes; and the Catholic Bishop of Winchester, Stephen Gardiner,
who had been confined in the Tower of London during Edward's
reign, joined the procession wearing his mitre, and was followed by
noblemen, ecclesiastics, and acolytes carrying crosses and tapers and
swinging censers. The Queen watched them from her bedroom
window as they went by singing *Salve Festa Dies*. Many were astonished that the Queen should look on and concluded that she had only
done so because of the widespread rumour in London and elsewhere
that she had died in childbirth.

As the time approached for her confinement the activity in the
Palace became very brisk. The nursery had already been got
ready; now 'a cradle, veri sumptuouslie and gorgeouslie trimmed',
was prepared for the infant and inscribed with the verse:

> The child which Thou to Marie,
> O Lord of might hast send,
> To England's joie in health
> Preserve, keepe and defend.

Midwives and nurses arrived. Passports were prepared for the
numerous messengers who were to convey the glad tidings to
English ambassadors and ruling monarchs in various parts of
Europe; and the documents they were to take with them had already
been signed by Philip and Mary—'Given under our signet at our
house of Hampton Court'; only the date was left blank and the word
fil was left uncompleted so that it could, by the addition of *s* or *le*,
indicate the sex of the child. One of these letters, to Cardinal Pole
in Rome, was more definite: it stated 'that God had been pleased,

amongst his other benefits, to add the gladding of us with the happy delivery of a Prince'. All these documents are preserved in the Public Record Office in London.

On 30 April, the day on which the child was expected, messengers sent in advance to various parts of England actually announced the birth of the child. *Te Deums* were sung in the churches, bells were rung, sermons of thanksgiving were preached, bonfires were lit, and salutes were fired by the ships in the river. Other messengers crossed the Channel. The great bell of the Cathedral in Antwerp was set ringing. At Hampton Court Princess Elizabeth, invited by her sister to witness the birth of the heir, arrived that morning: until then, after a term of imprisonment in the Tower of London by Mary for 'treasonable' activities, Elizabeth had been confined at Woodstock and came to Hampton Court with her chief warder and guards in attendance. Nor was she received by her sister when she arrived, but was conducted through a back gate to isolated apartments in the Water Gallery, built by Henry VIII by the river, and kept under guard there throughout her stay.

There was no child. The shock of disappointment suffered by Mary and Philip was very great. It was found that Mary had never been pregnant, but had been suffering from dropsy.

For some days Elizabeth was not allowed to leave her apartment or to receive visitors. Then, unexpectedly, a message from the Queen told her to wear her best robe as Philip was coming to see her. In order that he should not be seen, he came on 1 or 2 May by a private passage from the Palace. There is no record of what was discussed at their meeting in that isolated apartment. The fact that they had met and talked at all was kept a closely guarded secret. There is no mention of it in English records; but it was known to the Venetian and French ambassadors who reported it to the Doge of Venice and the King of France.

Nor were the rules relaxed after Philip's visit, for Elizabeth was kept under guard for a further fortnight. She was, however, allowed to receive Lord William Howard, first Lord Howard of Effingham, kinsman both of Catherine Howard and of Elizabeth's mother Anne Boleyn. It is recorded that Lord William 'used her very honourably, condoled with her, and raised her dejected spirits with comfortable speeches'.

This was followed by a visit from the Catholic Bishop of Winchester, Stephen Gardiner, who was accompanied by Lords Arundel and Shrewsbury and Sir William Petre, all members of Queen Mary's Council. They approached Elizabeth with a show of humility, but it failed to put her off her guard. She did not ask what was the purpose of their visit, but addressed them herself. 'My honourable Lords,' she said, 'I am glad with all my heart to see you, for methinks I have been kept a great while from you, desolately alone. Committed to the hands of a strict keeper, my humble request is to all your Lordships that you be the happy instrument of my further enlargement. It is not unknown to you what I have suffered now a long time. I beseech you, therefore, to take me into your loving consideration.'

The Bishop, on his knees before her, answered for them all: 'Let me request your Grace but to submit yourself to the Queen, and then I doubt not that you shall presently enjoy an happy issue of your desires.'

Elizabeth, always quick in her thinking, realised at once that they were advising her to confess complicity in the recent Wyatt rebellion to overthrow her Catholic sister and place her on the throne.

'No,' she said. 'Rather than I will so do, I will live in prison all the days of my life. If ever I have offended Her Majesty in thought, word or deed, then not mercy but the law is that which I desire. If I yield, I should then against myself confess a fault which was never on my part intended, by occasion whereof the King and Queen may then justly conceive an evil opinion of me. No, no, my Lords, it were much better for me to lie in prison for the truth than to be at liberty suspected by my Prince.'

Her answer was repeated to the Queen and the same four visitors came again to see Elizabeth on the following day. Kneeling once again before her, Gardiner stated that 'the Queen marvelled at her boldness in refusing to confess her offence so that it might seem as if Her Majesty had wrongfully imprisoned her Grace'.

'No,' said Elizabeth. 'I never had such a thought; it may please Her Majesty to punish me as she thinketh good.'

'Her Majesty willeth me to tell you that you must tell another tale before you are set at liberty.'

'Alas!' exclaimed Elizabeth, resolved not to be influenced by their promises. 'I had rather be here in custody, with honesty and truth, than abroad suspected of Her Majesty. And this which I have said I will stand to, for I will never belie myself.'

Gardiner was not to be budged either, so the duel went on. 'Why then, your Grace hath the advantage of me and the rest of the Lords for your "long and wrong imprisonment"', he replied.

'What advantage I had,' she rejoined, 'God and your own conscience can best tell, and here before Him I speak it: for that dealing which I have had amongst you I seek no remedy but pray that God may forgive you all.'

'Amen! Amen!' murmured the Bishop, and as they left, the door of Princess Elizabeth's apartment was locked again.

She was left in her solitary confinement for another week and then her sister sent for her. It was ten o'clock at night when she was escorted across the garden to the Queen's quarters by gentlemen ushers and grooms carrying lighted torches. Turning to her ladies-in-waiting who walked beside her, Elizabeth asked them to offer up their prayers, for none could tell whether they would ever see her again. Arrived at the foot of the privy stairway leading up to the Queen's chamber, she was separated from her personal attendants and was conducted by Mistress Clarence, Mary's lady-in-waiting, to the bedroom where she found her sister alone, seated in the Chair of State.

It was the first meeting of the sisters for nearly eighteen months. Elizabeth curtseyed three times and then, getting down on her knees, asked Mary not to mistrust or doubt her, for she would prove herself as true a subject towards Her Majesty as ever did any, and even so desired Her Majesty to judge her, and added that she would not find her to the contrary whatever report otherwise had gone of her.

The Queen's answer was short and sharp. 'Then you will not confess yourself to be a delinquent, I see; but rather stand stoutly on your truth. I pray God your truth may become manifest.'

'If not,' replied Elizabeth, 'I will request for neither favour nor pardon at Your Majesty's hands.'

Gazing at her sister in silence for a moment, the Queen gave her questioning a fresh twist. 'Well then—you stand so stiffly on your truth, belike you have been wrongfully punished and imprisoned.'

Unflinchingly Elizabeth answered: 'I cannot and must not say so to Your Majesty.'

'Why then belike you will report it so to others,' said Mary.

'Not so, as it please Your Majesty. I have borne and must bear the burden myself; and if I may but enjoy Your Majesty's good opinion of me, I shall be better enabled to bear it still, and I pray God when

I shall cease to be one of Your Majesty's truest and loyal subjects that then I may cease to be at all.'

Mary's inability to extort a confession of guilt from her sister, and possibly also the depth of feeling in Elizabeth's voice and the ring of truth in her words which the records are unable to convey, must have shaken Mary's doubts a little, for all she said was 'God knows!' using the Spanish words *Sabe Dios*! She then rose from her Chair of State and left. Elizabeth was taken back to her remote, guarded isolation. A week later she was allowed to leave Hampton Court and was granted complete freedom.

Reports, inevitably secondhand, of this famous interview by such contemporary writers as Foxe and Heywood reveal that during the talk King Philip was in the room concealed behind a curtain. This would have been in keeping with his character, for he was often seen creeping about the passages of Hampton Court to find out what was going on.

Early one morning, walking along a gallery, he peered through a small window into the bedroom of Lady Magdalen Dacre, a beautiful young maid of honour. Finding her at her toilet he pushed open the casement. The startled girl, although she saw that it was King Philip, quickly seized a stick and struck the royal arm at the window. Without a word either of pain or rebuke the intruder crept away.

Though weeks had passed since the expected birth of an heir, Mary still did not give up hope. The processions and the prayers went on at Hampton Court while Mary, swollen with dropsy, lay in her bed with the Book of Devotions in her hands open at the prayer for the safe delivery of a child: that book is still in existence and it is most moving to look upon that worn page.

She must in time have begun to realise that she would probably never have a child, for she allowed her sister to set up her own establishment and hold her own receptions at which she received ambassadors and even the Papal Nuncio. King Philip too went to some of them. It was a recognition by Mary that her sister was her heir; and for her part Elizabeth, submitting to her sister's wishes, attended the celebration of Mass in the Chapel and received the Communion from Bishop Gardiner.

But Mary, young enough at thirty-nine, still kept hoping that she would provide an heir, not only because she wanted England to maintain the restoration to Catholicism that she had brought about, but also because an heir that was Philip's would attach him more closely to her and to the country which he so longed to add to his vast European empire.

He was not often with her after that first awful disappointment, but wandered about Europe in quest of mistresses. Mary moved out of Hampton Court in the summer of 1555 shortly after giving her sister her freedom. She went no further than Oatlands, a few miles away, and stayed there for four months while Hampton Court was being cleaned.

Philip and she stayed together at Hampton Court for a time during the summer of 1557 'to hunt and to kill a great hart with certain of the Council'. Mary came only once after that, in August of the following year 1558, again in expectation of giving birth to an heir, but this time her hopes were not made public. Her health, never robust, had begun to fail. She made a will, appointing Philip Regent during the minority of their child. But no child arrived, she was not even pregnant. She died three months later in November 1558.

Despite the unhappy memories Hampton Court held for her during her stay there as her sister's prisoner, Queen Elizabeth often came to the Palace. The old Tudor display and extravagance, the festivities and the masques that had formed such a feature of her father's life at Hampton Court were not yet revived by her. She used the house as a place to which she could withdraw for rest and quiet.

Her first visit as Queen was in August 1559, nine months after her accession. The purpose of the visit was to meet in secret a man who had been suggested as a possible husband—James Hamilton, the Earl of Arran.

Elizabeth was twenty-five years old, red-haired, blue-eyed, aquiline-nosed and tight-lipped like her grandfather Henry VII. Arran had been suggested by William Cecil, because he was a Protestant. Grandson of Mary Stuart, the daughter of James II of Scotland, Arran was a member of the Scottish royal family and next in succession after Mary Queen of Scots; Henry VIII had wanted him to marry Elizabeth, and that was what Cecil was proposing now. Marriage with Elizabeth, Cecil felt, could lead to a union of the English and Scottish crowns: the more so because Mary Queen of Scots was married to François II of France and would doubtless in these circumstances be unacceptable as a possible successor to Queen Elizabeth.

Considerable thought was given by Elizabeth to the possibility of marrying Arran; she told De Quadra, the Spanish ambassador, that 'she would take a husband that would make the King of France's head ache'. Young Arran had been fighting for France against Spain in command of the Scots Guards and in 1557, aged twenty-seven, had distinguished himself in the defence of St Quentin. But the discovery in France that Arran favoured Protestantism made his arrest likely. He escaped to Geneva and was invited to come to England.

His first meeting with Queen Elizabeth took place in secret earlier in 1559 in Cecil's house in the Strand in London, where

Arran was in hiding. Elizabeth must have formed a favourable impression of him, for not long afterwards their second meeting took place at Hampton Court. Arran was smuggled out of Cecil's house by river so that nobody should know that a royal marriage was contemplated. After being hidden in a house on the Surrey side of the Thames, possibly at East Molesey, he was brought across the river to the tow-path by the old Water Gallery at Hampton Court. Cecil received him there and escorted him to the Queen's Privy Garden, where Elizabeth joined him. They sat in converse for some time. How the talk went is not known, nor what Elizabeth felt about the match.

Arran left for Scotland in the following month; but a year later the subject was brought up again and a formal proposal of marriage was made. It was, however, finally rejected by Queen Elizabeth in 1561. It is unlikely that this had any effect on Arran's mental state, but not long afterwards he showed marked signs of insanity and was confined in Edinburgh Castle for five years by his cousin Mary Queen of Scots, to whom he had proposed, equally unsuccessfully, on the death of her husband François II of France in December 1560. The power of speech was lost to him and his estates were administered by his bastard brother John, who later became the first Marquess of Hamilton. Arran died unmarried in 1609 at the age of seventy-nine and the title passed to his nephew the second Marquess of Hamilton: there is no link between this earldom of Arran and the later creation, an Irish title, which is held by the present Earl.

The purpose of the strict secrecy of the Queen's meetings with Arran was to prevent the French Ambassador, Noailles, from even suspecting that such a marriage was being considered, since the French link with Scotland, always close, had become even closer by the marriage of Mary Queen of Scots to the French king, and the possibility of the Scottish and English crowns being united in the near future would undoubtedly have caused considerable concern. All the letters sent on Queen Elizabeth's behalf to Arran were written in cipher and the code was constantly altered. The messengers were subjected to the sternest security tests; and not all the members of the Council were aware of what was going on.

On 6 September, five days after Arran had left Hampton Court, the French ambassador arrived there to see Elizabeth. He mentioned that Arran had escaped from France and conveyed the French king's hope that in the event of the fugitive arriving in England the Queen would take all steps to see that he was arrested at once.

Elizabeth declared that she had no news of him at all and asked the ambassador to reassure the French king that if Arran came to England she would certainly comply with the king's wishes. The ambassador did not know what to believe for, although he apparently suspected nothing, he was aware that whenever Elizabeth was confronted with a difficult question she managed to turn it aside, generally with a laugh.

The Spanish ambassador, De Quadra, who boasted to Philip II that his spies were everywhere, even in the Queen's court, knew within days of Arran's arrival in England. He must have voiced his suspicions to the Queen, for in a despatch to Philip he stated that the Queen had told him 'she would never have a husband who would sit all day by the fireside. When she married, it should be a man who could ride and hunt and fight'—a typically evasive generalisation which revealed nothing, for Arran could certainly ride and hunt and fight, as well as escape.

Philip II of Spain, her brother-in-law, whose marriage to Queen Mary had been so disastrous for England, was the recurrent suitor for Elizabeth's hand. He was not turned down out of hand, because Elizabeth wished relations with Spain to be friendly; but when it was obvious that she was not going to marry him, Spain put forward a new candidate, Philip's cousin, the Archduke Charles. On being told this, Elizabeth once again indicated that she was prepared to consider the proposal. Her lady-in-waiting, Lady Sidney, sister of Lord Robert Dudley, whose father the Duke of Northumberland had executed Somerset and was in turn executed by Queen Mary, sent a message to the Spanish ambassador De Quadra, asking him to come to Hampton Court to discuss it. The ambassador's despatch to the Spanish court reveals what happened. 'Lady Sidney,' he wrote, 'told a very strange story. She said that there had been a plot to murder the Queen and Lord Robert Dudley at a banquet given at Lord Arundel's. The frightfulness of the danger . . . had so alarmed Elizabeth that she had positively determined to marry. Sir Thomas Parry and Lord Robert were the only persons yet aware of her intention; it was with the Queen's knowledge that she was now speaking to him. He might assure himself that she would not risk her life in such a matter by telling an untruth; and De Quadra had but to take the first opportunity of speaking to the Queen himself to be satisfied of the sincerity of her good intentions.' Elizabeth granted the ambassador an audience and assured him that the Archduke would be most welcome at Court and led him to believe that she would accept the Archduke as a husband.

But before the Archduke was told of this Elizabeth was discussing the possibility of a marriage with the King of Sweden's heir, Prince Eric. The offer was brought by the King of Sweden's brother, the Duke of Finland, and Elizabeth left Hampton Court for London to discuss the project with him.

These were but some of the suitors, there were many more; but it became obvious in time that Elizabeth had no intention of accepting any of them. She kept toying with the idea of marriage to distract attention from the fact that she was in love with the tall, good-looking Lord Robert Dudley, who was constantly with her at Hampton Court and elsewhere. There was much gossip about their relationship, not only in England but also in the courts of Europe. De Quadra informed the King of Spain that the Queen was living with Dudley as his wife. The French ambassador reported that Dudley 'ayant l'entrée comme il a, dans la chambre de la Reyne, lorsquelle est au lit, il s'était ingéré de lui bailler la chemise au lieu de sa dame d'honneur, et de s'hazarder de lui même de la baiser, sans y être convié'. The scandal reached Mary Queen of Scots, who lost no time in writing to Elizabeth about it.

De Quadra states that during one of his talks with Queen Elizabeth, she referred to the gossip and showed him the distance between Dudley's rooms and her own royal apartments; but very soon after that, the ambassador adds, Dudley was moved to a room nearer her own, because, the Queen explained, his rooms being on the ground floor were damp and unhealthy. Robert Dudley's wife, Amy Robsart, was found dead at the foot of the stairs in her home at Cumnor near Oxford in September 1560, and it was expected that the Queen would now marry him, but the mystery surrounding Amy's sudden death made the Queen realise that marriage to him was now impossible.

The gossip became so extravagant that Elizabeth was said to be staying at Hampton Court in 1561 because she was pregnant and had given birth there to a son—all of which was reported in the despatches of the Spanish ambassador and may still be seen in the Spanish State archives. Many years later a man claimed that he was the son of Queen Elizabeth and Lord Robert Dudley. He added that the Queen declared that the infant was the child of one of her maids of honour, and that she had entrusted his upbringing to a former servant named Robert Sothern, who had been brought secretly to Hampton Court and was given the child in the gallery by the Royal Closet. At the Queen's suggestion, he added, the boy was named Arthur and was brought up by Sothern as his son. Only on his deathbed, he added, did Sothern reveal to him his true parentage. And that is all we know of it.

The proposals of marriage multiplied in the succeeding years, those from Catholics being out of the question, but one from the Protestant heir of the Elector Palatine was obliquely advanced by Sir James Melville, the envoy of Mary Queen of Scots, who had come to Hampton Court for that express purpose. The young Palatine heir Duke Casimir had made an earlier approach by letter, but had received an evasive answer. Undiscouraged, he begged Melville to show Elizabeth a portrait of himself. Regarding that as too obvious, Melville decided on an indirect approach. Equipped with portraits of the parents of the suitor and of other members of the family, he sought an audience of Queen Elizabeth and went to see her at Hampton Court, but did not take the portraits with him. He began by suggesting that many of the German Protestant princes would be worthy of her consideration and then launched on a glowing eulogy of the young suitor's father the Elector Palatine. Melville had been in his service and was loath, he said, to leave it. 'But to have the better remembrance of him,' the Elector had given him a picture of himself, another of his wife, and of all his sons and daughters. The Queen, on being told this, 'inquired', Melville states in his *Memoirs*, 'if I had a portrait of Duke Casimir'. He said he had not brought it with him; at which the Queen asked him to return to London and bring it.

A day or so later, when he showed all the pictures to her, she said she would like to keep them until the morning and made an appointment for him to see her in her garden. Overnight she showed them to Lord Robert Dudley, whose comments must have been unfavourable, for the Queen returned all the portraits 'unto me', states Melville, 'giving me thanks for the sight of them. I offered unto Her Majesty all of the pictures, so she would let me have the old Elector's and his lady's [a sly way of trying to get her to retain the portrait of the Duke only], but she would have none of them.'

Mary Queen of Scots was very much in Elizabeth's thoughts.

Widowed by the death of François II after a marriage of only twenty months Mary had returned to Scotland. Now only twenty, her youth, her much vaunted beauty, and her position as a reigning queen, made it obvious that many of the most important rulers of Europe would be striving to marry her or to arrange a marriage with their heirs. It disturbed Elizabeth that another great Continental power might soon link its fortunes with hers. A solution presented itself—Lord Robert Dudley, whom she could recommend from her own personal experience to be 'the most perfect and virtuous man she knew'. To make the proposition more attractive Dudley was created Earl of Leicester, a title hitherto borne only by members of the royal family.

She suggested it to Melville. He was horrified, but refrained from commenting or even betraying his feelings. He was well aware what Mary's reaction would be. When news reached her of Amy Robsart's death, she had said: 'How fortunate that my cousin of England can now marry her horse keeper.'

Mary angrily rejected the offer, writing 'I do not want your cast-off lover'. But some months later she sent Melville back to Hampton Court to apologise for her discourteous rejection of Dudley as a husband. How Elizabeth reacted to this is not known: but, possibly to cover her embarrassment and also to gratify her curiosity about her Scottish cousin, she asked Melville to stay at Hampton Court as her guest and saw him every day, often three times a day, during the nine days he spent there.

Endless questions about his Queen were asked. 'She expressed a great desire to see her,' Melville records, 'and because their so-much-to-be-desired meeting could not hastily be brought to pass, she appeared with great delight to look upon Her Majesty's picture. She took me to her bedchamber and opened a cabinet wherein were divers little pictures wrapped within paper, and their names written with her own hand upon the papers. Upon the first which she took up was written *"My Lord's picture"*. I held the candle and pressed to see the picture so named; she appeared loath to let me see it, yet my importunity prevailed for a sight thereof, and I found it to be the Earl of Leicester's picture.' Melville asked if the picture could be taken back for Mary to see, but Elizabeth refused, saying it was the only picture she had of him. To which he replied, 'You have here the original.' Elizabeth ignored the remark, picked up a miniature of Mary, kissed it 'and brought the audience to an end'.

Elizabeth made only one small structural addition to the Palace: a three-storeyed building to the south-east of Wolsey's lodgings. A stone bay rises to the very top: on its front, on slightly projecting stones, one can still see her initials E.R. and the date 1568.

On the north side of the Great Hall Elizabeth converted an adjoining room for the display of the large collection of horns and antlers at Hampton Court. It is still known as the Horn Room and the collection has been added to in the succeeding centuries. A Tudor doorway leads to it from the dais of the Great Hall.

No alteration appears to have been made by Elizabeth in the size and shape of the gardens at Hampton Court: they were left exactly as her father had laid them out. She saw to it that they were well kept. Bowers were set up at various points 'for recreation and solace' and for talks with her visitors. Rosemary was planted against the walls 'to cover them entirely'; and various other plants, we are told, were 'trained, intertwined and trimmed in so wonderful a manner and in such extraordinary shapes that the like could not easily be found'—referring presumably to topiary. Some of the plants in the herb garden and the flower garden were brought back for her by Hawkins, Raleigh, and Drake from the distant lands they visited. The tobacco plant was brought back from the New World in the 1560s, perhaps by Hawkins; it was valued for its medicinal properties, but before long men and even women were seen smoking it in long pipes. The potato plant was introduced some years later. Sir William Cecil, her Chief Minister, who took a keen interest in the gardens at Hampton Court, also had strange and rare new plants in his own gardens in the Strand and at Theobald's Park in Hertfordshire.

An excellent impression of gardens such as those at Hampton Court is given by Bacon in his essay on 'Gardens'. There should be 'things of beauty' for each month of the year—for the latter part of November, December, and January there should be holly, ivy, bays, juniper, cypress trees, yew, pine trees, fir trees, rosemary and lavender, periwinkle (white, purple, and blue), orange trees, lemon trees, and sweet marjoram. For the latter part of January and February the mezereon tree (which blossoms then), *crocus vernus* (both yellow and grey), primroses, anemones, early tulips, oriental hyacinths and *chamaeiris fritillaria* (spotted dwarf iris). For March violets (especially single blue which are earliest), yellow daffodil, daisy, almond tree in

74

The Great Gatehouse, the main entrance to Hampton Court, built by Cardinal Wolsey. Originally it had two extra storeys, which were removed in the late eighteenth century

The bizarre but attractive Tudor chimneys, which have been kept in splendid repair through the centuries

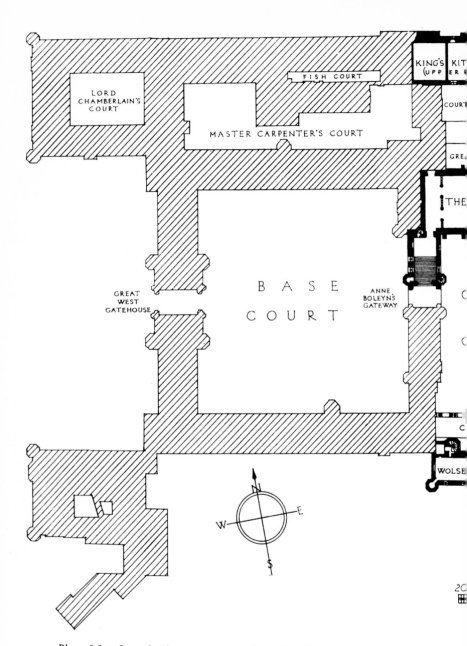

Plan of first floor, showing rooms open to the public. The Cumberland suite on the east side of Clock Court has been opened since this plan was made

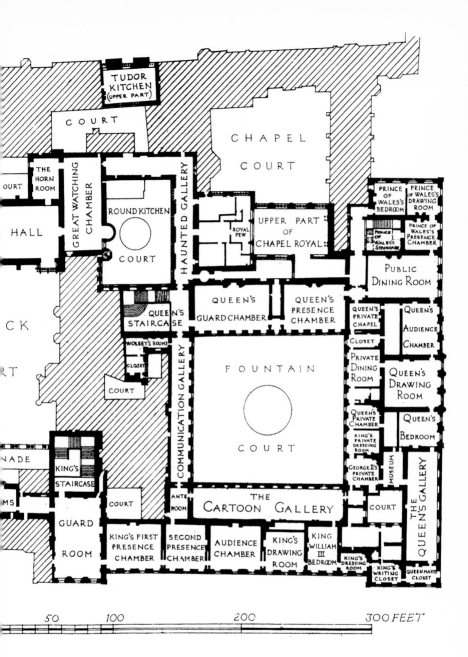

TUDOR KITCHEN (UPPER PART)

COURT

CHAPEL COURT

THE HORN ROOM

GREAT WATCHING CHAMBER

ROUND KITCHEN COURT

HAUNTED GALLERY

ROYAL PEW

UPPER PART OF CHAPEL ROYAL

PRINCE OF WALES'S BEDROOM

PRINCE OF WALES'S DRAWING ROOM

HALL

PRINCE OF WALES'S STAIRCASE

PRINCE OF WALES'S PRESENCE CHAMBER

PUBLIC DINING ROOM

QUEEN'S STAIRCASE

WOLSEY'S ROOMS

CLOSET

COURT

QUEEN'S GUARD CHAMBER

QUEEN'S PRESENCE CHAMBER

QUEEN'S PRIVATE CHAPEL

CLOSET

PRIVATE DINING ROOM

QUEEN'S AUDIENCE CHAMBER

QUEEN'S DRAWING ROOM

CK

FOUNTAIN COURT

QUEEN'S PRIVATE CHAMBER

KING'S PRIVATE DRESSING ROOM

QUEEN'S BEDROOM

RT

GEORGE II'S PRIVATE CHAMBER

MUSEUM

NADE

KING'S STAIRCASE

COURT

THE QUEEN'S GALLERY

MS

GUARD ROOM

ANTE ROOM

THE CARTOON GALLERY

COURT

KING'S FIRST PRESENCE CHAMBER

SECOND PRESENCE CHAMBER

AUDIENCE CHAMBER

KING'S DRAWING ROOM

KING WILLIAM III BEDROOM

KING'S DRESSING ROOM

KING'S WRITING CLOSET

QUEEN MARY'S CLOSET

50   100   200   300 FEET

Cardinal Wolsey. By an unknown artist

The famous astronomical clock, made for Henry VIII in 1540. It shows the hour, day, month, and days since the beginning of the year, the phases of the moon, and high water at London Bridge

blossom, peach tree in blossom, cornelian tree in blossom, and sweet briar. And so on through the months—wallflowers and stock, gilly-flowers and lilies, pale daffodils, white thorn in leaf and the lilac tree for April; pinks and roses, honeysuckle for May and June. The succeeding months are chiefly devoted to fruit—early pears and plums in July; apricots and more plums in August; apples, peaches, and nectarines as well as poppies of all colours in September; medlars in October, and so on. 'These particulars are for the climate of London,' he adds—Hampton Court was near enough; 'but my meaning is perceived, that you can have *ver perpetuum* [perpetual spring] as the place affords.'

One wonders if he was thinking of topiary at Hampton Court when he wrote: 'I for my part do not like images cut out in juniper or other garden stuff; they be for children. Little low hedges, round like welts, with some pretty pyramids, I like well.' Fountains he liked, 'but pools mar all and make the garden unwholesome and full of flies and frogs'. Water must never be at rest, he says, or it will become discoloured and gather putrefaction. This was avoided at Hampton Court.

Melville said Queen Elizabeth used to work in the garden for an hour every morning, working briskly when she was alone, but when others were present, 'she, who was the very image of majesty and magnificence, went slowly and marched with leisure'.

Of his further talks with her he says 'matters of gravity' were often avoided, for Mary Queen of Scots had warned him to keep to lighter topics. He spoke of his travels abroad and the dresses worn by women. Elizabeth was so pleased to find him interested in clothes that she wore a different dress every day. She asked him one evening which of them he liked best. 'The Italian dress,' he said. 'I found this pleased her well, for she delighted to show her golden-coloured hair, wearing a caul and bonnet as they do in Italy. Her hair was more reddish than yellow, curled in appearance naturally.'

Vanity, jealousy, and curiosity caused Elizabeth to ask questions about Mary's appearance and talents. 'She desired to know of me,' writes Melville, 'what colour of hair was reputed best; and which of them was the fairest.' His answer was adroit if evasive. 'The fairness of them both was not their worst fault,' he said. It did not satisfy Elizabeth. She asked for a direct answer and got, still evasively: 'You are the fairest Queen in England and mine is the fairest Queen in Scotland.' But Elizabeth pressed further, so he adjusted the phrase a little. 'Both are the fairest ladies in their countries; Your Majesty is whiter, but my Queen's very lovely.' Elizabeth shook her head. 'She is too high; for I myself am neither too high nor too low.'

Next she wanted to know what sort of diversions Mary had and was told that she went hunting, read historical books, played the lute and the virginals. The inevitable question followed: 'Does she play well?' to which Melville replied: 'Reasonably well for a Queen.' Elizabeth said nothing, but decided to let Melville hear *her* play. Not to make this too obvious, she got her cousin, Henry Carey, Lord Hunsdon (he was the son of Anne Boleyn's elder sister Mary, who had been Henry VIII's mistress and later married William Carey) to take Melville into one of the galleries at Hampton Court while she played the virginals in a chamber leading off it.

Melville, realising why he had been brought there, lifted up a tapestry hanging over the door of the chamber and found, as he had expected, that Elizabeth was playing. Noticing that she had her back to the door, he tiptoed in and listened for a while. He thought she played 'excellently well'; but, becoming aware of his presence, she stopped abruptly and, turning to him, asked with feigned surprise what he was doing there. 'I heard such melody as ravished, whereby I was drawn in ere I knew how,' he replied and apologised for the intrusion.

The Queen then left the virginals and sat down on a low cushion, and 'inquired whether my Queen or she played best. In that I found myself obliged to give her the praise.' She was so pleased that when Melville informed her some days later that he must take his leave and return to Scotland, she insisted on his staying 'that I might see her dance . . . which being done, she inquired at once whether she or my Queen danced best. I answered my Queen danced not so high or disposedly as she did.'

Elizabeth also played the lute 'handsomely' and occasionally she used to sing to the ladies and gentlemen of the Court, but being told afterwards that Lord Oxford (the son-in-law of Sir William Cecil) thought she had the worst voice and did everything with the worst grace, she was furious, and this was one of the charges against Lord Oxford when he was sent to the Tower.

The Earl of Leicester, escorting Melville in his barge from Hampton Court to London, inquired what Queen Mary thought of him and of the suggestion that he should marry her. 'Whereunto I answered very coldly,' states Melville, 'as I had by my Queen been commanded. Then he began to purge himself of so proud a pretence as to marry so great a Queen, declaring that he did not esteem himself worthy to wipe her shoes, and that the invention of that proposition of marriage proceeded from Mr Cecil, his secret enemy. "For if I," he said, "should have appeared desirous of that marriage, I should have offended both Queens and lost their favour." '

Some years later, in 1568, when Mary Queen of Scots fled from Scotland after the murder of her husband the Earl of Darnley and her surprising marriage to Bothwell, and came back to England to seek asylum, Elizabeth appointed a Commission of Enquiry to decide what should be done.

While at Hampton Court that autumn, Elizabeth held a meeting of the Privy Council to consider the Commission's report. Until recently she had appeared to be in sympathy with Mary and desirous of composing the differences between her and Mary's illegitimate half-brother the Earl of Moray, who was a Protestant and the leader of the rebellious Scots. During the battle Mary had been taken prisoner and her infant son was crowned King James VI of Scotland, with the Earl of Moray as Regent.

Elizabeth was faced with a difficult dilemma. To restore Mary to the Scottish throne would involve England in a war with Scotland; to let her escape to Europe would be to present a useful lever to England's enemies; to allow her to stay in England would be to make her a rallying point for the Catholics in the country. Already there were signs that the Catholics in England were planning to organise a rising in her support. There was evidence now of yet a further complication. The Catholic Duke of Norfolk, who had gone to see Mary as head of the Commission of Enquiry, was contemplating marrying her: Elizabeth saw in this a conspiracy to make Mary Queen of England with the support of Norfolk, his vast number of Catholic supporters, and the arrival of Spanish troops, for Mary was known to be in touch with Spain.

At the meeting of the Council it was decided to support the Earl of Moray. Elizabeth promised him her protection and at the same time ordered that precautions must be taken to prevent Mary escaping from England. The refugee Scottish Queen was moved to Tutbury, in Staffordshire, for greater security. The Duke of Norfolk was arrested and sent to the Tower of London: he was later tried for high treason and executed.

The Council left, but Queen Elizabeth stayed on at Hampton Court and occupied herself with other affairs of State. She received various foreign emissaries, among them the newly appointed French ambassador La Mothe Fénelon; and later the Cardinal de Châtillon, the envoy of Condé and the Huguenots. Each of them was received with the utmost pomp and ceremony. Fénelon was met at the foot of the great stairs by the Queen's Chamberlain and was taken through the Great Hall to the Presence Chamber, where Elizabeth sat in the Chair of State. Châtillon was conducted to the Park where Elizabeth, who had been hunting, dismounted and took him to a nearby cottage where they sat and talked for some time. To Fénelon at their second interview, while she reclined on a couch in her Privy Chamber because she had had an accident while out driving in her coach, she revealed that the Duke of Alba had sent her a letter that was tantamount to a 'Valentine'; at which the Frenchman flatteringly added that all the Princes of Europe were anxious to marry her.

On 14 December, the Great Council of Peers was convened again at Hampton Court and a casket, said to contain damaging evidence against Mary Queen of Scots, was produced. Inside the casket were eight letters from her to Bothwell which implicated her in the plot to murder Darnley, and a series of sonnets written by her to Bothwell. The handwriting in the letters was compared by Cecil and others with Mary's handwriting in the letters she sent to Queen Elizabeth and 'no difference was found'. According to the Spanish ambassador there was 'a difference of opinion' on this among the peers, some of whom criticised Cecil's violent denunciation of Mary. Whether this was based on reliable evidence or was invented by the ambassador to please his master Philip of Spain is not known. Mary had asked again and again to see Elizabeth to answer the accusations in person. This Elizabeth had refused; and the peers now merely recorded that 'they did not think it meet for Her Majesty's honour to admit the said Queen to her presence as the case did stand'.

Elizabeth told Mary to answer the accusations through her Commissioners; and added that if she agreed to her abdication from the Scottish throne and sought the protection of Elizabeth, she would be treated with friendship and kindness. Mary asked again to see the evidence against her, but was not allowed to have even copies of the letters in the casket. She thereupon refused either to answer the charges or to agree to her abdication.

At this Elizabeth sent for the Earl of Moray. He was received by Cecil at Hampton Court and was told that, 'as on their part they had seen nothing sufficiently produced nor shown against the Queen their Sovereign, whereby the Queen of England should conceive or take any evil opinion of the Queen her good sister from anything yet seen', they were given leave to return to Scotland. The casket and the letters were then handed back to them. Cecil gave Moray when he left the sum of £5,000 as a gift from Queen Elizabeth.

Mary was now moved to the strong castle of Fotheringhay in Northamptonshire where she could be closely watched. In February 1587 a plot to murder Queen Elizabeth and rescue Mary led finally to her execution. It was the year before the coming of the Spanish Armada.

17 CHRISTMAS FESTIVITIES AT HAMPTON COURT

In these first ten years of her reign Elizabeth, as we have seen, spent a great deal of time at Hampton Court. During the remaining thirty-five years she moved restlessly about the country, descending on nobles and merchants, not all of whom were rich enough to provide lodgings and board for the Queen and her enormous retinue and to give her jewels and horses as a parting gift. Often for her hosts her visits were ruinous.

It has been said that her method was to force the rich to contribute to the support of the Crown, that is, to maintaining her royal way of life. It was in fact a form of surtax. As a result of these constant tours Elizabeth became better known than any monarch had ever been before. Hampton Court was by no means neglected. Almost every year she went there for some weeks for rest and diversion. Usually she came for Christmas and the Palace was made gay with Yuletide festivities.

On one of these visits she had coach-houses built alongside Wolsey's stables on the Green beyond the Palace walls. Coaches had recently been introduced into England and the Queen used them for her longer 'progresses'; for her shorter journeys she preferred to travel on horseback or by royal barge from the stairs of the Water Gallery to the Palaces at Richmond, Whitehall, and Greenwich.

The Queen took a delight in the Christmas jollity and pageantry. The Great Hall, the long galleries, and the vast reception rooms were gaily and elaborately decorated. Not since the reign of her father had the Palace seen such lavish entertainment. There were banquets, sometimes in the Great Hall, or in the Great Watching Chamber, and after dinner when the guests moved to the Withdrawing Room the minstrels began to play and the Queen led the company in dancing the *corante* and the *galliard*. Masques, balls, masquerades, plays, revels—nothing was omitted; and there were endless outdoor sports such as tilting and shooting, hunting, of course, and always tennis. The Queen joined in most of them.

She was also fond of stag-hunting and went out with her own bow, attended by twelve ladies dressed in white satin and mounted on palfreys, and had a retinue of gentlemen in 'russet damask and blue embroidered satin, tasselled and spangled with silver, and bonnets of cloth of silver with green feathers. On entering the chase she was met by fifty archers, dressed in green with scarlet boots and yellow caps and gilded bows, who presented her with a silver-headed arrow, winged with peacock's feathers'.

The festivities went on from Christmas Eve until Twelfth Night. The Great Hall, where the plays were presented, is now the only surviving Elizabethan theatre in England. These theatrical performances were most elaborately mounted. In the *Accounts of the Revels at Court* published by the Shakespeare Society, the entries show that carpenters and joiners worked for days to get everything ready. The stage was erected in front of the screen and the minstrel gallery. 'Houses made of canvas' were built and 'framed and painted accordingly as might serve their several purposes'. For one of the plays the scenery required the 'painting of seven cities, one village and one country-house', and occasionally trees had to be brought into the Great Hall. The pantry behind the screens was used as a dressing-room by the players and the Great Watching Chamber beyond the other end of the Hall was used for rehearsals. Tailors, silk-weavers, and buskin-weavers were employed to make the costumes and a wardrobe department was set up for the 'airing, repairing, cleaning, putting in order, folding, laying up and safe bestowing of the garments, vestures, apparel, disguisings, properties and furniture ... which else would be mouldy, musty, moth-eaten and rotten'. Haberdashers, upholsterers, and other skilled artisans were on call to supply wings for angels, hair, vizors, wands, artificial fruit, flowers, and even fish.

Snow, since it could not be relied on to fall outdoors on the right date in the right quantity, was artificially provided by the artisans skilled in the craft of convincing deception. Instead of using torches in the hall, a more effective method of lighting was devised: wires were run from the beams at a safe level below the roof to carry small oil lamps, and silver sconces fitted with perfumed candles were placed high up on the walls.

During Christmas 1575 six plays were put on: they included *The Painter's Daughter*, the players drawn from the Earl of Warwick's staff; *Toolie*, with Lord Howard's servants; *History of the Collyer*, enacted by the Earl of Leicester's men; and the *History of Error* on

New Year's Day by the children of Powles: the nineteenth-century writer John Payne Collier in his *Annals of the Stage* thought Shakespeare's *Comedy of Errors* was based on this. Shakespeare was only eleven years old in 1575; plays by him were actually performed later at Hampton Court and Shakespeare himself may have acted in them, as we shall see.

The hospitality was lavish. Food was brought to Hampton Court every day in heavily laden waggons: the Queen's 'Book of Diet' lists tons of butter, milk, cheese, eggs; twenty varieties of fish; poultry and game such as venison, hares, partridges, pheasants, snipe, larks, chickens, capons. The Crown Accounts record that new hearths were made for the Great Kitchen for 'boyling brawnes against Christmas'. One can still see the rough inscriptions, made possibly by the kitchen staff, on one side of the enormous arched fireplace, near one of the old Tudor ovens, with the dates 1576 and 1578.

An enormous number of barrels of beer and hogsheads of wine were brought in—all of it needed for the house-guests who came with their retainers and servants and occupied hundreds of bedrooms. The cost was enormous. The figure given for a year's expenditure on eating and drinking at Hampton Court is £80,000, of this £30,000 was spent on the privy table—in present terms the figure would be nearly a million pounds.

These splendid, costly entertainments were not the only feature of Queen Elizabeth's stay at the Palace during the Christmas season. She also presented New Year gifts to the courtiers as well as to State officials and all the exalted guests. In 1577 these included such relatives of the Queen as Lady Margaret Lennox and Lady Mary Grey, various dukes, marquesses, earls, and other members of the peerage. Her presents consisted mainly of small silver-gilt articles. Their gifts to her were jewels, gold coins, and dresses. The Earl of Leicester gave her a 'carcanet' (collar) 'of gold, enamelled, garnished with sparks of diamonds and rubies and pendants of pearls'; the Lord Treasurer Cecil, by now Lord Burghley, gave her a purse containing £30: the Countess of Derby's gift was 'a petticoat of white satin edged with broad embroidery of divers colours'. It has been estimated that the gifts received by the Queen totalled £10,000 in value whereas the gifts she gave amounted to not more than £2,000.

In 1589 Queen Elizabeth removed the fountain her father had placed in the centre of Clock Court and put in its place one that was much more magnificent, crowned with the figure of Justice supported by columns of black and white marble. Her fountain provided a great deal of fun and doubtless some embarrassment, for the water could be directed on ladies in lovely dresses who had come up to admire it.

The Duke of Württemberg was delighted with it and enjoyed seeing the ladies get 'a thorough wetting'. He had come especially to look at the house and recorded in his diary: 'Now this is the most splendid and most magnificent royal palace of any that may be found in England or indeed in any other kingdom. It comprises ten different large courts'—there were in fact only five large courts, Base Court, Clock Court, Cloister Green Court, Chapel Court, and Round Kitchen Court; there were a number of smaller ones such as Fish Court, Master Carpenter's Court, and so on. The ducal diary continued:

> There is one apartment, belonging to the Queen, in which she is accustomed to sit in state, costly beyond everything; the tapestries are garnished with gold, pearls and precious stones—one table-cover alone is valued at above 50,000 crowns—not to mention the royal throne, which is studded with very large diamonds, rubies, sapphires and the like, that glitter among other precious stones and pearls as the sun among the stars. Many of the splendid large rooms are embellished with masterly paintings, writing tables inlaid with mother-of-pearl, organs and musical instruments which Her Majesty is particularly fond of. Among other things to be seen there, are life-like portraits of the wild man and woman whom Martin Frobisher, the English captain, took in his voyage to the New world and brought alive to England.

The French Ambassador was equally enthusiastic: 'I have seen in the palaces of Windsor and Hampton Court, but especially in the latter, more riches and costly furniture than I ever did see or could have imagined.'

Edmund Bohun, who also visited Hampton Court, wrote in his *Character of Queen Elizabeth*: 'She was a true lover of jewels and pearls, all sorts of precious stones, plate, plain, bossed of gold and silver, and gilt; rich beds, fine coaches and chariots, Persian and Indian carpets, statues, medals, etc., which she would purchase at great prices. . . . And here she had caused her naval victories obtained against the Spaniards to be represented in excellent tapestries, and laid up amongst the richest pieces of her wardrobe.'

During the Christmas festivities at Hampton Court in the winter of 1592, the Queen was confronted by an unexpected guest—Robert Carey, youngest son of her cousin Lord Hunsdon, a leading member of the Privy Council. Carey, who was thirty-two, had offended the Queen by marrying without her consent, an unforgivable affront in her opinion. He had been sent by the Queen on a mission to Scotland for a talk with Mary Queen of Scots' son King James VI, who was to become Elizabeth's successor. The Queen refused to see Carey before his departure for Scotland. On his return he insisted on seeing her, recording in his *Memoirs*:

> I made all haste I could to Court, which was then at Hampton Court. I arrived there on St. Stephen's Day in the afternoon. Dirty as I was, I came into the presence, where I found the lords and ladies dancing. The Queen was not there. My father went to the Queen to let her know that I was returned. She willed him to take my message or letters and bring them to her.
>
> He came for them; but I desired him to excuse me, for that which I had to say I must deliver myself. I could neither trust him nor much less any other therewith. He reacquainted Her Majesty with my resolution. With much ado I was called in: and I was left alone with her. Our first encounter was stormy and terrible, which I passed over with silence. After she had spoken her pleasure of me and my wife, I told her that she herself was the fault of my marriage, and that if she had but graced me with the least of her favours, I had never left her nor her Court: and seeing she was the chief cause of my misfailure, I would never off my knees till I had kissed her hand and obtained my pardon. She was not displeased with my excuse, and before we parted we grew good friends. Then I delivered my message and my papers, which she took very well, and at last gave me thanks for the pains I had taken. So having her princely word that she had pardoned and forgotten all faults, I kissed her hand and came forth from the presence, and was in the Court as I was ever before.

Robert Carey was made Earl of Monmouth by Elizabeth's successor.

A year later, not long after the Christmas festivities had ended and with the Queen still in residence, there was a robbery at Hampton Court, the victims of which were four 'gentlemen Pensioners'. The thieves broke into their room in one of the five towers of Tilt Yard while they were out, rifled their trunks and took jewels and money to the value of £400. One of the thieves, John Randall, was caught and hanged.

The Earl of Leicester, Elizabeth's favourite, died just after the defeat of the Spanish Armada in 1588. His stepson, the Earl of Essex, who was twenty-six and related to the Queen through his mother who was the granddaughter of Anne Boleyn's sister, took Leicester's place. Elizabeth had known him since his childhood and had watched him grow into a tall, elegant young man, with auburn hair and a dashing personality. His advancement was rapid. An adventurer by disposition, he had fought against the Spaniards and was strongly opposed to the Cecils (Lord Burghley and his younger son Sir Robert) who had been working for peace with Spain.

In 1593 Essex was involved in an intrigue against the Queen's trusted physician Dr Ruy Lopez, a Portuguese Jew, who was said to be party to a Jesuit plot to murder the Queen. The doctor was arrested. An investigation was ordered by Her Majesty and was partly carried out at Hampton Court by Burghley, Sir Robert Cecil, and the Earl of Essex. Dr Lopez's house was searched, but nothing was found to incriminate him. To every question the answer he gave was satisfactory. The Cecils declared that the allegation against him was completely unfounded; the doctor had served the Queen faithfully for many years and the attack on him was based on sheer malice. Elizabeth, still at Hampton Court, upbraided Essex, called him 'a rash and temerarious youth', declared that her honour was at stake, and ordered him to leave her presence.

Essex sulked for two days: his honour, he said, was also at stake. Spain had a hand in the plot, it was argued. Two Portuguese, arrested under suspicion, sought to exculpate themselves by incriminating Dr Lopez. They talked of letters, which they were unable to produce. But Essex succeeded in rousing the country into a fresh frenzy against Spain, and in the end Dr Lopez's fate was sealed. Elizabeth hesitated before allowing his execution to be carried out, for, having been served so long and faithfully by him, she still felt that he was innocent. In June 1594, however, she gave in. He was dragged on a hurdle to Tyburn, hanged, drawn, and quartered. Centuries later papers discovered in the Spanish archives supported Dr Lopez's innocence. He was in Shakespeare's mind, it is thought, when a year or two later he wrote of Shylock in *The Merchant of Venice*.

Elizabeth visited Hampton Court for the last time in the late summer of 1599, when she was nearing seventy. Riding there from the palace of Nonsuch in Surrey, she stayed at Hampton Court for a few days, danced the Spanish Panic to pipe and tabor, and then returned to Nonsuch. The weather was 'foul' on that day, the Scottish ambassador tells us, but the Queen insisted on riding, 'although she is scarce able to sit upright, and my Lord Hunsdon said "It was not meet for one of Her Majesty's years to ride in such a storm". But she answered in great anger: "My years! Maids, to your horses quickly" and so rode all the way. . . . As she passed Kingston one old man fell on his knees, praying God that she might live a hundred years, which pleased her so.'

She died at Richmond Palace on 24 March 1603. In general she had 'enjoyed her health very perfectly', says William Camden in his *Regnante Elizabetha*, 'for she never did eat meat but when her appetite served her, nor drink wine without some allaying'.

Twice she had smallpox, on both occasions at Hampton Court. The first time was in 1562, four years after her accession to the throne: she was twenty-nine then. Feeling faint, shivering a little, she felt she could throw off these symptoms by taking a walk in the garden. On her return she was found to have a cold and a high temperature and was put to bed. Two days later her condition was worse and the doctors said that, unless she improved, she was not expected to live. The Council was summoned to Hampton Court and found her in a state of coma, unable to speak. Their concern was over the succession. That night spots began to appear. The Council gathered round her bed and when at last she was able to speak, she told them that Lord Robert Dudley, not yet the Earl of Leicester, should be made Protector of the Realm. By the next morning there were signs of an improvement. The danger passed and a few weeks later she was able to return to London.

Mrs Sibell Penn, nurse and foster-mother to Edward VI, and still then living at Hampton Court, got smallpox too, and died of it. She was buried in Hampton Church. When the church was demolished in 1829 and her grave was disturbed, inhabitants of the Palace said they could hear a woman muttering as she worked a spinning wheel in the south wing. A search was made. The noise appeared to be coming through a wall. Behind it a forgotten chamber was found with a spinning wheel and the floorboard much worn by the treadle.

The Queen's second attack of smallpox occurred ten years later. Once again her condition caused alarm. Leicester sat by her bed all night nursing her. Elizabeth's own account of her illness is: 'After two or three days, without great inward sickness, there began to appear certain red spots on some parts of our face, likely to prove the smallpox; but thanked be God, contrary to the expectation of our physicians and all others about us, the same so vanished away, as within four or five days passed, no token almost appeared; and at this day, we thank God, we are free from any token or mark of any such disease.'

A very few weeks after ascending the English throne James I came to stay at Hampton Court. He was already King of Scotland, for he succeeded his mother Mary Queen of Scots on her abdication when he was only a year old. Now thirty-seven, ailing in health, his legs so weak that he had to lean on the arm of an attendant when he stood up and had to be strapped in the saddle when he went hunting, his unattractive appearance was not improved by the slovenly way he dressed. He had married Anne, daughter of the King of Denmark, when he was twenty-three and she not yet fifteen. As a dowry she brought the Orkney and Shetland Islands which were already pawned to Scotland. Blonde, sharp-featured, she was far from pretty. The marriage turned out to be a success: she tolerated his homosexuality and his lavishing of wealth on his handsome young male favourites, and he indulged her passion for dancing and amateur theatricals. They had three children, two sons and a daughter; had the heir Henry lived, Charles I would not have succeeded their father.

The change in atmosphere at Hampton Court was quite marked. Now it swarmed with Scots courtiers and retainers, and to their varied north of the border accents was added the guttural Danish of the Queen and her string of followers. To James it was an intoxicating change to come here from Edinburgh. Ruler until now of a tiny kingdom with a wild unruly population and a serious shortage of funds, England seemed to have been bestowed on him by Aladdin's lamp.

Within hours of his arrival at Hampton Court, James decided that his prime need was to raise funds. Acting on a suggestion said to have been made by Sir Robert Cecil, the ancient order of Knighthood, hitherto conferred personally by the sovereign for distinguished and gallant service, was put up for sale. 'You want the money, Sire,' Robert Cecil is said to have declared, 'and that will do *you* good. The honour will do *them* very little harm.' So on 17 July 1603 the new King issued a summons to all who received £40 or more a year from their land to come and purchase their knighthood at Hampton Court. The sum demanded was £30. If they declined the honour they were fined £40.

For three days nothing happened. Then two men arrived, Mr John Gammes from Radnor and Mr Willian Cave from Oxfordshire. They paid the fee and James knighted them. Finding the response disappointing, the King promptly put peerages up for sale. The price varied. What was taken into consideration was the degree of favour with which the King regarded the man, his usefulness to the Court, and how much he was able to pay. From many £5,000 was demanded. Others had to pay more. The sum was later raised to £10,000. Eleven men came forward and after paying £5,000 each they were conducted into the Great Hall where the Queen and the Court officials saw their ceremonial transformation into peers. The King then left for London and there found three hundred men waiting to be knighted. As the day was oppressively hot, they were assembled in the garden of the palace at Whitehall and there, with sword in hand, King James I went through the ennobling process and added an abundant sum to his exchequer within four months of his accession to the English throne.

Later in the reign, in May 1611, his greed led to the creation of a new honour, the baronetcy, half-way between a knighthood and a barony, but with this advantage over the knighthood that it was hereditary. The money was to be used for the support of English troops in Ulster. Each baronet had to 'defend and ameliorate the condition of the Province of Ulster, aid towards the building of churches, towns and castles there, and proffer their lives, fortunes and estates to hazard in the performance of this duty . . . and maintain thirty soldiers there.' The pay of the soldier was eightpence a day and had to be paid by the baronet for three years. Some of today's baronets are descendants of the purchasers of this honour.

In the course of the twenty-two years of his reign James I created one hundred and eleven new peers—seven times as many as Queen Elizabeth had created in her reign of forty-four years.

From the outset James and the Queen showed their intense delight in being at Hampton Court. It was admirably suitable for entertaining on a grand scale, for no other palace in England had such magnificent reception rooms, and it was their intention to maintain the festive gaiety that was such a feature of Queen Elizabeth's time there.

In December 1603 they returned to Hampton Court resolved to mark their first Christmas in England with splendour. The presentation of a masque, a form of dramatic entertainment that had begun to displace the old masquerades and mummings towards the close of Elizabeth's reign, was decided upon and the new young Queen, delighted to play a personal part in such diversions, got Samuel Daniel, already at forty a distinguished poet and Master of the Queen's Revels during the last months of Elizabeth's reign, to write a masque especially for her. Entitled *The Vision of the Twelve Goddesses*, it had a fine lyrical form that was later developed and perfected by the poet and dramatist Ben Jonson and attained its finest expression in Milton's *Comus*.

Daniel's was indeed the first of the great masques. The lovely Lady Arabella Stuart, a cousin of King James (she was a niece of his father the Earl of Darnley), refers to it in a letter from Hampton Court on 18 December. 'The Queen intendeth,' she said, 'to make a masque this Christmas, to which end my Lady Suffolk and my Lady Walsingham hath warrant to take of the late Queen's'—namely Elizabeth's—'best apparel out of the Tower at their discretion. It's said there shall be 30 plays. The King will feast all the Ambassadors this Christmas.'

This was not King James's first raid on Queen Elizabeth's wardrobe. Before leaving Scotland he wrote to the Council asking for robes as well as jewels belonging to Elizabeth to be sent so that Queen Anne should be suitably apparelled. The Council refused, saying that they had no authority to send the late Queen's possessions out of England. James was furious. But the situation was different now. Elizabeth is said to have had more than six thousand robes, all of great magnificence and enormous cost. One wonders how robes of the Elizabethan period were adapted for the twelve goddesses.

Another reference to the King's Christmas plans is made by Sir Dudley Carleton. 'We shall have a merry Christmas at Hampton Court,' he wrote, 'for both male and female masques are already bespoken.' There was plague in London and fogs and mists at Hampton Court, 'which make us march blindfold', Sir Dudley added in his letter, 'and we fear we shall now stumble into the sickness which till now we have miraculous scaped'.

His fears were unjustified. By Christmas conditions improved, and even in London, where the plague had been claiming a thousand victims a week, the toll went down to a few hundred a week.

When the ambassadors arrived with their staffs the bickering began. Protocol was quoted. The right of precedence was hotly disputed, with arguments as to who should have which suite of rooms and which seats at the tables. This went on all through Christmas, much to the annoyance of the King and his ministers.

To Inigo Jones, destined to be the outstanding architect of the early seventeenth century, was entrusted (it is said) the designing and building of the scenery. Though only thirty, he had studied design in Italy and, on his return to England with a warm letter from the Queen's brother King Christian of Denmark, was appointed designer to the Queen. Not content with just designing the scenery for the masques, he occasionally even acted as scene-shifter, for the machinery he had constructed for certain effects could only, he felt, be effectively handled by himself. He also trained the Royal children to act in some of the stage plays.

All the plays chosen had to be submitted to Samuel Daniel. Writing to thank Sir Thomas Egerton for securing him this office of authority, Daniel said: 'It seemeth to myne humble judgment that one who is the author of playes now daylie presented on the public stage of London and the possessor of no small gaines, and moreover himself an actor in the King's Companie of Comedians'—by which he obviously meant Shakespeare, who was the only playwright in the company—'could not with reason pretend to be Master of the Queene's Majesty's Revells, forasmuch as he wold sometimes be asked to approve and allow his own writings.'

The twelve noble ladies who were the goddesses in the masque used the old pantry behind the screens at the lower end of the Hall as their dressing-room—the Queen, who appeared as one of the goddesses, used it too. Among the papers at the Record Office is this entry: 'Item, Paid for making readie the lower ende, with certain Roomes of the Hall at Hampton Court for the Queens Majesty and ladies against their masque by the space of three dayes'—the sum paid has been obliterated by damp, decay, and worms.

Sir Dudley Carleton wrote at the end of the Christmas festivities to his friend John Chamberlain: 'We have had a merry Christmas and nothing to disquiet us save brabbles amongst our ambassadors, and one or two poor companions that died of the plague. ... We had every night a public play in the Great Hall, at which the King was ever present and liked or disliked as he saw cause: but it seems he takes no extraordinary pleasure in them. The Queen and the

Prince [their elder son Henry] were more the players' friends, for on other nights they had them privately and have since taken them to their protection. On New Year's night we had a play of *Robin Goodfellow*.'

The plays were performed by the King's Company of Comedians, which had been incorporated by royal warrant only a few months earlier: Shakespeare's name was on the list of players and it is likely that he was at Hampton Court with the rest of the company and even possible that some of *his* plays may have been performed there that Christmas. Thirty-nine at that time, Shakespeare had been acting at the Playhouse at Newington Butts and at the Globe at Bankside in some of Ben Jonson's plays as well as his own *Hamlet*, in which he played the ghost.

Robin Goodfellow was followed by a *Masque brought in by a Magician of China*: for this a Heaven was built, out of which a magician emerged and gave 'a long sleepy speech', Carleton says, describing 'the country from whence he came and comparing it with ours for strength and plenty'. Then 'Knights from China and India' emerged from behind a curtain, led by two boys and two musicians, who played and sang while the knights presented escutcheons and letters to the King. The knights were impersonated by various exalted members of the Court, richly dressed in robes of crimson satin, embroidered with gold and bordered with broad silver laces, which they found too heavy and cumbersome to dance in comfortably.

On Twelfth Night, after the banquet to the French ambassador, there was a masquerade in which some Scotsmen did the familiar sword dance, possibly an acknowledgement of the centuries-old link between Scotland and France. Then the King, tiring possibly of these diversions, left to take part in gambling; but after losing five hundred crowns at a game of dice he was never seen at the tables again.

Hampton Court was filled to overflowing for these festivities. All the one thousand two hundred rooms were occupied and many guests had to sleep in beds put into the outbuildings. For their retainers and servants tents were erected in the park. There were banquets, balls, and masquerades every day. The weather was not too inclement and the King himself took part in a tilting match.

But the *pièce de résistance* of that first Christmas at Hampton Court was *The Vision of the Twelve Goddesses*. From nine o'clock in the evening the guests began to emerge from their scattered lodgings, some of which were outside the Palace gates, and walk along the cloisters with attendants lighting their way with torches. Some used the wooden staircase which led to the minstrel gallery; others came up the stone staircase. The King, Prince Henry, Ministers and Lords of State entered the Great Hall from the Watching Chamber. Under an enormous canopy of state was the King's Chair.

The Queen and her group of ladies who played the goddesses wore headdresses to indicate which goddess each represented. The Queen as Pallas Athene, wearing the only short dress which revealed the legs, had buskins set with rich stones, a helmet studded with jewels and further jewels scattered over her entire attire. Pages dressed in loose gowns of white satin carried the torches to light their way to the Temple. There were prayer offerings and songs and finally dancing, in which the goddesses were partnered by the Duke of Suffolk, the Earl of Pembroke, and other noble lords.

It was an unforgettable evening. All those who witnessed it wrote long letters to tell their friends of it; and it was talked of for months afterwards. As it was performed on a Sunday night, it met with a great deal of criticism from those who felt that 'so profane' an entertainment should not have been presented on the Sabbath. The King did not share the Puritanical attitude to Sunday observance and replied to the critics in his *Book of Sportes*, which was published shortly afterwards; in it he pointed out that a large number of diversions, including bear-baiting, revels, dancing, and plays were lawfully acceptable on Sundays and had been so for a long time; to alter this now by accepting the demands of the Puritans would only lead 'to a filthie tippling and drunkennesse'.

The masque of the goddesses presented that last night was followed by a banquet at which there was 'the accustomed confusion', which involved a general scramble for food, the collapse of tables and trestles, the loss of jewels, and 'many great ladies were made shorter by their skirts'.

James's clash with the Puritans began long before *The Vision of the Twelve Goddesses*; it had been quiescent for a time because of the King's recent accession to the English throne. But now with signs of its flaring up again, James decided to deal with it firmly and finally.

A Puritan petition, known as the 'Millenary Petition' because it bore thousands of signatures, had been sent to him some weeks before Christmas. When the festivities ended His Majesty arranged a conference at Hampton Court at which the Church of England was represented by bishops, deans, and other dignitaries of the Anglican church and the Puritans by four of their divines.

The conference began on Saturday, 14 January 1604. The King received them on the preceding evening 'in an inner withdrawing chamber, where in a private manner and in as few words but with most gracious countenance', he told them of the purpose of the meeting and what they were expected to discuss and resolve.

The hopes of the Puritans were high because the King had been brought up as a Presbyterian, which was closer to Puritanism than to the Anglican Church, and the Puritans, feeling that the reformation of the Church under Elizabeth had not gone far enough, were pressing for the removal of certain forms and ceremonies. But James was insistent on having uniformity in religion, the uniformity imposed when the Book of Common Prayer was adopted half a century earlier.

At the first formal meeting, held in one of the large rooms of the Henry VIII suite of State apartments, the Puritans were not included; what was to be discussed with them was decided by the King and eight bishops, five deans, and the Lords of the Privy Council.

Opening with an hour-long speech, the King, removing his hat on referring to God, said 'the Lord hath brought me into the *promised land* where religion is purely professed, where I sit amongst grave, learned and reverend men, and not as before, *elsewhere*, a King without state, without honour, without order, where beardless boys would brave us to the face'. He was opposed, he said, to all innovation, but 'like a good physician', he was prepared 'to examine and try the complaints', and 'if anything should be found meet to be redressed it might be done without any visible alteration'.

From this it was obvious that the four Puritans, seated on a bench outside the barred doors, were not likely to get any concessions. Some of the bishops disagreed with the King, but James 'disputed with the Bishops so wisely, wittily and learnedly, with the pretty patience as I think never man living heard the like', wrote Dean Montagu in a letter to his mother, adding that: for Ireland 'the conclusion was (the King making a most lamentable description of the state thereof) that it should be reduced to civility planted with schools and ministers, as many as could be gotten'.

Forty-eight hours later, on the Monday, the four Puritan divines were admitted by the King to the conference. All the Anglican deans and doctors were there, but only two of the Anglican bishops were allowed to be present; Patrick Galloway, a former minister of Perth, attended only as a spectator. The heir to the throne, Prince Henry, sat on a low stool and listened to the proceedings. After a brief speech from the King, Dr John Reynolds—who was President of Corpus Christi College, Oxford—speaking for the Puritans, began to set out the concessions they hoped the King would make. The other three Puritans got down on their knees to listen. He was rudely interrupted by the Bishop of London, who chided the Puritans 'for appearing before His Majesty in Turkey gowns and not in your scholastic habits, according to the orders of the University'; but the bishop was rebuked by the King for his 'sudden interruption' and told that each party must be allowed to state its case. Interruptions from the bishop and others went on, with quite audible sneers such as 'A Puritan is a Protestant frayed out of his wits'.

Yet Dr Reynolds, unperturbed and undaunted, kept on talking, and suddenly made a suggestion which was of immense importance. He said: 'May your Majesty be pleased that the Bible be new translated, such translations as are extant not answering the original.'

The Bishop of London broke in with a sneer, but King James quietened him and added: 'I wish some special pains were taken for a uniform translation, which should be done by the best learned in both universities, then reviewed by the bishops, presented to the Privy Council, and lastly ratified by royal authority to be read in the whole church, and no other.' It was as a result of this suggestion, made by the Puritans at Hampton Court, that the compilation of the Authorised Version of the English Bible was put in hand. James I's enthusiasm was so great that no opposing argument was put forward by the Anglicans and it is greatly to the King's credit that he was himself able to sketch out the project on the spur of the moment so effectively in a few words.

The work started that same year, 1604. The new translators of the Bible were selected with great care. The best available scholarship was enlisted, forty-seven in all: divided into groups, they were allotted sections, one group dealt with Job, the Psalms, the Proverbs, the Chronicles and Ecclesiastes; and so on. Dr Reynolds was appointed to the committee which revised the translation of the Prophets. The revision took nearly three years to complete and was published four years later in 1611. And for centuries it has been in use in every country where English is read.

The arguments of the Puritans for concessions, such as the abandonment of the use of the Cross in baptism, of the wearing of the surplice, and of the words in the marriage service 'with my body I thee worship', were dismissed curtly by the King with the words: 'Some in whose behalf you speak think themselves able to teach me and all the bishops of the land'; then, asserting his authority as Defender of the Faith, he ended by saying that at a recent conference in Scotland he had been told by a 'beardless boy that he would hold conformity with me for matters of doctrine; but for matters of ceremony they were to be left in Christian liberty to every man. . . . But I will none of that; I will have one doctrine and one discipline, one religion in substance and ceremony; and there I charge you never to speak more to that point when the Church hath ordained it.' Sir John Harington, who was at the meeting, stated in a letter to his wife that King James used upbraiding rather than arguments and bade them 'away with their snivelling'.

The Puritans left convinced that they could not hope to get anything from the King. The Anglicans were jubilant. The servile Bishop of London called for a thanksgiving to God. Thus the discussion ended with the two religious groups as far apart as ever.

The King, chortling with delight at what he had achieved, wrote boastfully to a friend in Scotland: 'We have kept such a revel with the Puritans here this two days, as was never heard the like: quhaire *I have peppered thaime as soundlie* as yee have done the Papists thaire.'

Feelings hardened on both sides and developed in time into the crisis which sealed the fate of his son, Charles I.

Shortly after the conference the King left Hampton Court and stayed for a time in the King's House in the Tower of London. But his eleven-year-old heir, Henry, spent the entire spring and summer at Hampton Court. Attended by only a few tutors and retainers, he divided his time between his studies which his keen brain welcomed, and outdoor diversions including hunting. He is said to have been an unerring shot with the bow: there is a contemporary painting in the Queen's Audience Chamber at Hampton Court showing him drawing his sword from its scabbard; kneeling beside him holding a dead stag by the antlers is the young Earl of Essex, the son of Queen Elizabeth's favourite who was executed by her in the Tower only three years earlier. The boys are dressed in hunting green and the Prince's horse and groom and dog are also in the picture. For the other diversions of the Prince there were tennis and bowls, tossing the pike and shooting at the butts. It is sad that Prince Henry died young: he was gentle, kind, considerate and always eager to understand the problems of others and to try to help them. Things might have been very different if he had lived to succeed James.

The King and Queen joined their son in the autumn. With them was the very lovely Lady Arabella Stuart. James kept her within his circle so that every move of hers could be observed. His resolve was to prevent a marriage which might endanger his throne. The Earl of Pembroke, at Hampton Court at the time, wrote to her uncle the Earl of Shrewsbury: 'A great embassy is coming from the King of Poland, whose chief errand is to demand the Lady Arabella in marriage for his master. So may your Princess of the Blood grow a great Queen.' To every suitor there were objections. James would not even countenance her marrying a foreigner whether king or commoner. To allay His Majesty's anxiety, Lady Arabella kept rejecting every approach with 'I will not hear of marriage'; but she contrived nevertheless to make a clandestine marriage five years later.

When the King learned of it he was enraged, for her choice had fallen on William Seymour, grandson of Lord Hertford and Lady Catherine Grey, Lady Jane Grey's sister, which brought her claim to the throne so very much nearer. The bridegroom was arrested and sent to the Tower; Lady Arabella, despatched to Durham Castle to be kept as far from her husband as possible, managed to escape and, in male clothing and a wig, set out for France in a French ship which her husband had arranged to join, but he missed the ship and followed in another. Outside Calais, while waiting anxiously for her husband, she was seized, brought back to England and imprisoned in the Tower of London, where she died eleven years later.

It is not clear whether the King and Queen were at Hampton Court for Christmas in 1604. They were certainly there early in the New Year, and the Queen's delight in plays and masques was again indulged. One of the comedies the Court enjoyed was *The Fayre Mayd of Bristoe* (Bristol) presented by His Majesty's Players.

After their usual stay in London for the spring and summer, they were back at Hampton Court by the end of September, bringing the Archbishop of Canterbury with them, and went to London only for the opening of Parliament on the fateful fifth of November when the blowing up of the King and Parliament was only averted by the timely discovery of Guy Fawkes' Gunpowder Plot. Throughout the trial of the conspirators the Royal Family remained at Hampton Court.

The Queen's brother, King Christian IV of Denmark, spent the summer there, bringing a bodyguard of a hundred men dressed in blue velvet with silver trimmings, twelve pages and twelve trumpeters. He had already been shown by James 'with immense pride' the other royal palaces in and around London. The King of Denmark, we are told, 'dyned at Hampton Court and there killed deare, with great pleasure'; and the wine flowed freely. A play was put on for him, but the name of neither the play nor the players is now known; it is possible that Shakespeare, one of His Majesty's Players, was there, and these lines in *Hamlet* seem relevant:

> The King doth wake to-night, and takes his rouse,
> Keeps wassail, and the swaggering up-spring reels;
> And, as he drains his draughts of Rhenish down,
> The kettle-drum and trumpet thus bray out
> The triumph of his pledge.

Sir John Harington, who was present, records this in more lurid detail: 'We had women and wine too of such plenty as would have astonished each beholder. Our feasts were magnificent and the royal guests did most lovingly embrace each other at the table. I think the Dane hath strangely wrought on our good English nobles; for those whom I could never get to taste good English liquor now follow the fashion and wallow in beastly delights. The ladies abandon their sobriety and are seen to roll about in intoxication.'

A portrait of King Christian by Van Somer hangs in the King's Second Presence Chamber at Hampton Court: it shows him to be, as an eye-witness at the merriment describes, 'a man of goodly person, of stature in no extremes', and in appearance good-looking 'so like his sister', King James's Queen Anne, who derived the same joy from gaiety and entertaining.

After the Danish King's departure, King James arranged another theological conference at Hampton Court largely to taunt the Scottish Presbyterian divines, who had to listen to the long-winded sermons of Anglican bishops on the duty of passive obedience and the divine origin of arbitrary power. But the Scots, aware how the Puritans had been treated, skilfully avoided being entangled in any argument, and James was cheated of his delight in embarrassing them.

These discourses were interrupted by the arrival of the Duke of Lorraine's son, the Prince of Vaudemont, with a retinue of seven earls, ten barons, forty gentlemen of quality, and one hundred and twenty common persons. 'All the Lords and gentlemen,' we are told, 'were very brave and cumlie in their apparel and as civil in their behaviour'—how different from the Danish guests!

They arrived by coach from London and were taken out hunting by the King. The stag was found and killed and its head was brought with great pomp into the Privy Chamber.

The French Prince stayed at Hampton Court for a fortnight. There was some argument in private as to whether James or his princely guest should pay for the lavish entertainment. The King refused at first to meet the heavy cost, but finally agreed to do so. 'They were all very royally entertained and feasted,' we are told, 'a diet of two hundred dishes being appointed to be served all the while he abides here.' The diversions were many. In the Queen's Presence Chamber they danced the lively *corante* with its high hops and springs, and then the *galliard* with its even brisker high jumping.

Not many months later the Queen came alone to Hampton Court. She had just lost her infant daughter Mary and spent her time in complete seclusion. The Court officials, however, were given leave to divert themselves and did so in their own quarters. The King's Chief Minister, Sir Robert Cecil, by now Lord Salisbury, occupied quarters near the Queen's in order to comfort her.

Hunting was such an obsession with James that affairs of State often had to wait. On one occasion Lord Salisbury went down on his knees and begged His Majesty to postpone a hunting party for a few days as the business before the Council was both important and urgent.

The King refused and worked himself up into a great rage. 'You will be the death of me,' he bellowed. 'You had better send me back to Scotland.' It was the threat he made whenever he was displeased. If large numbers of people came out to watch him hunt, he would shout angrily that he would leave England if he could not take part in the sport without 'the barbarous insolency of multitudes of vulgar people'.

It was an idle threat: he was much too pleased with his exalted position, king not merely of a small, poorly developed country, but also of a highly civilised and wealthy nation, recognised as one of the most powerful and influential in Europe.

His contempt for the common people was constantly and blatantly expressed. In an angry proclamation issued from Hampton Court on 9 September 1609, he said: 'We must acknowledge that we have found *the gentlemen and persons of the better sort* (who know best what becometh their duetie) have restrained their owne contentment: yet falleth it out, notwithstanding, that neither the example of them, nor respect of Lawes, nor duty to us, hath had power to reforme *the corrupt natures and insolent dispositions of some of the baser sort,* and some other of a disordered life.' It showed his complete lack of understanding of the ordinary people of England, one of whom, in an anonymous letter to the King, threatened to poison all his hounds if he did not stop 'for ever running after wilde animals' to give a little more thought to the good government of the people.

The satirist Anthony Weldon declared that the King loved 'beasts better than men, took more delight in them, and was more tender over the life of a stag than of a man'. Weldon was more generous to the King in this statement than the facts support, for James often went into the park and took pot shots from behind a tree at the tame deer as they grazed in the shade. Even while engaged in hunting it was the King's practice to single out the deer he wanted, get the hounds to sniff the spot on which it had grazed and follow the scent of that animal and that one only, which did not make the sport particularly attractive for his guests; and when the mood took him, after pursuing the chosen deer, he as often as not shot it with a longbow.

His costume was often laughed at by his guests. One of them described him at the meet dressed in a suit 'green as the grass he trod on, with a feather in his cap and a horne instead of a sword by his side. How suitable to his age, calling or person I leave to others to judge.' His manner of hunting was described as 'tame' and far from enjoyable.

The park at Hampton Court was always well stocked with game and the fences were kept in excellent repair so that the deer should not get out of the enclosure. The Keeper of the adjoining park at Bushey was not allowed to hunt any of the deer there without express permission from the King. Every visitor from abroad was, as a special privilege, introduced to what they came to regard as *Le sport anglais* when they came to Hampton Court.

It was not only hunting and other outdoor sports that the King wanted his guests to enjoy. He was so proud of the Palace that he insisted on his visitors being taken round on a conducted tour of the galleries and State rooms by the Vice-Chamberlain. One of the visitors was Prince Otto, the seventeen-year-old son of the Landgrave of Hesse, who spent a great deal of his time with Prince Henry. He was so fascinated by what he saw that he compiled a list of what the rooms contained. His manuscript, which covers many pages, has been preserved in the library at Cassel. 'Many beautiful pictures in the galleries,' he noted, 'one of our Saviour with an inscription testifying that the Sultan (Bajazet II) had sent it to the Pope to liberate his brother (Zim) from captivity.' Among the 'Curiosities' a 'Map of the World, woven in cloth most cunningly, and dedicated to Edward VI', and 'a very fine musical instrument of glass', upon which were inscribed some verses in Latin. This instrument was presented to Princess Elizabeth 'by an English melord'—it had belonged to Queen Elizabeth and except for the strings was made entirely of glass.

A portrait that has sometimes hung at Hampton Court shows King James's wife Anne as 'The Huntress Queen'. Painted by Van

Somer, it shows her standing beside a fat sorrel steed with a cream mane, and a Negro groom dressed in red holding the bridle. The Queen's skirt is of dark-green velvet, with a bodice of the same material, very tight at the waist. On her head is a conical hat with a red plume.

Like her husband, when she hunted she shot the deer. But on one occasion while trying to shoot the deer she shot the King's favourite hound Jewel. The King 'stormed exceedingly awhile; but after he knew who did it, he was soon pacified, and with much kindness wished her not to be troubled with it, for he should love her never the worse, and the next day he sent her a diamond worth £2,000 as a legacy from his dead dog'.

Despite James's tenderness, one might even say devotion, to the Queen, he was passionately drawn to good-looking young men, the first of whom was a young Scot named Robert Carr, who had come to England with King James as his page in 1603. Carr was about thirteen at the time, the exact date of his birth is unknown. He left the royal service but, after a few years in France, returned to England and was recognised by the King while taking part in a tilting contest.

By now about seventeen, very good-looking and with a skill in the various sports the King admired, but completely lacking intellectual gifts, he was immediately knighted and attached to His Majesty's household and was of course with the King at Hampton Court for the Christmas festivities. When a year or two later, Sir Walter Raleigh was sent to the Tower for suspected plotting to put Lady Arabella Stuart on the throne, James gave Raleigh's extensive estate in Dorset at Sherborne to Carr, who was not yet twenty.

On the death of the Earl of Salisbury two years later, Carr was appointed to succeed him as Secretary of State and was raised to the peerage as Earl of Somerset. He was quite incapable of carrying out any of his important State duties and got Sir Thomas Overbury, who had been infatuated with Carr for some years, to undertake the work.

Overbury hated the King's relationship with the attractive young man, but put up with it because it helped his own advancement. The triangle soon had a fourth side to it. Somerset began a liaison with the divorced Frances Howard, Countess of Essex.

Disaster quickly followed. Overbury knew too much about the lady's earlier life and, driven by jealousy, threatened to reveal everything. To prevent this she persuaded the King to send him on a mission to Russia. When Overbury refused to go, he was sent to the Tower. The besotted King spent a vast sum of money on his favourite's marriage to the woman Overbury had described as 'nothing but a whore'. To put a stop to any further disclosures, the bride had him poisoned in the Tower. Her accomplices talked. Somerset was

Henry VIII. After Holbein

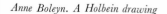

Anne Boleyn. A Holbein drawing

Antonius van den Wyngaerde's panoramic sketch of Hampton Court made in 1558, showing Wolsey's Great Gateway on the left, then Henry VIII's Great Hall with its tall louvred chimney, since removed, and the King's State Rooms, later replaced by Wren's impressive work

Jane Seymour. A Holbein drawing

Queen Elizabeth I as a young girl

The attractive Fish Court, one of the small Tudor courts on the north side of the Palace

implicated and both he and his wife were arrested and sent to the Tower where they were kept as prisoners for seven years.

In no time at all the King found a new favourite, George Villiers, a little younger than Somerset, good-looking of course, but much better educated than his predecessor and blessed with a delightful sense of humour. Appointed cup-bearer to His Majesty to begin with, he was next made Gentleman of the Bedchamber and given a knighthood, and eventually took over the high office of Secretary of State that Somerset had held. Honours were showered on him: within three years he was made Marquess of Buckingham and a Dukedom followed; the King's gifts of vast estates and money made him at the age of twenty-five the richest nobleman in England. Not content with all this, he obtained rank and fortune from the King for his numerous relatives. Advantageous marriages were arranged for them, and it is one of these marriages that concerns Hampton Court.

For Buckingham's elder brother Sir John Villiers an heiress to a vast fortune was selected. She was Frances Coke, daughter of Lord Chief Justice Coke, by his second and fabulously wealthy wife Lady Hatton. Shortly after the plan was set in motion, the Lord Chief Justice was dismissed from office for opposing Buckingham's uncontrollable avarice and recurrent encroachments on the King's prerogative. Coke was not in favour of his daughter's marriage to Sir John Villiers, but, with the promise of being made Lord Chancellor, he agreed but offered a dowry of only 10,000 marks instead of the £10,000 demanded and only £1,000 a year during his lifetime. This was unacceptable. The pressure upon him continued until it became unbearable. Eventually he agreed to pay £20,000 in cash and 2,000 marks a year, to be followed on his death by a bequest of land worth £2,000.

All was set now for the marriage, but his wife would have none of it. Neither she nor her daughter, who was madly in love with Sir Robert Howard, had been consulted. Taking Frances with her, Lady Coke fled from their home and hid in the house of a relative not far from Hampton Court.

The ex-Chief Justice, after a frantic quest, ferreted out where his wife and daughter were in hiding. He applied at once to the Privy Council for a search warrant; but, realising it would be a long-drawn-out affair, he took the law into his own hands. Collecting a band of armed men, his sons and his servants, and buckling on a breastplate himself, he set out with sword and pistols for the hiding-place.

They found the gate bolted and barricaded. It was forced open, but there remained yet another door, which was powerfully defended. To his repeated demand that his daughter should be handed over, 'in the King's name', he got no response. 'If death should ensue,' he warned, 'it would be justifiable homicide in him, but murder for those who opposed him.'

One of the invaders managed to get in through a back window and let the others in. In their quest for the ex-Chief Justice's daughter they had to break down still more doors and eventually found her and her mother in a small closet. Coke seized his daughter, wrenched her out of her mother's firm grasp and rode off with her to his home at Stoke Poges in Buckinghamshire; there he locked her up in an upper room and put the key in his pocket.

Proceedings were brought against the father in the Star Chamber, and he in turn prosecuted his wife for abducting his daughter. The girl meanwhile was placed in the custody of her proposed bride-groom's mother Lady Compton and was later moved into the care of the Clerk of the Council.

In the end Frances was induced by royal pressure to say that she liked Sir John Villiers better than anyone else in the world and she was made to sign a document stating that 'being a mere child she had not understood what was good for her' but agreed to marry Sir John.

By further pressure the mother's consent was also obtained, but she refused to attend the wedding. Coke arrived with his daughter, a great many relatives and friends for whom as many as nine coaches were needed. The marriage was solemnised in the Chapel at Hampton Court in the presence of the King and Queen.

It was a strange evening. After a banquet and a masque which finished very late, the King and his courtiers wandered in their night clothes along the galleries, broke into numerous bedrooms, sewed up the sheets in the beds, and finished by entering the bedroom of the bride and bridegroom, jumped on them and rolled them about.

The marriage was a failure. Before long the bride left her husband and went to join Sir Robert Howard, the man she had always loved.

The Queen, so gay and often boisterous, who loved the masques put on at Hampton Court and took part in so many of them, was suffering from a complication of ailments that led to her death. The diagnosis showed that she had tuberculosis as well as gout and dropsy: her legs began to swell and slowly her body got bloated. She died at Hampton Court on 2 March 1619. James, said to be ill in London, was not with her; their only surviving son Charles was at her bedside.

In his own strange way the King was devoted to her. Married when she was not yet fifteen, the ship bringing her to Scotland was driven by a violent storm to Norway, where James hurried to join her; many Danish and Scottish witches were rounded up and burned to death for causing the storm. Anne was vain and extravagant. Not content with appropriating all Queen Elizabeth's lovely dresses she spent vast sums on buying a great many more. Her passion for jewels was also insatiable. She kept aloof from affairs of State, interfering only to try to save the life of Sir Walter Raleigh whom she greatly admired and visited often when he was a prisoner in the Tower of London: in an earlier illness he had given her a cordial of his concoction which cured her. She begged Buckingham to plead for Raleigh's life, but without avail. He was executed a few months before her death.

A lady in attendance on the Queen described in a letter to a friend the Queen's condition before her death. Her Majesty had been staying at Hampton Court for some time because 'the air seemed to suit her so well. She was reasonably well recovered to the eyes of all that saw her, and came to her drawing-chamber and to her gallery every day almost; yet still so weak of her legs that she could not stand upon them, neither had she any stomach for her meat the space of six weeks before she died. . . . On the 22nd February she took a flux [cough] vehemently, which she has had all this winter, which is now seen to be the cough of the lungs by a consumption.'

On March first it was obvious that the end was near. Many lords and ladies came hurriedly from London to Hampton Court but were not admitted into her room. Only the Archbishop of Canterbury, the Bishop of London, and the Lord Privy Seal were allowed in. They knelt by her bedside and said a prayer. Then her son Charles, who was nineteen, was brought in. She died in the small hours of the next morning 'just as the old clock struck four'.

It is not clear whether she did leave a will: she certainly signed a document on her deathbed, which is said to have been her will; but the King disposed of her property as he thought fit. Though saddened by her death, he set off almost at once for the races at Newmarket and joined in a round of festivity and fun. A large quantity of her jewels was given to Buckingham by James as well as £1,200 of her land and the use of Somerset House in the Strand in London which had been the Queen's.

The total value of her estate was estimated at £800,000, half of this being the value of her jewels, which were conveyed to the King in London in four large carts. After checking the items it was found that £36,000 worth of her jewellery was missing. Two of the Queen's personal attendants, Pierrot and Anna, both Danish, were arrested and charged with theft. They were later released as their complicity in the theft could not be proved. What placated James, indeed greatly gratified him, was that by his wife's death he was saving £90,000 a year, for that is what it had cost to run her household.

Convinced that her death was caused by the appearance of a comet in the sky, James expressed his feelings in a rhyming epitaph:

> Thee to invite the Great God sent his star;
> Whose friend and nearest kin good princes are;
> Who, though they run the race of men and die,
> Death serves but to refine their majesty.
> So did my Queen her Court from hence remove,
> And left this earth to be enthroned above;
> She is changed, not dead, for sure no good prince dies,
> But like the sun, sets only for to rise.

There is a hint in this of his belief in the divine right of kings.

He had a portrait of himself painted by Van Somer dressed 'in a melancholy suit of solemn black'; it hangs in the Queen's Bedchamber at Hampton Court. The following year he had a second portrait painted by Van Somer which may also be seen at Hampton

Court. James is dressed in royal robes, lined with ermine, the crown on his head, the sceptre in his right hand and the orb in his left.

During these years, from 1615 until King James's death ten years later, Inigo Jones was his Surveyor and had Hampton Court under his supervision: in his copy of Palladio's sketches at Worcester College, Oxford, there is an entry giving measurements of some of the courts and cloisters at Hampton Court. There is also a letter—said to be the only surviving letter written by Inigo Jones—which refers to Hampton Court.

King James, unlike his predecessors, had a violent objection to any ambassador staying at the Palace; they were put up in other nearby buildings. But an exception was made in the case of Count Gondomar, the Spanish ambassador, because of the King's desire to marry his heir Charles to the Infanta Maria, daughter of the King of Spain. Yet the rooms allocated to the Count were found to be unsatisfactory, because they were not in the main building, but in one of the detached towers, which did not at all please the ambassador.

Inigo Jones wrote to the Earl of Arundel:

In my journey to London I went to Hampton Court, where I heard that the Spanish ambassador came to Kingston and sent his steward to Hampton Court, who looked on the lodgings intended for the ambassador, which were in Mr. Huggins his rooms; but the steward utterly disliked those rooms, saying that the ambassador would not lie but in the house (meaning the Palace); besides there was no furniture in those rooms, or bedding, or otherwise, neither for the ambassador or his followers. So the steward returning to his lord, he resolved only to hunt in the park and so return. But the Keeper answered he might not suffer that, he having received no order for it; so the ambassador went back discontented, having had some smart sport in the warren. But since, my lord of Nottingham hearing of this, sent to the ambassador to excuse the matter, which the ambassador took very well and promised to come and lie at Hampton Court before His Majesty's return.

A few months later the French ambassador, hearing of this, had to be shown the same courtesy and was 'nobly entertained with hawking and hunting', but was not apparently given lodgings inside the Palace itself.

Gondomar made all the arrangements for Prince Charles's visit to Madrid with the Duke of Buckingham. But the marriage did not take place because of the Spanish King's insistence on Charles's conversion to Roman Catholicism. Negotiations were begun shortly afterwards for the Prince's marriage to the sister of Louis XIII of France, but a similar difficulty arose there. Louis wanted very large concessions to be made to all the Roman Catholics in England, but James would not hear of this. In the end Buckingham, who was by now virtually ruler of the country, persuaded James to go back on the promise he gave the House of Commons that he would make no concessions. But in March 1625, before anything could be done James I died.

During his last visit to Hampton Court, in September 1623, the King was displeased with a sermon delivered in the Chapel by Dr Whiting. What angered the King has not been recorded, but Dr Whiting had to appear before the Council, who 'found him penitent and submissive; yet his offence requiring exemplary justice, they had him committed'.

Charles I, a small, elegant figure, only five feet tall, his handsome features set off by a well-trimmed pale brown beard, and sadly afflicted by a stammer, went to stay at Hampton Court three months after his accession. He had just married Henrietta Maria, Louis XIII's sister, and had decided to spend his honeymoon there. The bride, not yet fifteen, was also small and swarthy complexioned, with large black eyes and an abundance of black curly hair. She bore a strong resemblance to her father Henri IV, not only in her features but in her speech and gesture and above all in her temper. She arrived in England with a large French retinue numbering no less than a hundred and six people. They included a Lord Chamberlain (the Comte de Tillières), two ambassadors, the Bishop of Mende, thirty Roman Catholic priests, a father confessor, numerous ladies-in-waiting, and lords-in-waiting, and male and female servants.

One of her ladies-in-waiting, Madame de Saint-Georges, had been exercising a powerful influence over the young Queen since her childhood: Henrietta Maria never made a decision without consulting her.

That this was going to make life difficult was obvious at once to Charles; he decided to be firm. As they were setting out for Hampton Court, he ordered that the large coach should be taken away and a small one brought for him and the Queen; only two English Court ladies were allowed to travel with them. Madame de Saint-Georges was furious and the Queen did not conceal her own resentment. Using Buckingham as his confidant, Charles told him of it and asked him to explain to the Queen that her full co-operation with the King was essential. The Duke sought an immediate interview and told her bluntly that the King found her reliance on Madame quite intolerable. Though the Duke's manner was that of a headmaster towards a truant child, Her Majesty took it calmly. She was not aware, she said, that she had done anything to displease her husband, and added that she was eager to establish a good relationship with the Duke too if only he would behave towards her in a friendly and respectful manner.

Feeling that he might have been too severe, Buckingham called again next day to see the Queen and asked if she could honour him by appointing his wife (he had married Lady Katherine Manners, daughter of the Earl of Rutland), his sister, and his niece as Ladies of the Bedchamber: clearly his purpose was to introduce an English influence into her immediate circle. But the Queen avoided the trap by saying that she had brought three such ladies with her from France and would have to discuss the matter with the French ambassador.

Buckingham forestalled her by going to the ambassador himself. He said firmly that what he had suggested would be of service not only to the Queen but to France. They discussed the matter with Her Majesty's Roman Catholic bishop, who turned down the offer, saying that it would be wrong to expose the young Queen to the influence of heretical English women: it would scandalise all Catholics in England and abroad, and the Pope would certainly not approve of it. Buckingham was very angry but had to abide by the bishop's decision.

A few days later the King and Queen moved to Windsor Castle, as the plague raging in London was by now thought to be approaching Hampton Court. Once again, as they were about to get into the coach, Charles, to exclude Madame de Saint-Georges, invited the Marquess of Hamilton to get in. But Madame was not to be deterred; she attempted to get in too and the King seized her by the arm and pushed her back. The Queen's annoyance was obvious. She regarded it as a slight on her and had much to say about it in her *Memoirs*. She records that the Comte de Tillières heard Buckingham talk to Charles about the plan to prevent Madame from riding in the coach.

The plague did not affect Hampton Court, but reached Windsor. Two deaths occurred in a house in Windsor where some of the Queen's priests were living. They were quickly sent back to Hampton Court, where they were put into quarantine in one of the towers in the Tilt Yard, while the King and Queen went to Beaulieu and Titchfield in Hampshire.

The quarrel between the King and Queen over the treatment of Madame de Saint-Georges went on during the two months they were away and continued after they returned to Hampton Court. By now fresh causes of contention were added. Clearly set out in her marriage treaty was her right to practise the Roman Catholic religion with her attendants. But the King felt that these practices should not be flaunted in the presence of guests.

On one occasion, while the King and Queen sat down to dinner with a large company in the Presence Chamber at Hampton Court, the Queen's confessor, Father Bérulle, always near her Majesty and often aggressive, insisted on saying grace. 'Mr. Hackett, Chaplain to the Lord Keeper, being there to say grace', a letter to Sir Martin Stuteville dated October 1625 informs us, 'the confessor would have prevented him, but that Hackett shoved him away; whereupon the confessor went to the Queen's side, and was about to say grace again, but that the King, pulling the dishes unto him, and the carvers falling to the business, hindered. When dinner was done the confessor thought, standing by the Queen, to have been before Mr. Hackett, but Mr. Hackett again got the start. The confessor, nevertheless, begins his grace as loud as Mr. Hackett, with such confusion that the King in great passion instantly rose from the table, and taking the Queen by the hand retired to the bedchamber.'

Charles was also concerned about his wife's coldness and indifference towards him. The Comte de Tillières reveals in his *Memoirs* that this was caused by the malign influence of Madame de Saint-Georges. Finally the King resolved to get rid of the Queen's entire French retinue of women and priests. But he did nothing about it until he and the Queen returned to Hampton Court from London early in November.

The French ambassador, the Marquis de Blainville, followed the King and Queen there and asked to be lodged at the Palace, but was told that lodgings had already been found for him at Kingston, over a mile from the Palace. But the ambassador was not to be put off. He pointed out that there had been cases of plague in that town. Argument over this went on for some time. In the end the ambassador approached the Queen and was given rooms in the Water Gallery in the garden where Queen Elizabeth was housed when she was the prisoner of her sister Queen Mary. This made the ambassador a guest of the King, who was not at all pleased as it involved him in providing not only lodging but also board for the ambassador and his suite. The cost to the King was more than £2,000.

The final quarrel between the King and Queen over her retinue now began. The Queen insisted, firmly and angrily, that under the marriage treaty it was her prerogative to appoint her own French staff for the management and collection of the revenues of her dowry.

The King was not prepared to agree. He wrote to her mother, Marie de Médici, in Paris, complaining of his wife's undutiful conduct and blaming Madame de Saint-Georges for 'taking it in distaste because I would not let her ride with us in the coach (when there are many women of higher quality), claiming it as her due (which in England we think a strange thing), and setting my wife in such a humour against me, as from that very hour to this no man can say she has behaved two days together with the respect that I have deserved of her'. He continued:

> As I take it, it was at her first coming to Hampton Court that I sent some of my Council to her with regulations that were kept in the Court of the Queen my mother and desired the Comte de Tillières that the same might be kept. The answer of Queen Henrietta to this deputation was 'I hope I shall be suffered to order my own house as I list.' Now if she had said that she would speak with me herself, not doubting to give me satisfaction, I would have found no fault in her, for whatever she had said I should have imputed it to her ignorance of business; but I could not imagine her affronting me so by refusal publicly. After this answer, I took my time, when I thought we had leisure, to dispute it out by ourselves, to tell her both her fault in the publicity of such answer and her mistakes; but she gave me so ill an answer that I omit to repeat it. Likewise I have to complain of her neglect of the English tongue and of the nation in general.

It is possible that the King had talked the matter over with the Duke of Buckingham before writing this letter to his mother-in-law; Buckingham might even have drafted it. The Queen Mother's reply (if she did reply) is not known; we have, however, a second letter from Charles to her.

One night, after I was a-bed, my wife put a paper in my hand telling me 'It was a list of those she desired to be officers of her revenue.' I took it, and said that 'I would read it next morning'; but withal I told her 'that, by agreement in France, I had the naming of them.' She said 'There were both English and French in the note.' I replied that 'Those English whom I thought fit to serve her, I would confirm; but for the French it was impossible for them to serve her in that capacity.' She said 'All those in that paper had breviates from her mother and herself and that she would admit no other.'

Then I said, [the King added] 'It was neither in her mother's power nor hers to admit any without my leave; and if she relied on that, whomsoever she recommended should not come in.' Then she plainly bade me 'take my lands to myself, for since she had no power to put in whom she would into those places, she would have neither lands or houses of me'; but bade me 'give her what I thought fit by way of pension'. I bade her remember to whom she spoke and told her 'she ought not to use me so'. Then she fell into a passionate discourse, 'how miserable she is in having no power to place servants'; and that business succeeded the worse for her recommendation. When I offered to answer she would not so much as hear me but went on lamenting, saying 'that she was not of such base quality as to be used so'. I both made her hear me and end that discourse.

Later that month Buckingham set out for France. His purpose was to see the young French Queen Anne, daughter of the King of Spain and sister of the Infanta Maria, whom Charles had hoped to marry. On that earlier journey Charles and Buckingham had stayed in Paris for a few days during which Buckingham was greatly attracted to the young Queen; Charles had caught just a brief glimpse of Henrietta Maria, who was only thirteen then. Henrietta, hearing that he was on his way to Spain in quest of a wife, had remarked: 'He might have found one nearer at hand.'

On reaching Holland, Buckingham was handed a letter from Charles. It had been written (doubtless at Buckingham's dictation) for the express purpose of being shown to the Queen Mother, Marie de Médici, to make her well disposed towards Buckingham and further his romantic hopes of a love affair with Queen Anne. The letter added that despite Buckingham's continuous plea in favour of the Queen keeping her French retainers, the King would have to take action. The Queen Mother never got the letter. Cardinal Richelieu, knowing well Buckingham's purpose in wanting to come to Paris, forbade his coming to France at all. This so enraged Buckingham that he was more than ever determined to send Henrietta Maria's attendants back to France.

On returning to England he went at once to Hampton Court and did all he could to stir the King to action. The rows with the Queen were kept on the boil. Indeed he went a great deal further than that, warning the Queen, as Madame de Motteville records in her *Memoirs*, that 'Queens of England have been "beheaded before now"'. Had it not been for King Charles's great affection for Buckingham, he would certainly not have tolerated such behaviour towards the Queen of England, who was only fifteen at that time, living in a foreign land, where the language, the customs, and the religion were quite different from her own and her attendants were the only people who could offer her any sympathy and support.

Henrietta Maria was so upset by the whole affair, which had haunted her for months, that she refused, as a conscientious Catholic, to be crowned with the King by the heretic Archbishop of Canterbury. The King was shocked and deeply offended. The Coronation took place at Westminster Abbey on 2 February 1626. The Queen refused to attend although a latticed chamber had been erected for her inside the Abbey. She was the first Queen of England to refuse and it was regarded by the people as an international insult to their religion; the Puritans in particular never forgave her for it.

The atmosphere between the King and Queen worsened and Charles decided on the immediate removal of the Queen's French followers. His order to Buckingham was in this harsh form: 'I command you to send all the French away by tomorrow out of the Towne. If you can, by faire means (but stike not long in disputing), otherways, force them away, dryving them away *lyke so manie wylde beasts*, until ye have shipped them, and so *the Devill goe with them*. Let me heare no answer, but of the performance of my command.'

The Queen, told of it, wept, then got down on her knees and begged Charles to let her keep some of her retainers. But Charles was adamant: all would have to go, he said. When told that he would not allow her to say goodbye to them, Henrietta Maria began to scream. Hearing her screams, some of her French entourage ran out into the courtyard under her window. The Queen rushed to the window and smashed the panes of glass with her fists. Charles seized her and tried to drag her away, but her hands, badly scratched and covered with blood, clung firmly to the metal frame of the casement and she kept sobbing agonisingly. His Majesty had got his way at last.

The French entourage was thrown into a state of confusion and anger. They swore and howled and resisted, but the Yeomen of the Guard dragged them out and locked the doors of their lodgings. It was regarded by the French ambassador and others as a flagrant breach of the treaty of marriage. The Comte de Tillières' comment was: 'La facilité des anglais à tout promettre et leur effronterie à rien tenir.' Some wondered if it would lead to a war between England and France, but Cardinal Richelieu was not in favour of adopting such a drastic course. He sent instead the brilliant diplomatist Maréchal de Bassompierre, brother-in-law of the Comte de Tillières, to try and work out an acceptable compromise.

Bassompierre stayed in London to discuss the matter with Buckingham and some other ministers, while Charles was busy giving audiences to other emissaries at Hampton Court. He received Paul Rosencrantz, the Danish ambassador, on 11 July; Bethlem Gabor, the Prince of Transylvania, on 21 September in the Privy Chamber; and on 6 October, William Laud, who took the oath as Dean of the Chapel Royal and was later appointed Archbishop of Canterbury.

While Bassompierre waited in London, having 'gotten no audience with the King', it was discovered that the French retainers had made off with the Queen's entire trousseau. All she had left were two smocks and one gown. The Lords of the Council demanded the return of the beautiful and costly wardrobe. Only one old satin gown was returned: Madame de Saint-Georges stated that the dresses had been presented by the Queen to her friends; it was also claimed that a great many dresses had been bought for the Queen, at her request, by the staff who had never been paid for them.

Henrietta Maria was deeply distressed at the loss of her trousseau and swore to Charles that she had never asked for clothes to be bought for her and never owed her staff any money. The staff moreover had left their quarters 'so defiled' that 'a week's worke would not make it cleane'.

At last on 11 October 1626 Bassompierre was brought to Hampton

Court in one of the King's coaches. An excellent dinner had been prepared for him, but he arrived too late for it, purposely it is thought; a lighter meal was hurriedly got ready, but neither he nor his suite would eat any of it. It puzzled Buckingham, who went at once to see Bassompierre and told him that the King wanted to know beforehand what he wished to say. The reply, to quote Bassompierre's own record of it, was: 'I said to him that the King should know what I had to say to him from my own mouth and that it was not the custom to limit an ambassador in what he had to represent to the Sovereign to whom he was sent, and that if he did not wish to see me I was ready to go back again.'

Buckingham then found it necessary to explain the King's attitude. 'He swore to me,' Bassompierre goes on, 'that the only reason which obliged him (the King) to this, and which made him insist upon it, was that he could not help putting himself in a passion in treating the matters about which I had to speak to him, which would not be decent in the chair of state, in sight of the chief persons of the kingdom, both men and women; that the Queen his wife was close to him, who, incensed at the dismissal of her servants, might commit some extravagance and cry in sight of everybody. In short that he would not commit himself in public; and that he was resolved sooner to break up this audience and grant me one in private than to treat with me concerning any business before everybody.'

Eventually the King received him formally that same day, with the Queen seated beside him on a dais in the Audience Chamber. 'The company was magnificent,' Bassompierre states, 'the order exquisite. I made my compliment to the King, gave him my letters and said my words of civility.' The public audience was over. The rest was to be in private. But no arrangement was made as to where or when the King was to see him. Bassompierre then got into the coach and left Hampton Court. Four days later he was asked to return and was received by the King in one of the galleries. The Queen, still at the Palace, was not present at the interview. Charles, the ambassador records, 'put himself into a great passion,' complained of the intrigues of the French staff, their attempts to wean the Queen's affection from her husband and setting her also against everything English. 'Why,' the King asked, 'do you not execute your commission at once and declare war?'

Bassompierre replied: 'I am not a herald to declare war, but a Marshal of France to make it when declared.' Charles quietened down after a time and personally escorted the ambassador to the Queen's apartments. In the end not much was achieved. The King made a few concessions: the Queen was allowed to have two priests—an Englishman and a Scot—and three women attendants who could speak French, one of whom, the Duchesse de Thouars, was the daughter of William the Silent, Prince of Orange, and therefore a Protestant.

War did break out between France and England a few months later, but it was not directly connected with this. Of course Louis XIII strongly resented Charles's stern action against English Roman Catholics, whom by the marriage treaty he had solemnly undertaken to protect; but much more serious was the seizure by the English Navy of French ships which were attempting to evade the blockade of the Spanish Netherlands—that led to French reprisals and the capture of a fleet of English merchant ships.

Buckingham set out with six hundred sail and seven thousand men for La Rochelle, but the expedition ended in failure. Not long afterwards, as Buckingham was setting out once again for La Rochelle from Portsmouth, he was stabbed to death by John Felton, one of the men who had served under him in the previous expedition.

The relationship between the King and Queen began to improve shortly after Bassompierre's return to France. A letter to the Queen from her mother advised her to obey her husband at all times absolutely and completely; and the King, missing the warmth and familiarity of Buckingham, sought more eagerly the companionship of his young wife.

For the first time they found themselves falling in love with each other. If he was away for a few days she placed a small portrait of him by her bed, or if she went to a spa to rest or recuperate, nothing could stop him from hurrying to join her. The French ambassador, the Marquis de Châteauneuf, was surprised to see Charles kissing the Queen 'a hundred times in an hour. . . . You do not see that in Turin, nor even in France.' Henrietta described herself now as 'the happiest woman in the world'.

By disposition Henrietta was lively and gay: she loved dancing, never missed a chance of putting on a play and often played one of the parts in it. A tutor was engaged to teach her to speak English. When Ben Jonson wrote a masque for her she spent days learning the lines. But she preferred the lighter productions of Walter Montague and kept on reciting the lyrics of Edmund Waller, especially his 'Go, lovely rose'. The Scottish poet Sir Robert Aytoun was brought in as her secretary; he is said to have written the original version of 'Auld Lang Syne'. Card games and billiards helped to pass the time and she was fond of collecting dwarfs and black servants to add to her household; monkeys and dogs were her further joy. But what absorbed her most was the decoration of her own suites of rooms in the various royal palaces.

In the autumn of 1628 she became pregnant and gave birth to her first child in May 1629; the boy, born prematurely, was christened Charles James, but died an hour later. A second son born a year later was the future Charles II. No fewer than nine children were borne by her; the youngest, Henrietta Anne, was only four and a half when Charles was executed. The Queen's devotion as a mother was the subject of admiring comment; those who happened to overhear her singing lullabies to her children praised the arresting beauty of her voice. She began to display an interest in dress and made many alterations in style. Hoops and wires and the high ruff that was such a feature of the Elizabethan age were abandoned and all Europe soon began to adopt the simple style she introduced; even men's clothes were influenced by it.

The King and Queen loved being at Hampton Court and went there two or three times a year. They always stayed long enough to entertain and have plays performed in the Great Hall. In November 1630 a play, based on a Persian story, which the Queen had seen at Christ Church, Oxford (the college Wolsey built), was performed at Hampton Court by a group of the Queen's Players; they were fortunate to have the costumes and scenery used at Oxford lent to the Palace for the performance. Two years later two plays were put on at Hampton Court; for one of them £20 was paid to Mr Joseph Taylor and Mr Swanston; for the other 'a like sum was paid to Mr Christopher Beeston and the rest of the Queen's Players'.

Plague in London in 1636 kept their Majesties in residence at Hampton Court for many months. A proclamation was issued prohibiting anyone from London coming within ten miles of the Palace: even barges were barred from that section of the River Thames. Those who ignored the order were taken before the Lords of the Privy Council and punished. To escape the plague some Londoners had rented houses near Hampton Court; but the law instantly intervened and ejected them. The normal residents of the neighbourhood were warned not to go to London or allow their servants to go there, or they too would be ejected from their homes. The plague nevertheless reached the nearby town of Kingston: although no one cared to touch a plague victim, it is said that these were moved into shacks built on the common and their homes disinfected. At Hampton Court itself plague claimed a victim in one of the outer staff buildings.

During the long months of autumn and winter the King relaxed some of these rigorous regulations and allowed players to come from London and give performances in the Great Hall. A number of plays were presented during the three months from the first of November 1636 to the end of January 1637. They included *The Moore of Venice*; *The Platonick Lovers* by Sir William Davenant, who claimed to be Shakespeare's natural son and succeeded Ben Jonson as an unofficial poet laureate; *The Royal Slave* by William Cartwright; and *Hamlet*, which Shakespeare had written more than thirty years earlier. A warrant, dated 11 April 1637, has this entry: 'To pay £154, being the charge of the alterations and additions made in the scene, apparel and properties employed in setting forth the new play called "The Royal Slave", lately acted at Hampton Court, together with the charge of dancers and composers of music, the same to be paid as follows: viz., to Peter le Huc, property-maker £50; to George Portman, painter £50; and to Estienne Nau and Sebastian la Pierre for themselves and 12 dancers £54.' In the autumn of 1638 when the Court was again at Hampton Court another play by Davenant, *The Unfortunate Lover*, was put on for the King and Queen.

Though one can hardly regard it as a diversion the King and Queen sometimes dined in public in the Great Hall, which meant that there was just the one table at which they ate while the public stood at some distance and watched the long procession of servants bringing in the heavily laden and very appetising dishes from the kitchens for their Majesties. There is a painting by Van Bassan at Hampton Court; at one end of the table one can see Prince Charles as a small boy. The architecture of the room looks highly imaginary. Sometimes, we are told, there was more than just the one royal table. 'The King's table had 28 dishes; the Queen's 24; 4 other tables 16 dishes each, and so on.' Occasionally there were as many as '86 tables well furnished each meal: in all about 500 dishes each meal, with beer, bread, wine, and all things necessary'.

Charles detested the jovial vulgarity and drunken romps which had so delighted his father. Court life, he insisted, must have propriety and elegance. He approved of his wife's love of gaiety and often took part himself in some of her frolics and also occasionally in some of the Christmas masques. His intense interest in music led to the forming of a small private orchestra of Italian musicians who played to him while he had his meals and even provided sacred music in the Chapel.

But his greatest enthusiasm was for works of art. He commissioned portraits by Anthony Van Dyck, who painted no fewer than thirteen pictures of the Queen ('La Reyne—dressed in blue, price £30; dressed in white, price £50', and so on); no less a painter than Rubens was commissioned to decorate the ceiling of the Banqueting Hall built by Inigo Jones in Whitehall; Daniel Mytens, Wenceslas

Hollar, Gerard van Honthorst, and Balthasar Gerbier, the minia-
turist, were also engaged to work for him.

His elder brother Prince Henry, who had died at the age of
eighteen, had started the art collection to which Charles added so
magnificently and abundantly. His taste for pictures began during
the six months he spent in Madrid waiting to marry the Infanta
Maria. On leaving he was given many costly paintings by the King
of Spain: they included Titian's famous 'Antiope' and three more
by the same artist. Charles got Velazquez to paint his portrait; and
on the birth of his daughter Elizabeth, the Dutch sent Charles 'four
rare' paintings by Tintoretto, china ornaments, and a curious clock.

His most notable achievement was purchasing the entire collection of art treasures assembled over the years by the Dukes of Man-
tua, for which he paid £28,000. He also bought the collections of the
Count of Villamediana and the sculptor Pompeo Leoni. Among
Charles's acquisitions were Tintoretto's 'Nine Muses', Correggio's
'Marriage of Saint Catherine', Titian's famous 'Entombment', portraits by Raphael, and some outstanding pictures by Giorgione,
Bassano, the Carracci, and a great many more. Balthazar Gerbier,
who bought pictures for him in Brussels and the Hague, was knighted
at Hampton Court on 2 October 1638. Charles's agents were always
told to 'obtain free transportation for such pictures, paintings, statues
and other rarities as had been provided in those parts for ye adorning
of His Majesty's cabinet'. He also bought from English collectors,
one of whom was Sir Kenelm Digby.

While they delight those who now visit Hampton Court and other
palaces, Charles was criticised at the time for 'squandering away
millions of pounds upon old rotten pictures and broken-nosed
marbles'. These are now beyond value.

A catalogue compiled in 1639 shows that nearly four hundred of
the pictures Charles purchased were at Hampton Court, among
them the nine pictures by Andrea Mantegna on 'The Triumph of
Julius Caesar'. Painted in tempera on linen between the years 1485
and 1492, this series is generally recognised as among the artist's best
surviving work and one of the most precious possessions of the
Royal Family.

Strikingly attractive furniture, Florentine bronzes, carved ivories
and cut crystal were bought for Hampton Court and King Charles's
other palaces; statues, both ancient and Renaissance, were bought
for the parks and gardens at Hampton Court. Fountains, ornamental

stretches of water, and ponds were designed and water was brought to them from a great distance. This involved cutting a channel twenty-one feet wide, two feet deep, and eleven miles long, from Longford to the Palace. Some of this water was used for drinking and added to the supply brought in earlier for Cardinal Wolsey by the conduits from Coombe Hill. The cost was £4,102 and was paid out of the revenues of the Court of Wards and Liveries. Many people objected strongly to the channel being cut through their property, causing damage to their land, the collapse of banks, and decay of bridges. But Charles ignored their complaints.

His next project was to make a vast park stretching from Hampton Court to Richmond, enclosing an expanse of country ten miles in circumference, and to stock it with red deer as well as fallow deer, thus providing a magnificent hunting ground for the sport he enjoyed so much. This too was met with fierce opposition. Farmers and gentlemen who had residences in the area were furious. The King was advised by Lord Cottington, the Chancellor of the Exchequer, and other ministers to abandon the project, for apart from the anger of the people, it would also cost a vast sum of money to carry out. But the King rejected their advice. He declared that he was resolved to go on with it and had in fact already begun the work: bricks had been made and much of the wall was already being built on his own land. Eventually the Archbishop of Canterbury intervened. His chief desire, he said, was that the King should be on good terms with the people; it took time but His Majesty finally yielded to persuasion and the project was abandoned.

Exactly a hundred years earlier, in 1539, it will be recalled, Henry VIII was confronted by a similar predicament when he created an extensive enclosure to have all his hunting within easy reach of Hampton Court. Then too the inhabitants were incensed, but they were careful not to give voice to their objections while Henry VIII lived. On his death they petitioned Edward VI's Council and redress was granted: the Royal Chase was 'dechased'.

But by now much more serious trouble had begun for the King. Interference with Scotland's independent religious rights, flaunted when the King used the Anglican ceremonial in defiance of their wishes at his Scottish coronation at Edinburgh in 1633, was taken further when he insisted a few years later on the adoption of confession and threatened to excommunicate all those who refused to accept the new Prayer Book. There was a riot in St Giles Cathedral in Edinburgh; national committees, known as 'Tables', were set up by the people, and a covenant was signed to defend their religion to the death. The rebellion had begun. Charles arrived in Berwick in May 1639 with a small armed force, but confronted by a large Scottish army, the King agreed to refer all disagreements to the general assembly in Scotland and returned to London.

He came to Hampton Court early in August 1640 because plague had again broken out in London. After a time it reached Hampton Court, where three deaths occurred in the stables.

But plague was not the only thing that disturbed the King's peace of mind. Far greater anxiety was caused by alarming developments in England. He had been trying to raise a powerful army to deal with the Scots. Needing money for the troops he summoned Parliament for the first time in eleven years, but found Parliament to be in sympathy with the Scots. He nevertheless prepared for war, scraping together such money as he could and obtaining a grant from Ireland through his Chief Minister Strafford. But it was ineffective. His army was unequal to the contest and the Scots crossed the River Tweed into England on 20 August and occupied the towns of Newcastle and Durham.

In despair Charles assembled a fresh Parliament but the House of Commons was not prepared to give him any money until certain reforms were carried out. Meanwhile they impeached Strafford, whom they blamed for most of the King's actions, cast him in the Tower of London and forced the King to have him executed.

In the following year, on 10 August 1641, Charles went to Scotland, hopeful that he might persuade the Scottish army to support him against Parliament. The request was bluntly refused and he returned to Hampton Court on 26 November to consider what his next move should be.

Four days earlier, Parliament had set out, in what they called the 'Grand Remonstrance', the chief points of the King's misgovernment and insisted on the appointment of acceptable ministers and on the setting up of an assembly of divines to deal with religious problems. The Puritans in England, like the Presbyterians in Scotland, were violently opposed to having bishops and were vigorously supported in a rousing pamphlet written by a young man fresh from Cambridge named John Milton. There were disorderly demonstrations in Palace Yard where bishops and even ordinary peers had to fight their way through noisy crowds to reach the House of Lords.

The document of remonstrance was presented to the King at Hampton Court on 1 December. The King was much concerned at the harshness of it, but promised an answer as soon as the weight of business would permit, and desired 'there should be no publishing that declaration till they had received his answer to it'. The request was ignored and the Grand Remonstrance was immediately made public.

With a view to adjusting the damaging effect of the publicity, especially in London, King Charles invited seven aldermen from the City to visit him at Hampton Court. He spoke of 'his extraordinary love of London' and promised to come there in the next day or two. As the aldermen were leaving Hampton Court, he knighted all seven of them, feeling no doubt that it would make a good impression on the City council.

Whatever good effect it might have had was completely undone by the King's action not long afterwards. On 4 January 1642 he went into the House of Commons, where no monarch has ever been allowed in the entire history of Parliament. With His Majesty was an armed force which he had brought to arrest Pym, Hampden, and three other members of the House who were his most prominent critics. Warned in advance of the King's plan, the five members fled to the City of London and Charles followed them there and demanded their surrender. His demand was refused.

The King found the streets filled with people shouting 'Privilege of Parliament'. The shops had been shut and men stood at their doors with swords and halberds. Alarmed by their hostile demeanour, Charles went back to Hampton Court with his wife and children. Their hurried, unexpected arrival found the staff completely unprepared. One bedroom was quickly got ready for them and in it the King and Queen slept that night with their three eldest children—Charles Prince of Wales, James Duke of York, and Princess Mary, who was already at the age of ten betrothed to the heir of the Prince of Orange.

The attitude of the Londoners made it clear that the capital and the formidable Tower of London were in the hands of the Parliamentarians. Civil war was now inevitable and the King began to prepare for it. Colonel Lumsden, who had escorted His Majesty and his family safely to Hampton Court with a force of two hundred men, went to Kingston and seized the magazine of arms stored there. The next morning Lord Digby went over from the Palace to convey the King's thanks for what had been done and to urge Lumsden to strengthen his force by collecting still more recruits.

The King stayed at Hampton Court until 12 January and then went with his family to Windsor Castle for greater security. He and the Queen returned to Hampton Court for just one night at the end of the following month and left early the next day for Dover, whence Her Majesty sailed for Holland, taking her daughter Mary with her to deliver her to her future husband. The Queen took also all the available Crown Jewels to pawn in order to obtain money for troops and munitions for the King.

It was Charles's last visit to Hampton Court until he was brought back as a prisoner five years later.

Both sides, Parliament and the King, now began to prepare for war. On 24 August Charles set up his standard at Nottingham and eight weeks later the first battle of the Civil War was fought at Edgehill, which the King only just managed to win. The Royal forces then occupied Oxford and advanced on Brentford, a few miles from London. It was thought that if he had gone and taken the capital the result might have been decisive. But Charles hesitated and finally withdrew. There were some further Royal victories, but after the disastrous battles of Marston Moor in 1644 and Naseby in the following year, it became clear that Charles would not win the war.

He travelled north to Newark and surrendered to the Scottish army, who sold him to the Parliamentarians. On 24 August 1647 the

King was brought to Hampton Court as a prisoner. It had been left as a Royal Palace and had been in the care of the King's retainers until shortly after the battle of Naseby when Parliament took it over and put seals on the doors of the State apartments.

That was, however, not all that was done to it. The Puritans, roused to a frenzy by religious symbols and paintings, attacked the lovely Chapel with sledge-hammer and axe. To quote a contemporary report in one of the earliest newspapers:

> Sir Robert Harlow gave order for the putting down and demolishing of the popish and superstitious pictures at Hampton Court, where this day the altar was taken down and the table brought into the body of the church, the rails pulled down, and the steps levelled, and the popish and superstitious images that were in the glass windows were also demolished, and an order was given for the new glazing them with plain glass; and among the rest, there was pulled down the picture of Christ nailed to the cross, which was right over the altar and the pictures of Mary Magdalen and others weeping by the foot of the cross, and some other such idolatrous pictures were pulled down and demolished.

Just before the King was brought to Hampton Court, the Palace was prepared for him with considerate forethought. The things he had at Oxford, and the servants who waited on him there, where he had lived at Christ Church (Wolsey's foundation) for ten months during the war, were brought to Hampton Court. While he was at Oxford, the Queen returned from Holland and was provided with accommodation at Merton College, so that he could visit her at night without having to walk through the streets. The Queen had found herself pregnant while at Oxford and left for the West Country, where her daughter Henrietta Anne, known later as 'Minette', was born at Exeter in June 1644. Shortly after the confinement the Queen, who had been found guilty of high treason by the House of Commons and was terrified of being taken by the Parliamentarians, fled in disguise to France and was never to see her husband again. Unable to take her fifteen-day-old baby with her, she left the child in the care of the Countess of Dalkeith for the time being.

Charles was treated as a privileged guest rather than a prisoner at Hampton Court, but was under constant surveillance: soldiers of the Parliamentary army under the command of Colonel Whalley were posted on duty and a number of Parliamentary commissioners were also in residence to keep a watch on his activities.

The King dined in the Presence Chamber where the public were admitted, as in the old days, to look on while he ate; he was also allowed to receive visitors and many came to kiss his hand. Six weeks after he was brought here, the diarist John Evelyn came to see him. 'I went to Hampton Court,' Evelyn records, 'where I had the honour to kiss his Majesty's hand and give him an Account of severall things I had in charge, he being now in the power of those execrable Villains who not long after murder'd him.'

Quite a number of people came from London to pay their respects. All his former servants, in addition to those brought there from Oxford, were allowed to visit him; and even those who had fought for the King were given access to him. Two of his most intimate friends, John Ashburnham and Sir John Berkeley, who had fled to France, were granted permission to return and reside with the King at Hampton Court. A frequent visitor was Jane Whorwood, whose father lived at Kingston-upon-Thames, a mile or so from Hampton Court. She was tall, attractive, and red-haired. Now aged thirty-two, she was married to Brome Whorwood, eldest son of Sir Thomas Whorwood, of Holton in Oxfordshire, and had often been to see Charles when he was in Oxford. Many believed that she was the King's mistress and the letters from the King to her read like those of a lover to his mistress; he certainly saw much of her during the months Queen Henrietta was away. A dedicated Royalist, she served as a link between the King and the Royalists in London and often brought him gifts of money from them.

Charles was allowed to play tennis and to hunt in the park, but the most pleasing concession of all was to have his children living in Syon House, about five miles away. Only three of his six surviving children were there—James, Duke of York, aged thirteen; Elizabeth, eleven; and Henry, Duke of Gloucester, eight. Charles, Prince of Wales, now sixteen, had been sent by his father in 1645 to take charge of affairs in south-west England, but after the defeat of the Royalists there in the following year, he left for Jersey and later joined his mother in Paris. Mary, fifteen and a half, was already married to Prince William of Orange; and Henrietta, aged three and a half, was with Lady Dalkeith at Exeter when the town was captured by the Parliamentarians. After being moved to London, Lady Dalkeith was informed that the child would be taken from her and kept with Charles's other children as a prisoner at Syon House. Only by acting swiftly was Lady Dalkeith able to prevent this. Disguising herself in tattered clothes, she left with her *valet de chambre*, similarly disguised, and set out on the long walk from London to Dover, each carrying the child in turn. Seemingly a poor French family on their way home, they talked only French and called the child 'Pierre'. Puzzled and cross, little Henrietta said angrily: 'Not Pierre. Princess. And why am I wearing these torn clothes?' Efforts to calm her with 'Shoosh!' and '*Tais toi, mon enfant!*' were unheeded; though her voice was shrill, no passers-by intervened; and she was delivered safely to her mother in Paris.

The three children in Syon House came from time to time to see their father, and occasionally the King was allowed to ride over and see them.

The Parliamentary army's headquarters were at Putney, midway between London and Hampton Court. From there Oliver Cromwell, General in command of the Parliamentary Army as well as a Member of Parliament, came to see the King; so did two of his senior officers, General Fairfax and General Ireton, who was Cromwell's son-in-law: the officers always kissed the King's hand, but Cromwell did not. Charles said he would be glad to meet Cromwell's wife; she was brought to Hampton Court and dined with him and the wives of Ireton and Whalley.

The purpose of Cromwell's visits was to come to some sort of settlement whereby the King could return to the throne with diminished authority and power. Charles gave the impression that he was prepared to negotiate, but he was in fact negotiating at the same time not only with the Scottish Commissioners to invade England, but was also striving to get better terms from Parliament than Cromwell's army seemed ready to concede. When these manœuvres were discovered, the visits of Cromwell and the senior army officers ceased. Ireton sums up the talks at Hampton Court in these words: 'He gave us words and we repaid him in his own coin when we found he had no real intention to the people's good, but only to prevail by our factions and to regain by art what he had lost by fight.'

The damage thus done to the negotiations at Hampton Court could never be repaired. Little more than a year remained to him of life and some of those who came to see him became aware of his sense of foreboding. Lady Fanshawe, whose husband Sir Richard Fanshawe had been the King's Secretary at War, states in her

Memoirs: 'During the King's stay at Hampton Court my husband was with him to whom he was pleased to talk of his concerns. I went three times to pay my duty to him, both as I was the daughter of his servant and wife of his servant.' Her father was Sir John Harrison, one of the most devoted supporters of the King.

'The last time I ever saw him', Lady Fanshawe adds, 'when I took my leave, I could not refrain from weeping; when he had saluted me, I prayed God to preserve His Majesty with long life and happy years; he stroked me on the cheek and said, "Child, if God pleaseth, it shall be so; but both you and I must submit to God's will, and you know in what hands I am"; then, turning to my husband, he said, "Be sure, Dick, to tell my son all that I have said, and deliver those letters to my wife; pray God bless her! I hope I shall do well"; and, taking him in his arms, said, "Thou hast ever been an honest man, and I hope God will bless thee and make thee a happy servant to my son."'

Charles wrote numerous letters to his wife, using in part a complicated cypher. Often the Queen waited for weeks without receiving a letter from him. Some letters fell into the hands of the Parliamentarians and were published in the newspapers, guesswork and even fiction being used for the sections in code. Before long the Queen too began to detect her husband's foreboding of doom. 'If I should miscarry' is a phrase he used more than once: its true meaning becomes clearer when he says: 'I conjure thee, by thy constant love to me, that if I miscarry (whether by being taken by the rebels or otherwise) to continue the same active endeavours for Pr. Charles as thou hast done for me, and not whine for my misfortunes, but, like thy father's daughter, vigorously assist Pr. Charles to regain his own.'

Charles's acute depression and rumours that an attempt was to be made to assassinate him, are thought to have prompted his decision to escape. He had given his word to Colonel Whalley that he would not do so without formally withdrawing his promise.

In October, 1647, after being a prisoner in the Palace for nearly two months, Charles sent John Ashburnham to tell Whalley that the King could no longer be bound by his promise. Asked why, Ashburnham said: 'the multiplicity of the Scots about the Court was such, and the agitators in the army so violently set against the King, as (for ought I knew) either party might as well take him from Hampton Court'.

Whalley immediately informed army headquarters. Ashburnham was dismissed from the Palace and forbidden to enter it again; and the guards were doubled to prevent Charles escaping.

His children were still allowed to come and see him. In a letter to his daughter Elizabeth, written on 27 October, Charles said: 'Dear Daughter—This is to assure you that it is not through forgetfulness or any want of kindness that I have not, all this time, sent for you, but for such reasons as is fitter for you to imagine (which you may easily do) than me to write; but now I hope to see you upon Friday or Saturday next, as your brother James can more particularly tell you; to whom referring you, I rest, your loving father Charles R.' What the King had wanted James to tell her we do not know.

Elizabeth came by herself at the end of the week and was given a room near the King's quarters off the Long Gallery, where two guards were kept on duty night and day. Their noisy pacing disturbed her sleep and the King asked Colonel Whalley if the guards could avoid making a noise. But the noise continued. When the King mentioned it again Whalley said: 'If His Majesty would be pleased to renew his engagement, I will place the sentinels at a more remote distance.' Charles replied: 'To renew my engagement were a point of honour. You had my engagement; I will not renew it. Keep your guards.'

Indeed the plans for his escape were already being made. Not only had Ashburnham been dismissed from the Palace, but the King's other faithful attendant Sir John Berkeley had also by now been turned out and forbidden ever to return. With Colonel Legge the only attendant he could rely on, Charles now took him into his confidence and sent him to see Ashburnham and Berkeley, who, he knew, were living near Hampton Court. On 10 November they were smuggled in by Legge and taken to see the King. Both vowed their readiness 'to apply themselves to the discharge of their duties, and therefore if His Majesty would be pleased to say whither he would go, they would carry him thither, or lose themselves in the endeavour of it'.

The King revealed that he had 'some thoughts of going out of the Kingdom'. He had told Jane Whorwood that he intended to escape and she had asked the astrologer William Lilly where His Majesty should hide when he fled. Lilly advised him to hide in Essex. But, after talking to Ashburnham and Berkeley, Charles decided that delay would be dangerous and it was arranged that the escape would be made on the following day, 11 November. That day was chosen because, being a Thursday, it was the day on which the King remained alone in his bedchamber writing letters.

Early that morning, just as Charles was settling down to write his letters, Colonel Whalley asked to see him and showed him a letter from Oliver Cromwell, which read: 'For my beloved cousin Colonel Whalley at Hampton Court, These—Putney, November 1647. Dear Cos. Whalley—There are rumours abroad of some intended attempt on His Majesty's person. Therefore I pray have a care of your guards. If any such thing should be done, it would be accounted a most horrid act—Yours Oliver Cromwell.'

Whalley then withdrew and the King knew that he would not be interrupted until five or six o'clock in the evening, when it was his practice to leave his bedchamber and attend evening prayers; after which he would have supper and then retire to his bedchamber, where extra guards would be put on duty for the night.

At about five o'clock Colonel Whalley came to the anteroom adjoining the King's Bedchamber. The Parliamentary Commissioners and the bedchamber-men were there as usual waiting for the King to emerge from his room. In his report to the House of Commons Whalley stated:

I asked them for the King; they told me he was writing letters in his bedchamber. I waited there without mistrust till six of the clock; I then began to doubt, and told the bedchamber-men, Mr. Maule and Mr. Murray, I wondered the King was so long a-writing; they told me he had (they thought) some extraordinary occasion. Within half an hour after, I went into the next room to Mr. Oudart and told him I marvelled the King was so long a-writing. He answered, he wondered too, but withal said, the King told him he was to write both to the Queen and the Princess of Orange, which gave me some satisfaction for the present.

But my fears with the time increased, so that when it was seven o'clock I again told Mr. Maule I exceedingly wondered the King was so long before he came out. He told me he was writing and I replied, possibly he might be ill, therefore I thought he should do well to see. . . . He replied, the King had given him strict commands not to molest him, therefore he durst not, besides he had bolted the door to him. I was then extreme restless in my thoughts, looked oft in at the keyhole to see whether I could perceive His Majesty, but could not; prest Mr. Maule to knock very oft, that I might know whether His Majesty were there or not, but all to no purpose. He still plainly told me he durst not disobey His Majesty's commands.

Many hours were lost while they waited in a state of indecision, hours of the utmost advantage to the King; for His Majesty had left the chamber as soon as darkness began to fall, which is early in November. The night was stormy and the trees swayed in the tempestuous gale. The King's apartments were on the first floor on the south side of Cloister Green Court, overlooking the Privy Garden. (These rooms were later replaced by the south range of Wren's Fountain Court building.)

Whalley finally decided to enter the King's bedchamber from the other side and went through the Privy Garden with the Keeper of the Privy Lodgings and then to the Privy Stairs, where guards were stationed. He continued:

We went up the stairs, and went from chamber to chamber, till we came to the next chamber to His Majesty's bedchamber, where we saw His Majesty's cloak lying on the midst of the floor, which much amazed me. I went presently back to the Commissioners and bedchamber-men, acquainting them with it.

He thereupon commanded Mr. Maule, in the name of Parliament, to go into the bedchamber, and finally Whalley, the Commissioners' and Maule went in together. The King was not there. They then looked in the closet but he wasn't there either.

> I then, being in a passion, told Mr. Maule I thought he was an accessory to his going; for that afternoon he came to London, it being a rare thing for him to be from the Court.

The discovery of the escape led to a swirl of activity. Guards rushed about the Palace, looking down corridors, opening doors of rooms and closets. Troops of horse and foot-soldiers searched the Park and the Lodge in the Park, others made for Ashburnham's house at Thames Ditton.

Meanwhile Colonel Whalley, who had found three letters on the King's writing table, opened one which was addressed to him. One of the others was addressed to the two Houses of Parliament; the third to the Parliamentary Commissioners. The one to Whalley, dated at Hampton Court, 11 November 1647, began: 'I have been so civilly used by you and Major Huntingdon that I cannot but by this parting farewell acknowledge it under my hand; as also to desire the continuance of your courtesie by your protecting my household stuffe and moveables of all sorts which I leave behind me in this house, that they be neither spoiled or embesled.' He then referred to 'three pictures which are not mine that I desire you to restore'—one of these was a portrait of the Queen dressed in blue and seated in a chair, which he wanted the Queen's dresser to have; another was of his eldest daughter Mary, the wife of Prince William of Orange, which he wanted to be given to the Countess of Anglesey; and the third, a portrait of Lady Stanhope, to be given to the late Sir Walter Raleigh's son Carew Raleigh. The letter ended with this Postscript: 'I assure you it was not the letter you showed me today'—he was referring to Oliver Cromwell's letter—'that made me take this resolution, nor any advertisement of that kinde. But I confess that I am loath to be made a close prisoner under pretence of securing my life. I had almost forgot to desire you to send the black grew bitch to the Duke of Richmond.'

The reference to 'protecting my household stuffe and moveables' suggests that he hoped to return one day and find his furniture and pictures there, for it was his intention to go to France and return with a large enough army to recover his kingdom. But he did not get as far as that.

How he managed to escape is not known exactly. It is thought that he left his bedchamber with Colonel Legge, went down the back stairs and then along the King's Long Gallery, which jutted out eastwards into the Park. At the end of this gallery was a room called Paradise, built above a cellar with a private passage to the Water Gallery on the river where Queen Elizabeth I had been a prisoner.

Berkeley and Ashburnham had apparently been waiting for him there with a boat to take him across the river where horses waited to take them to the south coast. But stormy weather in the Channel prevented his crossing to France; so he went to the Isle of Wight to stay with Colonel Hammond, the Governor of the island, who, he was confident, would give him a lodging until the weather improved. Unfortunately Hammond, being related to Cromwell and supporting the Parliamentary party, took him to Carisbrooke Castle and imprisoned him there.

While the search for Charles was going on in the Palace, Colonel Whalley sent a messenger to Cromwell in Putney to inform him of the escape. Without an instant's delay Cromwell mounted a horse and rode to Hampton Court to find out how the King had managed to escape. It was midnight by the time his enquiries were completed and he sat down at once and sent the following report to the Speaker of the House of Commons.

Hampton Court, Twelve at Night, 11th November 1647. For the Honourable William Lenthall, Speaker of the House of Commons, these—Sir, His Majesty withdrawn himself at nine o'clock. The manner is variously reported; and I will say of it at present but that His Majesty was expected to supper, when the Commissioners and Colonel Whalley missed him; upon which they entered the room. They found His Majesty had left his cloak behind him in the Gallery in the private way. He passed, by the backstairs and vault, towards the waterside. He left some letters upon the table in his withdrawing room, of his own handwriting; whereof one was to the Commissioners of Parl. attending him, to be communicated to both houses and is here enclosed. Oliver Cromwell.

When Parliament met the next day Charles's letter to them was read out.

Liberty [the King wrote] being that which in all time hath been, but especially now is the common Theame and Desire of all men; common Reason shewes that Kings, lesse than any, should endure Captivity; and yet call God and the World to Witnesse,

The Great Hall with its magnificent hammer-beam roof

Wolsey's Closet. The ceiling, picked out in gold on a blue field, is in an excellent state of preservation. The restored linen-fold panelling was probably covered with rich tapestry. The sixteenth-century painted panels above represent scenes from the Passion of Our Lord

The Great Kitchen, built in Henry VIII's time

The Chapel Royal, with its ornate fan-vaulted ceiling and carved and gilded pendants, was built for Wolsey and lavishly redecorated for Henry VIII

The family of Henry VIII. An extremely interesting picture which shows Henry with Edward and the Princesses Mary and Elizabeth. The Queen on his left hand is thought to represent Jane Seymour, as mother of the future King, although she died shortly after his birth

Charles I and Henrietta Maria leaving for the chase. From a painting by Daniel Mytens

Jeffery Hudson, the dwarf, only 18 in. tall when he was given to Charles I and Henrietta Maria by the Duchess of Buckingham. The portrait, by Daniel Mytens, is in the Queen's Audience Chamber

with what Patience I have endured a tedious Restraint; which, so long as I had any hopes that this sort of my suffering might conduce to the peace of my kingdomes or the hindering of more effusion of blood, I did willingly undergoe; but now finding by too certain proofes, that this my continued Patience would not only turne to my Personal Ruine, but likewise bee of much more prejudice than furtherance to the Public good; I thought I was bound, as well by Natural as Political Obligations, to seek my safety by retiring my selfe, for some time, from the public view both of my Friends and Enemies.

And much more in like vein.

Colonel Whalley explained in self-defence that the most eminent officers in the army agreed that he, could no more keep the King if he had a mind to go than a bird in a pound. I was not to restrain him from his liberty of walking, so that he might have gone wither he had pleased; neither was I to hinder him from his privacy in his chamber, or any other part of the House, which gave him an absolute freedom to go away at pleasure. The House is vast, hath 1,500 rooms, as I am informed, in it, and would require a troop of Horse upon perpetual duty to guard all the outgoings. So that all that could be expected from me was to be as vigilant over the King as I could in the daytime; and when after Supper he was retired into his Bedchamber, to set sentinels about him, which I constantly performed, as is well known to the Commissioners and others.'

Some months later, in July 1648, while King Charles was still a prisoner in Carisbrooke Castle, there was a Royalist rising less than a mile from Hampton Court. A force of six hundred horse was involved, led by the Earl of Holland, who had with him the young Duke of Buckingham, son of Charles's friend, and his younger brother Lord Francis Villiers, aged eighteen. Lord Francis was killed in the fighting; on the Restoration of Charles II to the throne, his body was buried in his father's vault in Westminster Abbey.

Charles I was brought to Windsor in December 1648, was put on trial and found guilty of treason 'for levying war against the Parliament and kingdom of England'. On 30 January 1649 he was executed, stepping out on to the scaffold through a window of his beloved Banqueting Hall which Inigo Jones had built, with its splendid ceiling decorated for him by Rubens.

A few weeks after that cold January morning when the crowd gasped and many turned away as the King's severed head was held up, a Bill was introduced in Parliament, stating:

> Whereas the goods and personal estate heretofore belonging to the late King Charles and to his wife and eldest son have been and are justly forfeited by them, for their several delinquencies, the Commons of England assembled in Parliament, taking the premises into their serious consideration, have thought fit and resolved that the said goods and personal estate, heretofore belonging to the persons above named and to every and any of them, shall be inventoried and appraised, and shall be sold, except such parcels thereof as shall be found necessary to be reserved for the uses of the State.

It was further decreed that the proceeds of the sale should be devoted, in the first instance, to the payment of the King's and Queen's debts. The Bill became law on 4 July 1649.

The inventory of all the pictures, tapestries, furniture, plate, jewels, and carpets, running to about one thousand pages, still exists and can be seen at the British Museum: the section concerning Hampton Court runs to about seventy-six pages. Estimates are given of the price each article should fetch, to which was added later the price for which it was actually sold and the name of the purchaser. The inventory was not completed until the autumn of that year and the sale began in the winter of 1649 and went on for almost three years.

The costly tapestries at Hampton Court belonging to Wolsey and Henry VIII included 'Ten pieces of Arras hangings of the Story of Abraham', measuring a total of 826 yards, and valued at £10 a yard, which made their price £8,260. 'Ten pieces of rich Arras of Josuah at £3,399; nine pieces of Tobias at £3,409; nine pieces of Arras of St. Paule at £3,065; and ten pieces of Julius Caesar at £5,019.'

Fortunately these were all withdrawn from the sale and retained for Cromwell's use.

The famous paintings, a great many of which had been bought by Charles I, were given ridiculously low values: Titian's 'The Venus del Pardo', considered one of the best pictures painted by Titian, was valued at £600, his 'Herodias with the Head of John the Baptist' at a mere £150; Raphael's famous Cartoons at £300; and Mantegna's 'Triumph of Julius Caesar' series, among the most precious of the paintings, at only £1,000: fortunately the Mantegna as well as the Raphael Cartoons and Titian's 'Herodias' were withdrawn from the sale. The total value of the 332 pictures at Hampton Court was entered at £4,675 16s. 6d.

The furniture and other effects listed for the sale included many priceless items, such as Cardinal Wolsey's beds, chairs, chests, musical instruments, and looking-glasses. One of the looking-glasses, bearing Wolsey's coat of arms, fetched only £5. A cane belonging to Henry VIII went for five shillings; his hawking glass was sold for two shillings; and his gloves for one shilling.

Hampton Court itself, with all its buildings, was valued at £7,777 13s. 5d. The Parks, estimated to have a total of 1,607 acres, were separately valued at £10,765 19s. 9d.

The proceeds from the sale of this and the other Palaces, decided by Parliament after declaring that the office of King was 'unnecessary, burthensome, and dangerous', were to be used for the benefit of the Commonwealth, by which term the Kingdom was to be known in future. But a year later the Council of State withdrew Hampton Court and the palaces of Whitehall and Westminster from the sale, as well as some of the pictures, furniture, hangings, tapestry and 'distinguished works of art and curiosity' and 'reserved them for the use of the Commonwealth'.

In 1651, two and a half years after the execution of Charles I and six weeks after the shattering defeat of his son (Charles II) at the Battle of Worcester, Oliver Cromwell, now fifty-two, moved into Hampton Court: the Council of State had decided, chiefly because Cromwell liked it so much, that it would be a suitable place for him to live in and gave orders that the Palace should be got ready for him and his family.

Cromwell was born in the small town of Huntingdon, where his family were looked up to as great landowners. His great-great-uncle Thomas Cromwell was Wolsey's successor as President of Henry

VIII's Council, and arranged the King's marriage to Anne of Cleves, for which he was sent to the Tower and executed.

In the very beautiful Elizabethan manor house built at Hinching-brooke in Huntingdonshire by Oliver Cromwell's grandfather, King James I stayed on his journey from Edinburgh to London on the death of Queen Elizabeth, and he rewarded the then owner, Oliver Cromwell's uncle and namesake, with a knighthood.

Despite the family's wealth Oliver inherited very little from his father: but at the outbreak of the Civil War he had an income of about £500 a year, which was fairly large at that time. He was, moreover, connected with a number of important families; his great-great-grandfather, grandfather, and father had all been Members of Parliament and more than twenty of his relatives sat with him in the last Parliament of Charles I. He was a little above medium height, heavy in build, with a swollen, reddish face and the famous warts; he dressed poorly in a plain cloth suit, was slow in his deliberations, a visionary, and fanatically religious. His hard eyes and his set lips were eloquent of his determination. He had been planning to emigrate to America but the troubles in England made him change his mind.

Cromwell loved living at Hampton Court. He came again and again, making sometimes very brief stays, at others staying for quite long periods, having with him his family and friends, and was often gay, even boisterous in his jests. He was fond of playing bowls, hunting in the parks, as the Kings and Queens had been, and in the evenings when the candles were brought in, he would fill his pipe with tobacco and listen to music played by his favourite organist John Hingston on an organ presented to him by Magdalen College, Oxford, while his guests drank wine with him; he generally joined in the singing of glees and part-songs, and later withdrew to read the Bible.

On 31 December 1652 the House of Commons reversed the earlier decision not to sell Hampton Court; and passed a law that it should be sold with all 'the barns, stables, outhouses, gardens, orchards, yards, courts and backsides belonging to or used and enjoyed with the said mansion house, with the park commonly called the House Park, and the two parks there, the one called the Middle Park and the other called Bushey Park'.

It was a surprising turn about: the house had been reprieved for Cromwell and his family to live in and now notice to quit had been served on them. That he had many enemies in Parliament Cromwell knew; Parliament was no longer interested in the army after the Civil War was over. Doubtless at Cromwell's instigation, the friends he had in Parliament quickly got busy; and three and a half months later, on 15 April 1653, a resolution was passed that the sale of the house, parks and the rest 'should not be carried out until Parliament gave further orders'.

But on 23 August it was again decided to put Hampton Court up for auction because, it was declared, the country's need for money was urgent. This to-ing and fro-ing was becoming tedious. A month later Hampton Court was offered to Cromwell in exchange for New Hall, south of Thaxted in Essex, which had belonged to the Duke of Buckingham but had been bought by Cromwell. Cromwell refused to agree to that. So all the parks of Hampton Court, apart from the Home Park, were sold on 15 November by auction to Edmund Backwell for £6,638 7s.; and the Middle Park to Colonel Norton for £3,701 19s.; the Manor and Honour rights of Hampton Court were sold separately to John Phelps of London for £750.

But exactly a month later, when Cromwell became Lord Protector of the Commonwealth, all the land was bought back by the State for £2,000 more than its purchasers had given at the sale; and the entire Palace and its grounds were assigned to Cromwell for his use. The manor deeds were conveyed to Cromwell personally by Mr Phelps for the exact sum he had paid, namely £750. Oliver Cromwell thus, after abolishing the monarchy, became Lord of the Manor of Wolsey's Palace which had been the home of Kings and Queens for a century and a quarter.

Except when he came for a very brief stay at Hampton Court, 'His Highness', as Lord Protector Cromwell was called, was always accompanied by members of the Council. Like Cardinal Wolsey he had work to do and he was sufficiently self-disciplined and blessed with a sense of responsibility to apply himself to it.

To imagine that the Lord Protector lived in royal splendour in the Palace would be wrong. His mode of life was simple. His wife, a commonplace but pleasant woman, had an eye to economy; many critics called her mean because she insisted that the cook should not be wasteful with the victuals. Many contemptuous and even scandalous stories were put into circulation about her by Royalists, some sneering at her for being unequal to a life of grandeur, others presenting her as common and petty and ill-mannered.

In fact it was only when they entertained foreign ambassadors that the Cromwells provided hospitality in the princely style of their predecessors in the Palace. The Lord Protector felt that to depart from the lavish ceremonial and the banqueting so much enjoyed by foreigners would be gravely damaging to the reputation of England. Only in the presence of foreigners did he discard his boisterous playfulness: emissaries of exalted rulers from France and Spain and Sweden expected the head of the English Commonwealth to be dignified.

Bulstrode Whitelocke, who was in Parliament with Cromwell and had fought against the King, stated in his *Memorials of English Affairs* that Cromwell 'would sometimes be very cheerful with us, and, laying aside his greatness, be exceedingly familiar with us, and, by way of diversion, would make verses with us'. James Heath, a stern critic, said of Cromwell in his *Flagellum On the Life and Death of Oliver Cromwell*, that after hunting, 'he would sometimes coax the neighbouring Rusticks and give them a Buck he hunted, and money to drink with it. His own diet was very spare and not so curious, except in publique treatments, which were constantly given every Monday in the week to all the officers of the Army not below a Captain, where he dined with them and showed them a hundred Antick Tricks, as throwing of Cushions and putting live coals into their pockets and boots; a table being likewise spread every week for such officers as should casually come to Hampton Court. . . . With these officers he seemed to disport himself, taking of his Drink freely and opening himself in every way to the most free familiarity.' However familiar and coarse he may have been with his army friends, he would not tolerate blasphemy or swearing in the army: a fine of twelvepence was imposed for every swear word used by his troops.

There was another side to Cromwell, which should not be overlooked. He took a keen interest in the arts. Mantegna's nine wonderful canvases of 'The Triumph of Julius Caesar', which had been saved from the auctioneer's hammer, were hung in the Long Gallery adjoining his personal suite at Hampton Court; fine old tapestries were placed in the Great Hall; and he selected five others, though 'ungodly and carnal', for his own bedchamber. These belonged to the State. But the inventory drawn up after Cromwell's death, which is kept in the Public Record Office in London, lists items of his own purchasing, which were used in the bedrooms: 'Two window curtains, one of scarlet baize, the other of serge; one small couch of fly coloured [blue?] damask, cased with watchet [light blue] baize; two elbow chairs ditto; four black stools ditto; one black table with a turned frame; one pair andirons with double brass; one pair of creepers [small iron firedogs] with fire-shovel and tongs; one pair of bellows.' In his dressing-room he had 'one Spanish table; two small Turkey carpets; one pair of andirons with double brass; one pair creepers and a fire-shovel, tongs and bellows; and four black stools of Turkey work'.

His great love of horses sent his agents seeking for Arabs in Aleppo and Barbarys in Tripoli, just as Charles I's agents sought for paintings and art treasures all over Europe. Cromwell matched his coach-teams with care—his liking seemed to be for reddish-grey and snow-white.

Great attention was given to the parks and gardens at Hampton Court. The artificial river Charles had created, known as the New or Longford river, to supply the ponds and fountains with water, had been disrupted by the inhabitants of the parishes through which it flowed: their protests to the King having been ignored, they took advantage of the confusion during the Civil War and demolished banks and bridges, and filled the stream's course with stones and gravel. Cromwell gave orders for the damage to be repaired. The farmers who had suffered when the river overflowed its banks, ruined their crops, and drowned their sheep, were furious again, but as helpless as when Charles brought the water across their fields. But Cromwell went a little further, for he brought the water into 'Harewarren', a part of Bushey Park, to the north of the Kingston road, and laid out two attractive ponds there that are still known as Heron Ponds, sometimes referred to as Herring Ponds. Palings were erected to close the right of way enjoyed for centuries by the inhabitants of the neighbouring parishes. While resenting his interference with their traditional rights, the people were careful not to raise their voices.

A vast network of spies had been set up by Cromwell to ferret out the Royalists conspiring to murder him and restore Charles II to the throne. The Lord Protector went in constant fear of his life and was never without guards in attendance. His numerous visits to Hampton Court, mostly on horseback, were discussed publicly and assassins lay in wait for him along the route. He escaped them by varying his route, often going along quite unfamiliar tracks and always returning by a different way.

One attempt was planned by Captain Thomas Gardiner, who boasted later that he went to Hampton Court in 1657 with two loaded pistols and a dagger with the intention of assassinating Cromwell in one of the galleries of the Palace; but he was surprised, the weapons were taken from him, and he was imprisoned for twelve months.

Far more daring was the elaborate plot of Miles Syndercombe, who constructed a complicated machine consisting of seven blunderbusses, cunningly bound together to go off simultaneously. It was set up in a house in Hammersmith which Cromwell was likely to pass, but the machine failed to go off. Later Syndercombe erected his seven blunderbusses in Whitehall, but one of his accomplices betrayed him. He was arrested and imprisoned in the Tower of London, where he committed suicide.

The plots became so numerous that Cromwell always wore a shirt of mail under his doublet and refused to eat any food that had not been tasted by others; and it became his practice to change his bedroom every night.

The Hampton Court Chapel, where there had been so many changes in the service—the celebration of Mass under Wolsey,

Protestantism under Edward VI, back to Mass under his sister Mary, and Protestantism again under Elizabeth, James I and Charles I—was changed yet again for Cromwell. The Presbyterian form was now adopted. With his family and friends seated around him, His Highness listened to sermons preached by the minister of Hampton, 'who on one occasion, causing embarrassment possibly, drew a parallel between David cutting off the top of Saul's garment, and the cutting off of the late King's head; and how David was troubled for what he had done, though he was ordained to succeed Saul'.

Here in the Chapel Cromwell's daughter Mary—'Little Mall', Cromwell called her—was married on 17 November 1657 to Thomas Bellasis Viscount Falconbridge, a friend of the family and a frequent visitor to Hampton Court. The bridegroom, a widower, was a former Royalist, and there was some uneasiness whether a Presbyterian service would be recognised in the event of a Royal Restoration, for Mary was a staunch adherent to the Church of England; it was solved by their being married again that same afternoon by Dr Hewitt, an Anglican clergyman. The official gazette announced: 'Yesterday afternoon His Highness went to Hampton Court and this day the most illustrious lady, the Lady Mary Cromwell, third daughter of His Highness the Lord Protector, was there married to the most noble lord, the Lord Falconbridge, in the presence of Their Highnesses and many noble persons.' Earlier that same month Cromwell's youngest daughter Frances, pretty and high-spirited, was married to the Earl of Warwick's grandson Robert Rich: forty-eight violins and fifty trumpets delighted the guests on that occasion: they danced, we are told, until five o'clock. An equally lavish reception had been planned by her father for Mary, but Falconbridge said he would prefer to spend the money on something more useful. Though the couple made their home in London, they came frequently to Hampton Court where all the members of Cromwell's family had special apartments set aside for them.

Cromwell had four sons and four daughters. The eldest son, Robert, died just before the outbreak of the Civil War; the second, Oliver, was killed on active service. The third, Richard, who was to succeed him, was easy-going, casual, and regarded by many as lazy: 'I know my son is idle,' Cromwell wrote of him. The Lord Protector's family bore the courtesy titles given to sons and daughters of a Duke. Having abolished the House of Lords, he made Richard one of the first new Peers when the Upper House was resuscitated in 1657.

Preferring a quiet life in the country with his wife and family, Richard only occasionally visited Hampton Court. The official gazette noted all their visits: 'On the 17th July 1658 there arrived the most illustrious Lord, the Lord Richard, who being returned from the western parts, was received by Their Highnesses with the usual demonstrations of high affection towards his Lordship.' A few days later Falconbridge and his wife Mary, 'being safe returned from the North', also came to stay there.

That was a year of death for the Cromwell family. The Protector's favourite daughter, Elizabeth, who was married to John Claypole and had just lost her baby son, Oliver, had come to Hampton Court in a state of acute pain and was joined there by her father, who came hurrying from a Council meeting in Whitehall. The doctors had told him that Elizabeth was dying of cancer. She died in Hampton Court on 6 August, aged only twenty-nine. Andrew Marvell, the poet, in two lines described the attempt of daughter and father to hide from each other their agonised suffering.

> She, lest he grieve, hides what she can her pains,
> And he, to lessen hers, his sorrow feigns. . . .

Cromwell, already ailing, was so shattered by grief that he was unable to attend her funeral. Her body was taken by boat down the river to Westminster Palace where it lay in state in the Painted Chamber and was then buried in Westminster Abbey.

After a succession of sleepless nights at Hampton Court, he was violently sick; double ague followed and his condition was found to be critical. The Groom of his Bedchamber said that he called for his Bible 'and desired a person honourable and godly then present, to read unto him from the Epistle to the Philippians "Not that I speak under peril of want, for I have learnt in whatsoever state I am therewith to be content. I know both how to be abased and how to abound: everywhere and in all things I am instructed both to be full and to be hungry, both to abound and to suffer need", which read, he said: "This scripture did once save my life when my eldest son died, which went as a dagger to my heart, indeed it did."'

After this he appeared to have found strength. His health improved and a day or so later he was able to get out of bed and go for a walk. Soon he was able to ride again and in the park encountered George Fox, the founder of the Society of Friends, who was on his way to petition Cromwell to ease the persecution of the Quakers.

'Before I came to him,' Fox records in his *Journal*, 'as he rode at the head of his Life Guards, I saw and felt a waft of death go forth against him, and when I came to him he looked like a dead man.'

Fox, then aged thirty-five, was invited to come and see him at Hampton Court. After spending a night at nearby Kingston, he went to the Palace, but was told that the doctors (Cromwell had five physicians in attendance at the time) would not allow anyone to see him. Cromwell, however, sent one of his secretaries to see James Naylor, a Quaker, in prison to arrange for his release.

A little later he told the doctors: 'You think I am going to die'; then, taking his wife's hand, he added: 'I declare to you that I shall not die; of this I am certain. Don't think me crazed. I am telling you what is true; and I have better authority than your Galen or Hippocrates. God himself has vouchsafed this answer to our prayers—not mine alone, but those of others who have a closer intercourse and greater familiarity with Him than I have.'

The doctors seemed to be impressed; indeed one of them, Dr Goodwin, told the others that they should say in their prayers: 'Lord, we beg not for his recovery, for that Thou has't already granted and assured us of; but for his *speedy* recovery.'

But Cromwell steadily got worse. The fever increased and he was often delirious. On 24 August, the doctors feeling that a change of air might do him good, he was taken to Whitehall Palace. He knew now that he was going to die and before leaving Hampton Court wrote down the name of his son Richard as his successor.

On the night of 2 September London was shaken by a terrifying storm—the worst storm known for a hundred years; roofs were torn off and church spires were toppled.

The doctors offered Cromwell a sleeping draught, but he shook his head and said: 'It is not my design to drink or to sleep, but my design is to make what haste I can to be gone.'

He died the next day on 3 September, which he had regarded as his fortunate day because it was the anniversary of his victories at the battles of Dunbar and Worcester.

It took no more than a few months for Cromwell's son Richard to be found quite unequal to the task of governing the country.

He handed over to Parliament a list of his father's debts, which amounted to £29,000—a considerable sum at that time—and a House of Commons committee was set up 'to examine what furniture, hangings, and other goods in Whitehall Palace, Hampton Court, Somerset House and St. James's Palace, do, or ought of right to, belong to the Commonwealth'; the committee was ordered 'to take special care that the goods and household stuff at Hampton Court be kept from embezzlement and spoil, and to bring in an act for their sale'.

So once again some of the contents of Hampton Court were to be auctioned. It is thought that the sale of the furniture in these palaces had been decided on to prevent Richard Cromwell from living in them. This is supported by what occurred when Richard went down to Hampton Court to shoot deer in the park. A messenger from the House of Commons, who had followed him there, told him that he was not allowed to kill any of the deer.

Oliver Cromwell's widow claimed that the bulk of the contents in the palaces belonged to her husband, but it was discovered that a fruiterer's warehouse had been filled with a lot of furniture which she also claimed was hers, but which in fact belonged to the Crown. In the end she was compelled to surrender them all.

Richard Cromwell gave up the office of Lord Protector in May 1659 and retired into private life. His departure had been accelerated by one of Oliver Cromwell's generals, John Lambert, who was aspiring to take over the Protectorship himself. In the uncertainty and confusion of the ensuing months another of Cromwell's generals George Monk, who had no personal ambitions, made it clear that he was not prepared to serve under Lambert. Shortly afterwards he began secret negotiations for the return of Charles II from his exile.

While these moves were being made behind the scenes a resolution was passed in the House of Commons for the sale, yet again, of Hampton Court. But General Ludlow, a gruff republican, who had often criticised Oliver Cromwell, suggested that it should be retained by the State and used as 'a very convenient place for the retirement of those employed in public affairs, should they be indisposed'. The suggestion was accepted and Hampton Court with all its furniture and fittings was this time finally reprieved.

In February 1660, shortly after Monk arrived with his army in London, a Bill was introduced in the House of Commons to settle Hampton Court and its park on Monk and his heirs. But Monk urged his friends in the House to have the Bill rejected. The House gave him instead £20,000 and the custody and stewardship of Hampton Court.

Charles II was proclaimed King while still in exile; the proclamation was made in Westminster Hall, where his father had been tried and sentenced to death. On 29 May 1660, his thirtieth birthday, he arrived in London, welcomed with the wildest acclamation by his joyous subjects.

Quite unlike his father in appearance, he resembled in many ways his maternal grandfather Henry of Navarre, who was dark-skinned, with jet-black hair and black eyes. Charles I had been only five feet tall, his son was over six feet; and, far from being assertive and obstinate, the new King was easy-going, gay, witty, and blessed with infinite charm. Like Henry of Navarre he could not resist women; his court was soon filled with his mistresses.

During his long years of exile, of wandering and poverty, he had often thought that, when he returned to the throne—as he was fairly confident that he would—he would found an Order of the Royal Oak, to commemorate his escape after the Battle of Worcester in 1651, for it was in an oak tree at Boscobel that he had found shelter and escaped capture by Cromwell's army. The plan for such an Order was abandoned, but visitors to Hampton Court can see there today two old firebacks of cast-iron, each of which has a three-branched oak tree with a crown on each branch representing the kingdoms of England, Scotland, and Ireland, and underneath the words 'The Royal Oak' and the Royal initials 'C.R.'.

One of the first things he did on his return was to have Hampton Court redecorated. Many of the tapestries, pictures, and articles of furniture that had been sold were bought back and all were replaced in the Palace.

151

Charles II liked Hampton Court and often went there, sometimes to stay, at others just for a game of tennis. Among the earliest alterations he made was to build a new doorway at the north-eastern end of the Palace leading to Henry VIII's old covered tennis court. Attention was then given to the tennis court itself, which had been sadly neglected because the Puritans regarded the game as sinful and ungodly. Although it was the largest and quite the best tennis court in England, it lacked the numerous recent developments the King had seen in those he had played on in Paris and other Continental cities. The tennis court here, he decided, must be brought up to date. Masons, bricklayers, carpenters, and sawyers were brought in. A new floor was laid down, with lines of black marble to mark the chaces; the tambour (a sloping projection inside the tennis court) was mended; the galleries were renovated and the roof was completely rebuilt. The cost was considerable. In addition nets and curtains were bought and all the seats were covered with velvet cushions.

He was as fond of tennis as Henry VIII, but probably not quite as good at the game, though his courtiers constantly flattered him about the superb way he played. Pepys was more frank in his diary: 'To the Tennis Court and there saw the King play at tennis, and others; but to see how the King's play was extolled without any cause at all was a loathsome sight, though sometimes indeed he did play very well and deserved to be commended; but such open flattery is beastly.'

Another change made at Hampton Court was the building of a guard house for foot-soldiers in the large Tilt Yard where Henry VIII had his tilting matches and tournaments. Most of the Tilt Yard has gone, but Charles II's guard house was the forerunner of the barracks which were built later and can still be seen on the left of the main western approach.

Gardening claimed the King's unflagging interest. He made more changes in the gardens than Henry VIII did when he took Hampton Court over from Wolsey. Charles had seen the beautiful gardens of the Tuileries in Paris. The son of one of the gardeners who had helped to lay them out, André le Nôtre, had thought of becoming a painter and studied under Simon Vouet with Le Sueur, Mignard, and Le Brun as fellow students; their pictures won admiration and fame, but young Le Nôtre abandoned the brush to join his father in the garden. Eventually the splendour of his landscape gardening attracted Louis XIV and he was called in to help in laying out the impressive and very lovely gardens at Versailles.

Charles possibly saw Le Nôtre's early work in the gardens of the French Chancellor Fouquet and, taking his cue from it, moved away from the small enclosed garden of the Middle Ages and adopted the vast spacious style of landscaping that Le Nôtre had introduced. We know that he wrote to Louis XIV and asked if Le Nôtre could come to England and lay out the gardens at Hampton Court and elsewhere. Louis agreed. But there is nothing on record to show that Le Nôtre came. Neither Evelyn's diary nor Pepys's mentions that Le Nôtre came. The *Victoria County History* goes so far as to state that Le Nôtre 'is generally supposed to have *designed* the plan of St. James's Park [in London] and the alterations at Hampton Court'. Of this there is no doubt, for Charles II wrote in October 1664 to his sister Minette, who was married to Louis XIV's brother the Duc d'Orléans: 'Pray let le Notre go on with the model [plan] and tell him this in addition, that I can bring water to the top of the hill, so that he may add much to the beauty of the descent by a cascade of water.' The date suggests that Charles was referring to the garden being laid out at Greenwich, but Le Nôtre's influence is clearly evident in the gardens at Hampton Court. A great canal was dug, jutting eastwards from the Palace out into the Home Park; and the water was brought to it from the Longford river. Three avenues of lime trees were planted, radiating like attractive toes from a semi-circular *patte d'oie* or 'goose-foot'. An avenue of lime trees was also planted on either side of the canal. To achieve all this the park was encroached on. Formerly just a flat, naked piece of land, the appearance now of this end of the park, as John Evelyn, a dedicated gardener himself, records in his diary, was transformed into a scene of striking beauty.

The man who carried out Le Nôtre's plan was John Rose, who had studied gardening in France with Le Nôtre and is, incidentally, also remembered today for having grown the first pineapple in England. Two French gardeners associated with him at Hampton Court were the brothers Gabriel and André Mollet: Gabriel's reputation stands almost as high as Le Nôtre's in French gardening history; in André's book *Le Jardin de Plaisir* there is a design, stretching to a *demi-lune*, similar to the avenues of lime trees.

These lime trees were brought from Holland. Christian van Vranen was given a permit in 1662 to bring four thousand trees from Holland for the King. A hundred years later, in 1762, the accounts show that John Harrison, Edward Collyer, and others were paid sixteen pence a day for digging and picking out weeds from young lime trees in the Nursery at Hampton Court, and William Steele Gardiner was paid six shillings for planting them: they were probably cultivated in order to replace older trees that had died.

Encroaching on the Home Park made little difference to what remained, for the size of this park and Bushey Park was estimated to extend, together with the land on which the Palace was built, to two thousand acres in 1514, when Wolsey got his lease. Nor have the boundaries of the two parks been altered in the intervening four hundred and fifty years. The ancient road running from Kingston Bridge to Hampton Court still separates them. For the most part the parks are flat, with some very aged oaks and thorns, which must have been there when the Knights Hospitallers farmed the land for some centuries before Wolsey.

For their various sports both parks were divided: Bushey Park was divided into three sections marked by brick walls—the Upper Park on the west, the Hare Warren (or Harewarren) on the east, and between them the Middle Park; the Home Park was divided into two sections—the Course and the Home Park proper.

Charles II was not as attracted to hunting as Henry VIII and Elizabeth I; but he often joined the distinguished guests who were staying at Hampton Court. He did not neglect the game in the parks: the covers were restocked and he gave instructions that all dogs, guns, and nets used for the destruction of game should be destroyed.

Adjoining the gardens of the Palace Charles planted a number of yew trees, which have been admired as the finest in England.

Charles's two brothers, James Duke of York and Henry Duke of Gloucester, returned to England with him in May 1660. James, as tall as Charles, very fair, blue-eyed and now twenty-seven, had got himself involved with Anne, the very young, large-bosomed daughter of Sir Edward Hyde, Charles's Chancellor during his years of exile and confirmed now in that office. In October Anne was found to be pregnant and, to the horror of his family, James married her: Charles described his new sister-in-law as 'the ugliest girl I've ever met'.

Whether James visited Hampton Court that summer and autumn is uncertain, but the youngest brother, Henry, also tall, blue-eyed and very English, often went there to play tennis, doubtless with Charles, who was much more attached to Henry than to James. After a series of brisk games one afternoon Henry fell ill and was thought to have caught a chill, but unhappily it was smallpox, and a few days later, on 22 September 1660, he died, aged only twenty.

His mother and two sisters, Mary Princess of Orange and Henrietta Anne (Minette, not yet Duchesse d'Orléans), arrived in England at the end of the following month. It was Minette's first visit to England since being carried on that long walk to Dover thirteen years before.

The thought of spending Christmas at Hampton Court reminded Charles's mother of how she had shivered in the dark-panelled rooms there despite the large wood fires. Already her joy in coming to see her eldest son return to the throne which had been taken from her husband was clouded by the recent death of her youngest son; and a week before Christmas, on 18 December, her daughter Mary, who at twenty-nine looked like a Stuart with delicate features and chestnut hair, contracted smallpox and died on Christmas Eve in London; she was buried in Westminster Abbey beside her brother Henry. Her son was to rule as William III.

Eventually Charles went to Hampton Court with Minette, whom all England adored and called 'Our Own Princess': they did not want her to leave the country and marry the brother of the King of France. She was tiny, with an alabaster white skin, sparkling blue eyes, lovely golden brown hair, witty, roguish and very beautiful. Many courtiers fell in love with her. Poems were written about her. Charles and she walked together in the Home Park and talked of her coming marriage. The Duc d'Orléans sent messengers almost daily, begging her to return, but Charles was not prepared to let her go yet. Minette was herself uneasy at the prospect of marrying Orléans: he was very odd in his behaviour. Her mother had told her that she could mould him after marriage; but she replied: 'I would rather have one ready made, maman. . . .' In the chill winter evenings, Charles and she strolled in the courtyards of the Palace; and together they admired the lovely pictures on the walls of Hampton Court which their father had bought, most of which fortunately were still there. The Queen Mother stayed in London at Somerset House in the Strand (sometimes called Denmark House after James I's Queen), and joined them for only a brief visit; then she returned to France with Minette, who was married to the Duc d'Orléans two months later.

Charles had been giving some thought to getting married and providing an heir to the throne, but within a few hours of his arriving in England he met the very lovely Mrs Barbara Palmer and is said to have spent the first night of his homecoming with her. A member of the Villiers family and daughter of Viscount Grandison, she was not yet twenty and was already married to a complaisant husband, who was rewarded with the earldom of Castlemaine while his wife was Charles's mistress. Some years later, after she had left her husband and had taken many other lovers, including John Churchill, later Duke of Marlborough, as well as a common rope-dancer, the King raised her to the rank of Duchess of Cleveland. She had two daughters and three sons by Charles: the eldest son was made the Duke of Southampton and later inherited his mother's title as Duke of Cleveland; the second son, created the Duke of Grafton, is the ancestor of the present Duke. The younger of the two daughters married the Earl of Lichfield.

Barbara Castlemaine was by no means Charles's only mistress, and she regarded it as her right to adjust the balance by taking other lovers. Quite early in the *affaire* Charles, while busy laying out his gardens at Hampton Court, rebuilt the Upper Lodge in Bushey Park for Edward Progers, who had acted as messenger between

Charles I, when he was a prisoner at Hampton Court and at Caris-brooke, and his Queen, crossing and re-crossing the Channel frequently with their letters. He had recently been appointed Groom of the Bedchamber to Charles II and was not only a confidant of the King's but acted as a useful go-between with his mistresses. Progers was also made Keeper of the Middle Park and deputy to General Monk, Duke of Albemarle, whom Charles had appointed Keeper and Steward of Hampton Court.

Marriage, however, could not be avoided. The choice finally fell on Catherine of Braganza, daughter of King John IV of Portugal. Charles went to Portsmouth to meet her and they were married the next day. She brought as part of her dowry the port of Tangier on the north coast of Africa, the island of Bombay in India, the right of free trade with Brazil and the East Indies, and half a million pounds in cash. Not yet twenty-four, Catherine was by no means pretty, though Evelyn, who was at Hampton Court when the royal couple arrived for their honeymoon, expresses it more gently. 'The Queene arrived with a train of Portugueze Ladys or *Guarda-Infantas* in their monstrous fardingals. Their complexions olivaster and sufficiently unagreeable, Her Majesty in the same habit, her foretop long and turned aside very strangely. She was yet of the handsomest Countenance of all the rest, and the low stature prettily shaped, languishing and excellent Eyes, her teeth wronging her mouth by sticking a little too far out: for the rest sweete and lovely enough. This day was solemnly kept'—it was 29 May—'the anniversary of His Majesty's birth and Restoration.' Evelyn stayed there for the night with his wife in the Vice-Chamberlain's apartment, dined in the Hall, and was taken up afterwards to kiss the new Queen's hand.

The progress of the royal party from Portsmouth to Hampton Court was an impressive affair. For the King and Queen a chariot drawn by six horses was provided. In their wake came a great many carriages full of Portuguese ladies-in-waiting and very dirty monks, all of whom had brought their relations; behind came waggons and carts laden with their clothes. Crossing the bridge across the moat, the royal coach went through the Great Gateway and through the Base Court, and stopped under Anne Boleyn's Archway at the foot of the Great Hall stairs. Alighting, they went up the stairs, lined by guards in handsome uniforms, and up to the royal bridal bed of crimson and silver.

The Queen's Portuguese retinue did not create the complications and irritations Charles I had to suffer from his wife's French followers. The ladies-in-waiting, however, came in for a great deal of criticism. Lord Clarendon, the Lord Chancellor, described them as 'old, ugly and proud, and incapable of any conversation with persons of quality and a liberal education'; to which the Comte de Grammont added in his *Memoirs* that there were 'six frights who called themselves Maids of Honour, and a Duenna, another Monster, who took the title of Governess to these extraordinary beauties'. Nor did the male attendants make a better impression. De Grammont says that Taurauvédez, who called himself Don Pedro de Silva, though extremely handsome was 'a greater fool than all the rest of the Portuguese put together and more vain of his names than his person. On him the Duke of Buckingham fastened the nickname of "Peter of the Wood", which so enraged him that, after many fruitless complaints and ineffectual menaces, he left England in disgust.'

The virtue of the *Guarda-Infantas* was never in doubt. It was thought that they would not so much as sleep on sheets that a man had touched. To the surprise of the Court a few weeks after their arrival at Hampton Court one of these ladies was said to have given birth to a child. Pepys, in his diary entry for 22 June 1662, reports: 'This day I am told of a Portugall lady at Hampton Court that hath dropped a child already since the Queen's coming, but the King would not have them searched whose it is.' Her name was never revealed, but the father was identified as Edward Tildesley, a Catholic gentleman resident in Lancashire, who had been sent to Portugal by the King in the preceding autumn to escort the royal bride on her journey to England. The Queen ordered that Tildesley must give the lady-in-waiting he had seduced the sum of £1,500. To raise the money he had to mortgage his estate, and the priests, imposing a penance on the lady concerned, insisted that the entire sum paid to her must be handed over to them.

Charles did everything to make the young Queen happy. For months he had been redecorating Hampton Court for her, coming from London almost every morning and returning later in the day for Council meetings in Whitehall. He had resolved to be a faithful husband and was quite determined to keep his resolve when he found that his bride was in love with him. Their honeymoon was spent picnicking either on the Thames or in one of the parks; in the evenings there was music and dancing. Evelyn, who spent some days at Hampton Court, tells us that the gondola which had been sent to the King by the State of Venice was used during the honeymoon; and also of an evening when he listened to 'the Queen's Portugal music, consisting of fifes, harps and very ill voices'. Courtiers noticed that the King was 'very much taken with her and becoming fond of her'. But Lady Castlemaine was not prepared to let him go. She gave birth to his son during the honeymoon; a week later she left her husband and moved to nearby Richmond. The King stood sponsor at the christening and Lady Castlemaine's tears, as well as her beauty, shattered all hope of his keeping his resolution.

She begged him to make her a Lady of the Queen's Bedchamber. He put her name on the list for Her Majesty's approval; but the Queen had heard of what was going on and struck her name out. The King was angry and so was she. Clarendon tried to reason with him, but Charles brushed aside his arguments. 'I am resolved to go through with this matter, let what will come of it.' The Queen couldn't argue for she knew hardly a word of English, but she was in a jealous temper and that was quite clearly intelligible. They were by now barely half-way through their honeymoon. Avoiding the Queen by day, the King plunged into a life of gaiety and merriment. The scandal got about and so did news of the quarrels between the bride and bridegroom. Pepys heard of both in London.

The return of Henrietta Maria from France made things a little easier. Queen Catherine, escorted back to London by the King, found it easy to establish a warm relationship with her mother-in-law; for one thing they had their religion in common, for another Henrietta Maria remembered the difficulties she herself had to face during the early months of her marriage. She told Catherine that she would have to order her *Guarda-Infantas* to give up wearing their hideous dresses, which looked ludicrous in an English setting and were the subject of much ridicule in Court. Moreover she should not turn to them for advice and guidance: she had herself tried that and it brought disaster. Meanwhile Lord Clarendon, having failed to influence Charles, had been persuading the Queen that the only way to win the King's affection was to give way. What, he asked, were the morals of her own brothers in the Portuguese Court? It took some time for her to accept the situation.

Without warning, Charles attempted to force the issue. He walked into the Presence Chamber at Hampton Court one evening with Lady Castlemaine. The Queen, seated with her ladies around her, rose to welcome her without realising who she was. Charles gave no name in presenting his mistress and Catherine, suspecting who she was and overwhelmed by her humiliation, sat down. She wept for a while, then fainted and was helped by her ladies to her room.

The King was indignant. After a week or two the Queen agreed to Lady Castlemaine being her Lady of the Bedchamber; and in early September, less than four months after her marriage, guests at the reception given by the Queen Mother in Denmark House in London, saw the King arrive with the Queen as well as Lady Castlemaine and a boy aged thirteen, the son of Charles by an earlier mistress Lucy Waters, known now as James Crofts but later made the Duke of Monmouth. The boy had been brought up by his grandmother Henrietta Maria, but was now with Lady Castlemaine, the mother of his half-brother.

Lady Castlemaine moved into Hampton Court where she had her own apartments. The Queen saw her every day, 'was merry with her in public, talked kindly to her, and in private used nobody more friendly'. As with Louise la Vallière, the current mistress of King Louis XIV, Charles's mistress became *la mâitresse en titre*. Queen Catherine regained her husband's respect and affection and was treated by him with the deference due to her as Queen of England.

Life became easier and pleasanter after that. The King, who delighted in dancing, would first take the floor with the Queen in a *coranto*, and then with Lady Castlemaine. When the country dances followed, the King always announced that the first of these should be 'Cuckolds all awry', which was, as he phrased it, the old dance of England. There was gaiety and fun, with the fiddlers accelerating the pace while the dancers whirled in the light of the tall, flickering candles.

But as the months passed the gaiety and laughter were overshadowed by the misery of Queen Catherine, who showed no signs of providing the King with the expected heir, whereas Lady Castlemaine, having delivered one son, was to provide him with two more. Ill with worry over Charles's acute disappointment, for she had seen how happy he was with his illegitimate children, the Queen went to Tunbridge Wells, wondering if the waters of the chalybeate spring there would help her, but in vain.

Soon it was Lady Castlemaine's turn to be miserable, for a new beauty had caught the King's eye—Frances Stuart, often spoken of as 'the prettiest girl in the world', and now appointed Maid of Honour to the Queen. Though known as 'La Belle Stuart', she was only distantly related to the royal family. Her father was Dr Walter Stuart and her grandfather Lord Blantyre. Barbara Castlemaine, jealous and deeply distressed, kept sulkily to her room, but the King, who visited her and dined with her every night, told her bluntly that he would stay away unless Frances Stuart was invited too. Barbara gave in and soon she and Frances became close friends. Frances, moreover, managed to avoid responding to the King's advances. Deeply in love with the Duke of Richmond, she had been about to marry him when the King's eye alighted on her. To prevent the marriage he arrested Richmond and put him in the Tower. Later, relenting, he sent him as ambassador to Denmark. Charles wrote this song to give vent to his feelings for her.

> I pass all my hours in a shady old grove,
> But I live not the day when I see not my love;
> I survey every walk now my Phillis is gone,
> And sigh when I think we were there all alone;
> O then, 'tis O then, that I think there's no hell
> Like loving, like loving too well.
>
> While alone to myself I repeat all her charms,
> She I love may be locked in another man's arms,
> She may laugh at my cares and so false she may be
> To say all the kind things she before said to me:
> O then, 'tis O then, that I think there's no hell
> Like loving too well.
>
> But when I consider the truth of her heart,
> Such an innocent passion, so kind without art;
> I fear I have wronged her, and hope she may be
> So full of true love to be jealous of me;
> And then 'tis, I think, that no joys be above
> The pleasures of love.

Roettier, the Dutch engraver working in the Mint in the Tower of London, made for the King a design of her as Britannia, wearing a helmet and holding a trident: it was used on all halfpennies at the time and later on pennies as well. Eventually Frances Stuart married her Duke of Richmond.

During Henrietta Maria's stay in England she paid occasional visits to Hampton Court, generally staying for only two or three days. It was full of memories for her, sad ones of those early quarrels with her husband, good ones of the years of great happiness, and finally the awfulness of the months when Charles was a prisoner there far away from her, and the terrible ending. To dispel her sad recollections her son did everything he could to make her happy. Whenever she came, she found him waiting for her at the foot of the stairs of the Great Hall: he received her with filial devotion and the honour due to her status as the Queen Mother. On her first day there Charles and Catherine dined alone with her. They were joined in the afternoon by other members of the family, such as the King's brother and his wife Anne Duchess of York, usually in the Queen's Chamber, where the Portuguese band diverted them. Henrietta Maria had by now forgiven James his 'dreadful' misalliance and accepted Anne as her daughter-in-law.

In the summer of 1665, when the Great Plague was raging in London, the Queen Mother left England for the last time. She had aged greatly: her face was drawn, her cheeks sunken, and her dark eyes appeared to be larger than ever. Four years later she died in France at the age of sixty: her daughter Minette had died a few months earlier aged twenty-six.

Often Charles went to Hampton Court solely to entertain distinguished foreign visitors. In June 1663 the Duc de Monconys arrived in a coach and six and spoke delightedly of the beauty of the countryside between London and the Palace. He was greatly attracted by the enormous number of towers and turrets, cupolas and pinnacles at Hampton Court, admired the gardens and commented on the fountain in the Privy Garden 'composed of four sirens in bronze seated astride on dolphins between which was a shell, supported on the foot of a goat. Above the sirens, on a second tier, were four little children, each seated holding a fish, and surmounting all a large figure of a lady—all the figures being of bronze, but the fountain itself and the basin of marble.' The figure at the top, made by the sculptor Fanelli, was thought to be a statue of Arethusa, though, as she held a golden apple in her hand, it may well have been Venus. This fountain was moved by William III to the centre of the great basin in Bushey Park, where it is known as the Diana fountain, a still further confusion over the identification of the figure at the top. A curious bower in the garden, known as the Cradle Walk, also attracted the Duke's attention. Evelyn described it as being of hornbeam; it is, in fact, of wych-elm. 'Opposite to it,' said the Duc de Monconys, 'is a terrace along which, from the brick cloister, several little chambers, or cabinets, of various shapes—round, square and in the form of crosses, with little turrets—jut out into the Park.'

Evelyn had a look into a royal bedroom: 'The Queen's bed was an embroidery of silver on crimson velvet, and cost £8,000, being a present made by the States of Holland when His Majesty returned, and had formerly been given to the King's sister, the Princess of Orange. . . . The great looking-glass and toilet of beaten and massive gold was given by the Queen Mother. The Queen brought over from Portugal such Indian cabinets as had never been seen here.'

One summer the Earl of Bedford came to Hampton Court on the King's invitation. He stayed as a guest, but various charges were made for the servants and horses he brought. The bill handed to him

M

stated: 'Two grooms' board wages at Hampton Court for five days—
15 shillings; Horses hay and corn for five nights—£2; for the fal-
coners and their two horses for seven days—£2 2s. 0; for carriage of
pigeons from London to Hampton Court for the hawks—8d.; for
hogs' hearts for the hawks—8d.'

During the terrible Plague in London in 1665 death took a heavy
toll, often as many as a thousand a day in the city, and the nights
were filled with lamentation and terror. Even in the countryside
around the capital one saw corpses rotting in the fields. But Hampton Court being just far enough away, the King and Queen came to
stay there with the Duke and Duchess of York, Lady Castlemaine,
quite a number of other pretty women, and a host of courtiers. At
nearby Syon House and sometimes in the Palace itself the Council
held its meetings.

The quarantine was apparently not strictly applied, for Pepys
fairly frequently came from London to see the King. In his diary he
records:

Sunday, 23rd July—Up betimes, called by Mr. Cutler and with
him in his coach and four, over London Bridge to Kingston, a very
pleasant journey, and at Hampton Court by nine o'clock. ... I
followed the King to Chapel and there heard a good sermon; and
after the sermon with my Lord Arlington, Sir Thomas Ingram and
others, spoke to the Duke [of York] of Tangier, but not to much
purpose. I was not invited any wither to dinner, though a stranger,
which did also trouble me; but yet I remember it is a Court, and
indeed where most are strangers; but, however, Cutler carried me
to Mr. Marriott's, the housekeeper, and there we had a very good
dinner and good company, among others Lilly [Sir Peter Lely],
the painter. Thence to the Councill-chamber, where in a back
room I sat all the afternoon, but the Councill began late to sit.
They sat long and I forced to follow Sir Thomas Ingram, the
Duke and others, so that when I got free and came to look for
Mr. Cutler he was gone with his coach, so that I was forced with
great trouble to walk up and down looking for him, and at last
forced to get a boat to carry me to Kingston, and there, after
eating a bit at a neat inne, which pleased me well, I took boat and
slept all the way.

Three days later, on 26 July, the indefatigable Pepys went again to Hampton Court to see the King and Queen, who were about to move to Salisbury because the Plague seemed now to be approaching the Palace. After they had left, he stayed to talk to the Duke of York, who, as Lord High Admiral, was Pepys's chief in the Navy Office. On seeing the Duchess of York, he kissed her hand. 'It was the first time I did ever, or see anybody else kiss her hand, and it was a most fine and fat hand. But it was pretty to see the young, pretty ladies dressed like men in velvet coats, caps with ribbons and with lace bands, just like men.'

Lely was asked by the Duchess of York, not herself a beauty, to paint portraits of the lovely women in Charles's Court. De Grammont says: 'He could not have worked on more beautiful sitters. Each portrait was a masterpiece.' The portraits, still at Hampton Court, present languorous-eyed young women, their bare shoulders lightly draped, some with almost the entire bosom exposed, and their hair dangling in delightful curls. Lady Castlemaine is of course there in a loose brown dress, pale blue drapery and red hair; and Frances Stuart—said to be brainless, though, as we have seen, she managed rather well—beautiful in a yellow dress cut low. Lady Falmouth, who did yield to the King, is there too; and so are La Belle Hamilton, whom De Grammont married; Jane Middleton with a dish of fruit and an exposed right breast; and many, many more. Even the Duchess of York, plump and unattractive, is there. The pictures are not Lely's best work: they have a monotony of pose and treatment and the hands and draperies seem to have been done by his assistants. Louise de Kéroualle, Charles's pretty French mistress, who was made Duchess of Portsmouth, is in the gallery, but she was painted by Verelst, another of Charles's Court painters.

Towards the end of the following January the King, his brother James, and their cousin Prince Rupert (he was the son of Charles I's sister Elizabeth, who married the King of Bohemia, and uncle of the future King George I, who was then six years old) came to Hampton Court because of the Plague in London and were joined by the Council. Again Pepys came to see the King. In his diary entry for Sunday 28 January, he says he woke at six o'clock, went 'to my Lord Brunker's with all his papers and there took his coach with four horses and away toward Hampton Court. . . . We find the King and Duke and Lords all in Council, so we walked up and down, there being none of the ladies come and so much the more business I hope will be done. The Council being up, out comes the King and I kissed his hand and he grasped me very kindly by the hand. The Duke also, I kissed his and he mighty kind.' Later 'I went down into one of the Courts and there met the King and the Duke; and the Duke called me to him. And the King come to me of himself and told me. "Mr. Pepys," says he, "I do give you thanks for your good service all this year and I assure you I am very sensible of it." I walked with them quite out of the Court into the fields and then back.'

On the next day Evelyn came. Like Pepys he had stayed in London to carry on with his work: he had been appointed by the King to serve on various commissions—for regulating hackney coaches in London, for regulating the Mint, and to take care of the sick and wounded in the war against the Dutch, which had broken out a few months earlier and went on for three years. The King, he wrote, on seeing him 'ran towards me and in most gracious manner gave me his hand to kisse, with many thanks for my care and faithfulness in his service in a time of great danger when everybody fled their employment. . . . He said he was severall times concerned for me and the peril I underwent, though in truth I did but what was my duty. After this His Majestie was pleased to talke with me alone neere an houre of severall particulars of my Employment.'

While the Queen was at Oxford with her ladies, Charles stayed at Hampton Court for just over a week and then left for London when the Plague was over, where the Queen joined him after spending a night or two at Hampton Court on the way. During the Great Fire which devastated the City of London in September 1666 the King sent many of his precious paintings and finest furniture by boats up the Thames for safety to Hampton Court.

In the years that followed other foreign visitors who came to Hampton Court as Charles's guests left records of what impressed them most. Mandelslo, who had travelled over most of Europe, makes special mention of the ancient tapestries that are known as 'The Creation of the World', in which, he notes, the Trinity is represented by three men dressed as bishops with crowns on their heads and sceptres in their hands. Cosmo III, Duke of Tuscany, came in May 1669 and watched the stag-hunt in the Park. His secretary Magalotti, in his book *Travels of Cosmo III*, records: 'On first entering the Park, he was met by Prince Rupert, who was likewise come thither for the diversion of seeing the hunt.' It was a sport in a sense not unlike bear-baiting and cock-fighting, which one just watched; the Duke stayed with Prince Rupert 'under the shade of a tree on a stage a little raised from the ground, which is the same where the King stands to see this amusement'. The secretary describes what happened. 'When the huntsmen had stretched out the nets after the German manner, inclosing with them a considerable space of land, they let the dogs loose upon four deer which were confined there, who as soon as they saw them took to flight; but as they had not the power of going which way they pleased, they ran round the net, endeavouring by various cunning leaps to save themselves from being stopped by the dogs, and continued to run in this manner for some time to the great diversion of some of the spectators; till at last the huntsmen, that they might not harass the animals superfluously, drawing a certain cord, opened the nets in one part, which was prepared for that purpose, and left the deer at liberty to escape.'

A walk in the park was always enjoyed by the guests, who found it 'truly delightful by its numerous canals and amenities of every kind', Duke Cosmo's secretary adds. 'The gardens are divided into very large, level and well kept walks which, separating the ground into different compartments, form artificial pastures of grass, being themselves formed of espalier trees, partly such as bear fruit and partly ornamental ones but all adding to the beauty of the appearance. This beauty is further augmented by the fountains made of slate after the Italian style, and distributed in different parts of the garden, whose *jets d'eaux* throw up the water in various playful and fanciful ways. There are also in the gardens some snug places of retirement in certain towers, formerly intended as places of accommodation for the King's mistresses.' Of the Palace itself he thought that 'although the more elegant orders of architecture are not to be found in it, so as to make it a regular structure according to rules of art, yet it is, on the whole, a beautiful object to the eye. The numerous towers and cupolas, judiciously disposed at irregular distances all over the vast pile of building, form a most striking ornament to it, whether viewed near or at a distance.'

During the last years of his reign Charles came to Hampton Court much less frequently. In the summer of 1679, five and a half years before his death, he held a meeting of the Council there. He had been gravely ill and was not expected to live; in consequence a crisis confronted him over his brother James, who was next in succession to the throne because the Queen had been unable to have any children. After being a Protestant for years James had now become a Roman Catholic and the people had got to know of it. The country was shaken by a Popish Plot scare. The Scottish Covenanters were up in arms; the London 'mob' got busy demonstrating. Parliament met and the House of Commons passed a Bill to exclude James from the throne. Charles was strongly opposed to it. He discussed it with the Council and found that a large majority of the members were for James's exclusion. An attempt to nominate as his heir the Duke of Monmouth, now aged thirty, was rejected by Charles, who denied that he had ever been married to Monmouth's mother, Lucy Waters. Enraged by their persistent hostility to James, Charles promptly dissolved Parliament.

The people's opposition continued. All attempts at finding a compromise failed. Another Exclusion Bill was passed in the following year by the next Parliament. As a solution the King suggested that, in the event of a Roman Catholic succession, a Protestant could be appointed to administer the country. But this was unacceptable.

Eighteen months before the death of Charles II Judge Jeffreys informed the Council at Hampton Court of a plot (known as the Rye House Plot) to assassinate both the King and his brother James on their way back from the races at Newmarket. Charles's reaction to this was to banish Monmouth from the country.

The King died in February 1685, confessing that he too was a Roman Catholic. He was succeeded by his brother.

On his accession James II assured the people that he would 'make it his endeavour to preserve this government in Church and State as it is now by law established'. Many doubted that the promise would be kept. Now fifty-three, he had never been a likeable person: he was arrogant, stubborn, impatient, and so far as his religious faith was concerned utterly bigoted. But the people for the most part were prepared to see what course he would really adopt.

Within four months the Duke of Monmouth returned to England, landing at Lyme Regis in Dorset, which was strongly Protestant. Proclaiming himself King, he accused James of poisoning his brother Charles in order to gain the throne and restore Catholicism.

In a brief, swift battle at Sedgemoor, James's troops defeated Monmouth's seven thousand men. Monmouth himself was arrested, taken to the Tower of London and two days later executed. Few of those who had taken part in the rebellion escaped Judge Jeffreys' terrible vengeance. Even those remotely connected with it were savagely punished. According to the official figures three hundred and twenty were executed and more than eight hundred were sold as slaves in the West Indies. Among the victims were quite a number of women.

The people were rudely shocked. But James, delighted with these barbaric sentences, made Jeffreys his Lord Chancellor.

Flushed by his victory, James felt it was the right moment to restore the country to Roman Catholicism. Quite blatantly he had begun to celebrate Mass in public. He forbade any preaching against Catholics inside or outside the churches. Catholics, who had been forbidden by the Test Act of Charles II from holding any public office, were admitted now to many chief posts, even in the Army. Increasing the size of the standing army to twenty thousand men James encamped them at Hounslow Heath, near enough to London for prompt action if there were any signs of rebellion against his course of action.

Aware that he would be fiercely opposed by the entire Anglican

Church, James planned to win the support of the Nonconformists, who, like the Catholics, had been subjected to various restrictions. He issued a Declaration of Indulgence to dispense with all the prohibitory laws and grant liberty of conscience to all faiths. This, he hoped, would add their support to that of the Catholics and provide him with sufficient allies for the inevitable battle. Not only the Anglicans, but the Nonconformists too, saw through this at once. But James was prepared to face the consequences. He ordered all bishops and the clergy to read the Declaration of Indulgence in all the churches on Sundays. The Archbishop of Canterbury and six other bishops refused to do so and were promptly arrested and sent to the Tower.

The reaction of the people was instantaneous. There were angry demonstrations in the streets and a widespread display of support for the arrested bishops awaiting trial and doubtless also execution.

Unexpectedly, the new Catholic Queen Mary of Modena, whom James had married on the death of his first wife, had, after the loss of all her other children, given birth to a son who survived. The perpetuation of a Catholic monarchy was now likely; something had to be done quickly if it were to be prevented. Secretly a group of prominent persons got in touch with Prince William of Orange, who was married to King James's daughter Mary, and invited him to take over the government of England.

William landed at Torbay on 5 November 1688 and in December James fled. The claim to the English throne by Mary, James's elder daughter, was greater than that of her husband William, who was the son of Charles and James's eldest sister. But Mary insisted on their ruling jointly and consequently they became King William III and Queen Mary II. A Declaration of Rights presented to them by both Houses of Parliament, besides guaranteeing free elections and trial by jury, deprived the monarch of the power, which James II had exercised, to suspend the law of the country and maintain a standing army without Parliament's consent in time of peace. Among those who went over to William was John Churchill, who not long before had helped stamp out Monmouth's rebellion and been raised to the peerage and given the rank of General by James II. Churchill's sister Arabella had been James's mistress and was the mother of his son, the Duke of Berwick.

The new rulers visited Hampton Court on 23 February 1689, soon after their accession. The beauty of the setting, its seclusion yet

Charles II's lovely young sister Minette. A portrait by Claude Mellan

Etching by Dirk Stoop showing the arrival at Hampton Court of King Charles II and his bride, Catharine of Braganza

William III when Prince of Orange. The portraits of William and Mary were painted c.1685 for James II by Willem Wissing

Wren's South Front. The King's State Rooms are on the first floor

Mary II when Princess of Orange

Wren's East Front with the Queen's State Rooms

Sir Christopher Wren. From a portrait by Sir Godfrey Kneller

The King's Staircase, Wren's grand approach to the State Rooms. The walls and ceiling were painted by Antonio Verrio and the wrought-iron balustrade was designed by Jean Tijou

nearness to London, made them decide at once that it was the ideal place to live in. The flatness of the parks, with the long straight canal and its avenues of trees, appealed to them because it reminded them of Holland.

They spent three days inspecting it. The Queen went from room to room examining everything: she opened every closet door, turned over the quilts on the beds as one would on arriving at an inn, inspected the gardens and the parks. Evelyn records: 'She smiled upon all and talked to everybody.' After only a brief visit to London they returned to Hampton Court.

The new King was thirty-eight years old, of medium height, firm-chinned, hook-nosed and slightly hunchbacked; he was born on his mother's nineteenth birthday, a few days after his father's death. His wife Mary, aged twenty-six, was handsome rather than pretty, with pale blue eyes and a small mouth. She was fifteen when she married William, who could hardly speak English at the time, but though she wept on her wedding day, she gave her husband her complete loyalty and devotion.

Finding the royal apartments built by Henry VIII old-fashioned and uncomfortable, William and Mary engaged the distinguished architect Sir Christopher Wren to provide them with modern State rooms. The French Renaissance style of architecture, so fashionable in Europe, greatly appealed to Wren, who had spent some months in France in 1665 and had made numerous sketches of the buildings put up for the 'Sun King' Louis XIV and his nobles. With the existing Tudor Gothic style of Hampton Court he had little sympathy. It was his intention to tear it all down and build a completely new Palace. Plans for this were drawn up, but William and Mary wanted their new residential suites to be built first so that they could move into them as soon as possible. Wren accordingly pulled down the State apartments erected by Henry VIII round Cloister Green Court. The attractive old State rooms, the mullioned windows, the gables, the moulded chimney shafts, the fretted ceilings, the latticed casements with their lovely stained glass, the galleries, the towers and turrets of that part of the old Palace all lay in heaps of rubble.

On this site Wren was to erect four new ranges in the modern style round an entirely new court, known as the Fountain Court. The range providing a new south front facing the river contained the King's State apartments; the range facing the great eastward vista along the canal contained the Queen's State apartments. As the new east front required more space immediately before it to set it off impressively, some adjustment had to be made in Charles II's layout: the Long Canal, which pointed like a finger at the centre of this front, had to be shortened—more than two hundred yards were cut off—and in the middle of a semicircular parterre a large fountain was placed, with smaller fountains dotted around it.

The contrast between the old Tudor buildings and Wren's massive rectangular structures which adjoin them can be described as an unfortunate misalliance or as a happy conjunction of opposites. The Tudor section has infinite variety and charm; Wren's new wings, mathematically planned, with the distance between the windows carefully measured, strike a recurrently monotonous note. But by his use of red brick, with white Portland stone to frame openings and form string-courses, Wren neatly linked his new structure with the old and avoided too glaring an incongruity. It is fortunate for posterity that he did this, for although this structure was to be only a part of the Palace he planned to build, it is all that was in fact built—lack of money and the deaths of first the Queen and later of the King prevented his going on with the work. And so the bulk of the Tudor Palace still stands, with Wren's seventeenth-century addition attached to it. Whatever regrets one may have for what was destroyed, one can today admire both the old and the new.

The King and Queen had planned to stay in Windsor Castle until their new apartments were completed; but because of an outbreak of smallpox at Windsor, they went on living in the Palace despite the dust and noise. They were indeed so deeply attached to Hampton Court that they stayed there until their Coronation and came back a day or so later.

Not long afterwards they were joined by Mary's younger sister Anne, who was twenty-four. As Queen Anne she was to succeed William III, who outlived his wife. Anne was already married to Prince George of Denmark and expecting her first child. Daniel Defoe refers to their arrival at Hampton Court in his book *A Tour through England and Wales*: 'The Prince and Princess, I remember, came once down by water, upon the occasion of Her Royal Highness's being great with child, and near her time; so near that she was deliver'd within two or three days after.' The child was a boy, and at his christening—the first in the Chapel there since the christening of Edward VI—the King gave him the title of Duke of Gloucester. There was great public rejoicing, church bells were rung and bonfires lit all over the country.

But despite his courtesy and charm in honouring his Protestant nephew and, as it seemed, the eventual heir, William was not very kind or even civil to the child's mother. This was no doubt due to James II's original intention (before the birth of his own son) to exclude his elder daughter Mary from the throne, and to arrange, after converting Anne to Catholicism, for her to succeed him. Princess Anne's favourite lady-in-waiting and for years her closest friend, Lady Churchill, who became Countess and later Duchess of Marlborough, wrote later:

I could fill many sheets with the brutalities that were done to the Princess in this reign. William III was indeed so ill-natured and so little polished by education, that neither in great things nor in small had he the manners of a gentleman. I give an instance of his worse than vulgar behaviour at his own table when the Princess dined with him. It was in the beginning of the reign and some weeks before the Princess was put to bed of the Duke of Gloucester. There happened to be just before her a plate of green peas, the first that had been seen that year. The King, without offering the Princess the least share of them, drew the plate before him and devoured them all. Whether he offered any to the Queen I cannot say, but he might have done that safely enough for he knew she durst not touch one. The Princess Anne confessed when she came home that she had so much mind for the peas that she was afraid to look at them and yet could hardly keep her eyes off them.

The household books set out the meals served to the King and Queen: 'Dinner—Pottage of Capons i, *or* Pullets ii, *or* Chickens iii, *or* Partridges iv, *or* Boiled Beef 24 lb.' Then mutton roasted, followed by 'Turkey *or* Goose large, *or* Capons fatt ii'. The next course was 'Pigeons tame viii *or* Pheasants ii, *or* Partridges vi, *or* Cocks vi, *or* Quails viii, *or* Buck baked quarter, *or* Hen Pye'. Then 'Tarts of Sorts'. The dessert consisted of 'Morelles [an edible fungus], *or* Trouffles'; followed by 'Jelly *or* Asparagus'.

Supper was not so elaborate: 'Pigeons tame iiii, *or* Mutton roast, *or* Veale. Then Capons fatt ii *or* Pullets iii, *or* Plovers viii, *or* Snites [i.e. snipe] viii, *or* Pigeons field xii, *or* Larks ii dozen. Next Runners vi *or* Ducklings vi; followed by Lamb quar', *or* Tarts of Sorts'. And for dessert, 'Ragou of Sweetbread, *or* Pistachio Cream, *or* Hartichokes *or* Pease'.

A great deal of criticism began to be levelled against William III for spending so much of his time at Hampton Court. Even his great admirer and friend Bishop Burnet said: 'From that Palace he came into town only on Council days: so that the face of the Court (in London) and the rendezvous usual in public rooms was now quite broken. The gaiety and diversions of the Court disappeared.' Many complained that he was using Hampton Court as King Louis XIV used Versailles; 'and,' the Bishop adds, 'the entering so soon on so expensive a building affords matter of censure.'

One of the King's ministers, Lord Halifax, said that 'his inaccessibleness and living so at Hampton Court altogether, and at so active a time'—for there were numerous problems, mostly international, which had to be discussed—'ruined all business'. Often the King did not go to London even for Council meetings, and 'his ministers, every time they went to see him, lost five hours in going and coming'. The King's only answer to that was: 'Do you wish to see me dead?'

It is possible that his reply was prompted by news of a plot against his life of which Catherine of Braganza, Charles II's widow, warned him when he called to see her at Somerset House in London. She said that the Countess of Monmouth (in no way connected with the Duke of Monmouth whom James II had executed) had received an anonymous letter stating that the Catholics intended on the night of Sunday 21 July, to assassinate the King, set fire to his London home, the Palace of Whitehall, and seize the Tower of London. After reading the letter the King hurried back to Hampton Court and a powerful guard was put on the Palace. Troops of cavalry and several companies of infantry were brought in and were stationed all round the building. No one was allowed to come near the Palace without the strictest security. As the days passed and nothing happened the guards were eventually reduced.

Weary of the very slow progress with the new wing and driven almost to distraction by the dust and clatter, the King and Queen moved into the Water Gallery by the river. Some distance from the main building, it was large enough to be made comfortable. The Queen got Wren to redecorate it: the ceilings and panels were painted; new doorways and cornices made of limewood were put in, with delightful carvings of fruit and flowers by Grinling Gibbons; corner fireplaces with marble mantelpieces and shelves for the Queen's rare pieces of Oriental china were constructed: her Delft china was displayed in a separate cabinet made for her by Gerreit Johnson, an outstanding cabinet-maker. In a number of the State rooms her china may still be seen.

One of the rooms in the Water Gallery was known as the Looking Glass Closet, which James Bogdane (Jakob Bogdany, a Hungarian), a painter of animals and birds, decorated for her. There was also a Bathing Closet which, Defoe tells us, was 'made very fine, suited either to hot or cold bathing, as the season should invite'. She had also here 'a dairy, with all its conveniences, in which Her Majesty took great delight'.

Almost as a challenge to Lely's portraits of Charles II's Beautiful Women, Queen Mary got Sir Godfrey Kneller to paint a series of portraits of the Beautiful Women of her Court. Born in Lübeck, Kneller had studied art in Amsterdam, visited Italy, and come to England in 1674. Eventually, after the deaths of Lely and of Riley, he became sole 'Principal Painter'. His portraits possess dignity and elegance, if less charm than those of Sir Peter Lely. Horace Walpole, writing of them in his *Anecdotes of Painting*, says: 'The thought was the Queen's own during one of the King's absences'—William was in Ireland fighting the Battle of the Boyne, in which he defeated the forces of his father-in-law James II. 'The pictures contributed much to render her unpopular, as I have heard from the authority of the Duchess of Carlisle, who remembered the event. She added that the famous Lady Dorchester advised the Queen against it, saying: "Madame, if the King was to ask for the portraits of all the wits in his court, would not the rest think he called them fools?"'

Of the beautiful women in Kneller's pictures few seem to have possessed the loveliness of those Lely had painted; had Kneller depicted his sitters in transparent draperies, displaying bared shoulders, they might have been more admired. Defoe, however, liked them: 'This was the more beautiful sight because the originals were all in Being and often to be compared with their pictures.' The pictures were hung in the Water Gallery and remained there until after Queen Mary's death. When Wren's south and east fronts of the Palace were completed, the Water Gallery was pulled down because it obstructed the view of the river from the new State apartments. The portraits were then moved to the King's Guard Chamber where William often dined in private; they can now be seen in King William's First Presence Chamber: they include portraits of the Duchess of St Albans, wife of Charles II's illegitimate son by Nell Gwyn; Lady Margaret Cecil, Countess of Ranelagh; and the Duchess of Grafton, wife of one of Charles II's illegitimate sons by Lady Castlemaine.

During the King's absence in Ireland, the Queen sent him regular reports on the progress of Wren's work. 'The Queen pleased herself from time to time,' Wren says, 'in examining and surveying the drawings, contrivances and the whole progress of the present building and in giving thereon her own judgment, which was exquisite; and there were few arts or sciences in which Her Majesty had not only an elegant taste but a knowledge much superior to any of her sex in that or, it may be, any former age.'

There were problems. The cost of Wren's new apartments was enormous and England was at the time involved in two wars—against James II in Ireland and a joint action with the Dutch on land and at sea against the French. The Treasury declared that there was not enough money to spare for these building projects. The Queen wrote in a letter to the King: 'I spoke to Sir J. Lowther [later the first Earl of Lonsdale] this very day and hear so much use for money and find so little, that I cannot tell whether that of Hampton Court will not be the worst for it, especially since the French are in the Channel and at present between Portland and us, from whence the stone must come.'

And again a few days later: 'Want of money and Portland stone being the hindrances.' Portland stone was needed for the splendid Corinthian order on the two main fronts, for the framework of windows and doors, and other dressings. Prevented by the French from getting it, Wren used Bath stone, which weathers much less well, for the inner east range of the quadrangle. The Queen disliked the substitution. Two hundred years later it had to be replaced with Portland stone.

At an early stage of the construction, while William and Mary were in London, a wall fell down, killing three men and injuring others. An immediate inquiry was ordered by the King. Summoned to appear before the Lords of the Treasury, Wren was told to write a full report on what had happened. He did not like their attitude or their tone. After waiting in vain for nearly two weeks for the report, they ordered him to exercise 'some haste, for the King is of the opinion ye building is in a bad condition'. This fresh and more pointed criticism of his work as well as his suspicion that some of his colleagues on the board of the Office of Works were prejudiced against him, caused Wren to tell their Lordships that he was going to get on oath 'the affidavits of able men', no longer involved in the work—'bricklayers, carpenters and masons that have left off their aprons and are without suspicion of being influenced' by him: the report, he added, would be handed to them in a week's time.

After reading his report and that of William Talman, Comptroller of the Works, a difficult person who was critical of Wren's work, the Lords of the Treasury asked both men to appear together before them. It was an angry encounter. Wren, speaking with the authority of his position as Surveyor-General, objected to Talman's quotation of a comment by a Mr Latham, whom he described as a madman. The work, he added, had stood a new trial in a hurricane; Talman's rejoinder was: 'My Lord Chamberlain's lodgings kept the wind absolutely from this building, and Mr. Latham is not mad.' A member of the board of the Office of Works came to Wren's rescue. 'There are,' he said, 'twenty-four piers next the garden and only four stones were cracked, and the cracks are no bigger than a hair's breadth, and the building, each day it stands, grows stronger.' Talman disputed this: 'Every pier is cracked and one can put his finger in the cracks.' To end the argument their Lordships appointed their own inspectors, who finally declared that Wren was right. So the order was given for the work to be resumed and completed with all possible despatch. Time has justified Wren's contention: the solidity of his work is still apparent.

The accounts show that Sir Christopher Wren was paid only 4s. 10d. a day, whereas Talman was receiving a salary of 6s. 10d. a day.

Mary's considerable changes in the gardens were strongly influenced by gardens in Holland; there those of the middle-class were small, with hedges and tiny canals; and those of rich merchants, though somewhat larger but still restricted, were provided with the illusion of landscaping. This was achieved by putting up brick piers to support ornamental grilles through which one got the impression of a long vista. Mary adopted this for her intimate gardens at Hampton Court. She called in Jean Tijou, the brilliant French designer of wrought-iron screens, who erected a number of them in various parts of the garden. His delicate designs supplied a lovely cobweb beauty to the setting. Tijou's entrance gates in the centre of the east front, and his iron balustrades for the King's and Queen's Staircases in Wren's new wing are fine examples; but most delightful of all is the Tijou Screen, originally a magnificent set of twelve wrought-iron gates designed for Mary's Great Fountain Garden by the East front, but now re-erected at the river end of the Privy Garden. Poor Tijou had to wait nearly twelve years for the £1,982 0s. 7d. owed him for his delightful work.

Mary's other improvements in the gardens were carried out in the five years from 1690 to her death in December 1694. Many exotic and rare plants were introduced by her with the advice and help of the distinguished herbalist Dr Plukenet. Experts were then sent to the Canary Islands, to Virginia and other territories across the Atlantic to look for rare plants. The cost was high: the records show that 'For going to Virginia to make a collection of foreign plants' the sum of £234 11s. 9d. was paid. Plants were grown from seed in hothouses in the Privy Garden and the old Melon Ground (a part of the old Kitchen Garden) at Hampton Court.

Many splendid specimens of the *Agave americana variegata*, often called the Century Plant, because it was said to take a hundred years to flower (it took in fact two hundred years to flower at Hampton Court), growing at times as much as five inches a day and rising eventually to a height of sixteen feet, were brought and planted here. In the summer all these tropical specimens were planted along the south front; in the winter they were moved into the numerous greenhouses or the long Orangery which Wren built as part of the South front: in fact the whole of the ground floor of this section of the building was used as a greenhouse. Orange trees (an inevitable choice by the Royal house of Orange) as well as lemon trees were brought from the gardens of William's Palace at Loo. The greenhouses were divided into several small sections in each of which stoves were used to supply continual heat for the more tender foreign plants.

An unusual and attractive feature in the garden is Queen Mary's Bower, which she erected in the Privy Garden: raised above ground level, it is one hundred yards long, twenty feet in height, and twelve feet wide, with the branches of wych-elm interlaced overhead to form a completely enclosed avenue.

Mary's other great interest was needlework: she used to sit for hours in her Bower with her ladies, all of them chattering while busy with their needles. Her needlework was as fine as that of three other Queens at Hampton Court—Anne Boleyn, Mary I, and Elizabeth I.

In 1694, at the very early age of thirty-two, Queen Mary died of smallpox at Kensington Palace in London. Wren's State apartments at Hampton Court, the building of which she had watched with such interest and expectation, had not yet been completed and she was deprived of the joy of furnishing them and moving into the vast, high-ceilinged rooms.

After her death the King, deeply grieved, took no further interest in either the Palace or the gardens. Wren's work came almost to a complete stop. But William returned to Hampton Court four years later, when the Palace of Whitehall (the nucleus of which Wolsey had once built for his town house, and which Wren had expanded), burned down. Only Inigo Jones's Banqueting Hall, through the windows of which Charles I had stepped out for his execution, survived the fire and still stands.

In the spring of the following year, 1699, the King's State apartments were nearing completion. Just before leaving for Holland William insisted that they must be ready for occupation by the time he returned at the end of September, as a number of foreign princes would be coming to stay with him there. It did not give Wren much time: he engaged more than four hundred additional men who worked night and day, but, despite the King's delayed return, much still remained to be done. Fortunately William stayed at Kensington

Palace, his London residence since the Whitehall fire, and did not arrive at Hampton Court till the end of October. He was delighted with the new State apartments and kept exclaiming ecstatically as he walked through the large, impressive rooms. He even admired the mechanism of Joseph Key's superb locks and their decorative brass setting—their excellence cannot be disputed even after nearly three centuries.

To prepare the visitor entering the courtyards for the transition from the old architecture to the new, Wren built an Ionic colonnade along the southern wall of the Tudor Clock Court, opposite the heights of Henry's Great Hall. (As the gatehouses in the other two ranges were already off-centre, there was no symmetry to destroy.) The colonnade leads to the large and magnificent staircase with the Tijou balustrade, which takes one up to the King's State apartments on the first floor. Climbing it, one can see Antonio Verrio's decorative paintings on the walls and ceiling, which depict scenes of Roman gods feasting and enjoying other diversions. Evelyn declared that Verrio's 'design and colouring and exuberance of invention' were comparable to the greatest Old Masters; but Alexander Pope, who thought otherwise, dismissed them in a couplet:

> On painted ceilings you devoutly stare,
> Where sprawl the saints of Verrio and Laguerre.

Louis Laguerre was Verrio's assistant: he painted the Twelve Labours of Hercules in twelve exterior circular spaces of the round-windowed upper half-storey overlooking Fountain Court: they have been greatly damaged by time and weather.

The first of the State rooms is the King's Guard Chamber. Like all the other main rooms, it is not only large but lofty, rising into the half-storey with circular windows. The walls are oak panelled halfway up and over the fireplace are King William's arms carved in wood. On the long walls no fewer than 3,141 weapons are massively and most ingeniously displayed in two large circular patterns. For his work on this arresting display a gunsmith named Harris was given a pension. High up on one of the walls there are three trophies of five drums each between the circular windows. In this room the Yeomen of the Guard used to be on duty when the sovereign was in residence.

Each State room has a connecting door to the next: this one leads into the First Presence Chamber, where the lesser guests waited before being admitted into the Royal presence. Here on the casing of the oak doors and cornice you see some of the delicate and delightful carving of fruit and flowers and foliage, and at times of birds and cherubs, in limewood by that great master of the craft, Grinling Gibbons. Described by Horace Walpole as 'an original genius', Gibbons, born in Rotterdam of an English father, had been introduced by the diarist John Evelyn to Charles II, who admired the delicacy of his work and its elaborate detail. His carving, regarded by many 'as equal to anything of the ancients', has rarely been equalled and never surpassed. He was not quite fifty when he began to work for Wren on King William's Hampton Court.

On the wall of this room is a canopy of crimson damask, with its valance bearing the cypher W.R. and, at intervals, the rose, harp, fleur-de-lys, and thistle, each with a crown above it; under it is the Chair of State. A cast-iron fireback with the Royal arms of James II, bearing the initials J. R. and the date 1687, stands in the fireplace. Many of the firebacks in the other rooms are Dutch in style, decorated with scriptural and mythological subjects. Among the pictures on the walls is one by Kneller of William III on horseback, commemorating his return to England after the defeat of the French. Here too is Queen Mary's 'Gallery of Hampton Court Beauties' painted by Kneller.

Next we come to the Second Presence Chamber, where the more important visitors waited. A portrait of King Christian IV of Denmark over the fireplace has a very beautiful carved frame by Grinling Gibbons. There is also a picture of 'The Lovers' by Titian bought by Charles I and another, a portrait of Jacopo Sannazaro, also by Titian, which was presented to King Charles II. Other outstanding pictures in this room are by Giorgione and Palma Vecchio. Between the windows are long attractive mirrors with engraved borders. The immense gilt chandelier hanging from the ceiling is the loveliest of the chandeliers at Hampton Court.

After passing through the two Presence Chambers one comes at last to the Audience Chamber. Above the fireplace hangs yet another example of Grinling Gibbons' delicate woodcarving on the frame of a portrait by Honthorst of James I's daughter Elizabeth (the grandmother, through her marriage to the Elector Palatine, later known as the King of Bohemia, of King George I of England). There are also four Tintorettos. The canopy of State, covered with crimson

Genoa damask, was used for State receptions right up to Georgian times.

From here we go on to the Drawing Room with Grinling Gibbons' strikingly beautiful heads of cherubs; and then to the King's State Bedroom, the most lavishly decorated of the rooms: the ceiling was painted by Verrio and is regarded as his best work. It depicts various mythological gods in attitudes intended to encourage repose, but the elaborate canopy of the King's four-poster bed with its enormous plumes at the four corners completely obscures a view of the painting from the bed. A ten-foot high clock, made by the celebrated Daniel Quare, stands near the bed. The main dial is sixteen inches by fourteen, and there are three other dials, one of which indicates the rising and setting of the sun. The pier glass between the windows has a blue border bearing the King's monogram.

These five rooms, each thirty feet in height, include the half-storey: the three rooms beyond are small and lack this loftiness: they are the King's dressing-room, with a ceiling painted by Verrio; the King's writing closet from which there is a private staircase leading to the ground floor and the garden; and one built at the south-eastern corner which is known as Queen Mary's closet, although it was built after her death.

In a letter to King William dated 28 April 1699, Wren gives an estimate of the cost for finishing and furnishing most of these rooms: 'The expense of this work thus performed by good Artists will amount to the sum of £6,800.' But with the addition of 'the Communication Gallery, the King's Eating-Room, the lobby between the two galleries, with ye smoking room to the guard chamber, fixing the arms there etc.', *plus* some back-stairs rooms, the total cost was £7,092 19s. 0½d. This did not include the fees paid to Verrio.

Now that he was back at Hampton Court and living in the State apartments, King William was able to give his personal attention to the gardens. Every detail was attended to by him.

In the Great Fountain Garden, the semicircular section originally laid out for Charles II, William had placed a large fountain in the centre with others grouped around it; he now increased their number to twelve, indicating what their size should be and what quantity of water was required for the jets. Round these fountains grass plots were laid out with flowerbeds in the form of scrolls; and clipped yew and white holly alternated around them.

The semicircle of limes was enlarged and the base was given two long wings of lime trees, one running to the north, the other southward. At the same time he laid out a terrace or Broad Walk, 2,300 feet in length, along the eastern façade, the section containing the Queen's apartments on which Wren was now at work.

The Privy Garden, which stretched to the Thames from Wren's south front, was altered. The box and the flowering shrubs as well as the cypresses and hornbeams which lined the paths were moved to a new garden called the Wilderness, on the north side of the old Tudor Palace built by Wolsey and King Henry VIII. Talman records that in December 1699 the sum of £400 was paid for 'taking up all the plants and lines of Box, putting them in Baskets, with the charges for the Baskets, carrying them into the Wilderness and planting them there till such time as the ground is made, new gravelling and making the walks, turfing all the verges, quarters and slopes.' Yew trees were also planted there on the 'tops of the slopes'; and a section called Troy Town was marked out for a topiary garden, oval in shape and formed of tall espaliers. Defoe, who was ecstatic about Wren's new buildings and did not like the old Tudor Palace, wrote: 'On the north side of the house, where . . . the view of the Chapel and some parts of the old building required to be covered from the eye, the vacant ground, which was large, is very happily cast into a Wilderness with a labyrinth, and espaliers so high that they effectually take off all that part of the old building which would have been offensive to the sight.'

The labyrinth or maze was constructed at the far end of the Wilderness. It is almost triangular in shape, the base two hundred and twenty feet wide, the paths meandering for nearly half a mile and covering in all about a quarter of an acre. It is thought to have been inspired by King Louis XIV's maze at Versailles, which is much more elaborate and has at intervals groups of statuary representing 'The Fox and the Crow', 'The Hare and the Fox', and other familiar fables of the time; water was spouted by some of these sculptured animals. Mazes were common in the larger Dutch gardens. The chief gardeners in charge of these alterations at Hampton Court were George London and Henry Wise.

The Tilt Yard, where Henry VIII had his jousts and tournaments in a setting of unparalleled splendour, was carved up by William into six kitchen gardens with high walls to separate them. Four of these are now open to the public—one is a hard tennis court, another provides putting-greens, the other two are tea-gardens.

William, like James I, tended to have male favourites. He sought their advice in most of the things he undertook, including the furnishing of Wren's new State rooms and the making of the new gardens. Mary believed that he had homosexual tendencies and to this has been attributed his aloofness towards his wife for many years after their marriage: he not only neglected her, but was often most insulting. Not until after their accession—as joint rulers because of her insistence—did his affection for her develop: they worked closely together and on her death his grief was evident to all. Yet for many years he had a mistress too. Elizabeth Villiers, his wife's lady-in-waiting, became his mistress before he came to England. She was ugly and had a shapeless figure, but was said to be intelligent. When Mary found out, she dismissed 'Betty', but later took her back and shut her eyes to what was going on.

The first of his male favourites, Hans Willem Bentinck, a member of the Dutch provincial nobility, came into the royal household as a page: William was only thirteen at the time and Bentinck about eighteen. In the years that followed they became inseparable. They had many interests in common—hunting, landscape gardening, and of course war. When William sought Mary's hand in marriage Bentinck went to England to ask James II for it. Shortly after the marriage, Bentinck got married too; and in 1688, crossed to England with William. Within a very few months he was made a Privy

Councillor, Viscount Woodstock, and Earl of Portland, was with the King at the Battle of the Boyne, and later represented him on various diplomatic missions.

Not only were titles heaped on him. William gave him estates as well—135,000 acres of land in Ireland—and was about to give him yet another vast estate in North Wales when Parliament intervened and prevented it. That a foreign favourite should be honoured and so abundantly endowed roused the wrath of the English people.

But a new favourite, also Dutch, had by now come into King William's life. His name was Arnold Joost van Keppel; he was not only handsome but twenty-five years younger than Bentinck. A page to begin with, he too came to England with William in 1688. His rise too was rapid. He was made Groom of the Bedchamber, Master of the Robes, and Earl of Albemarle—and the King gave him a large estate in Ireland but was forced by Parliament to cancel it. As compensation William gave him £50,000 and eventually made him a Knight of the Garter: he was then only thirty years old.

Portland, who had enjoyed the King's friendship and affection for thirty years, was beside himself with jealousy and did everything he could to break up the association. Albemarle was often absent from Court. His private life was pried into and it was found that he had a pretty brunette as his mistress in Chelsea, and quite a number of other women for his dissolute diversion, which had given him gonorrhea. In a personal letter to the King, Portland pointed out that if the King intended to preserve his reputation, Albemarle must be dismissed; and added that if His Majesty did not do so he would be forced to withdraw from the royal service. William kept Albemarle on and Portland changed his mind about leaving.

Hardly any part was played by William III in the social life of the country. He indulged in hunting with his close companions, entertained ambassadors when necessary, but the lavish entertaining at Hampton Court by the Tudors and the Stuarts and even by Cromwell was no more. His bad health often made him irritable; but he gave his time to the affairs of State untiringly and was involved in a number of wars against France and also in Ireland where James II was backed by French troops and money. By the people he ruled he was regarded as a foreigner. His small circle of friends were Dutch. Mary had been genial and friendly, but, though both were of Stuart descent, neither had the family flair and charm, and after her death William's unpopularity increased.

While living in the State apartments, the King was able to keep an attentive eye on the further progress of Wren's work. Only the south front had so far been completed. Mary being dead, the completion of the east front, where the Queen's State apartments were to be, was no longer urgent. Wren's attention was focused now on two new galleries. One of them ran along the inner side of the King's State apartments and overlooked the new Fountain Court. It was called the King's Gallery, but was often referred to as the Great Council Chamber, for the Privy Council usually met there. It is one hundred and seventeen feet long and twenty-four feet wide and was designed to take the seven surviving cartoons painted by Raphael for tapestries in the Vatican, representing scenes in the lives of St Peter and St Paul. The cartoons are now in the Victoria and Albert Museum in Kensington, but Brussels tapestries made from them hang in this gallery.

The other gallery, called the Communication Gallery, overlooks Fountain Court from the west side. On its panelled walls hang Lely's portraits of the Beauties of Charles II's Court. In addition to these galleries Wren was working on the King's Backstairs, the King's Wine Cellar and the King's Chocolate Room. Above the Royal apartments were Lord Albemarle's lodgings and kitchen.

Meanwhile the furnishing of the King's rooms continued. Damask curtains were hung at the windows, tapestries on the walls, carpets were laid on the floor. Stools, chairs, settles, covered with crimson damask and embroidered with silver and gold, were brought and placed in position, also marble tables and china cabinets. The chandeliers hung from the ceilings are strikingly beautiful.

The Queen's Great Staircase, begun by Wren, was not actually finished and decorated until the reign of George II. It lies to the north of the King's Great Staircase and leads up to the Queen's State apartments. It is admirably proportioned and has Tijou's fine iron balustrade, and the allegorical painting by Honthorst on the west wall has become more colourful since a recent cleaning. From the ceiling hangs an old-fashioned lantern and the cornice carries George II's monogram.

Later, in the autumn, the King discussed with Sir Christopher Wren his plan to tear down the rest of the lovely old Tudor buildings and make Hampton Court a Versailles on the banks of the Thames. Wren had already drawn plans for this that still exist and can be seen in the Ministry of Environment (formerly Works). His proposal was to provide a stately new entrance to the Palace on the north side, that is to say from Bushey Park.

After his talk with the King the first stage of this transformation was begun. A mile-long drive, sixty feet wide, was laid out across Bushey Park. As it approached Hampton Court it bellied out into a circle, in the centre of which a vast pond was dug, four hundred feet in diameter; this is called the Diana Basin, the fountain sculpture having been moved here from the Privy Garden. All the way along the drive and round the circle, four rows of lime trees were planted, with two rows of horse-chestnuts beyond them: a total of seven hundred and thirty-two lime trees and two hundred and seventy-four horse-chestnuts. The drive stopped short at the Kingston Road, on the other side of which the Lion Gates, put up by Queen Anne, lead to the Wilderness.

It was Wren's purpose to take this magnificent drive right across the Wilderness and the moat, approaching the Palace by way of a vast, new rectangular Entrance Court, three hundred feet long and two hundred and thirty feet wide, flanked by an impressive Renaissance structure on each side, and a new entrance to the Palace itself leading to Henry VIII's Great Hall, the only part of the Tudor building that was to be retained. All the rest would have been torn down—the towers, the turrets, the State rooms used by Wolsey, Henry VIII, Charles I, and Charles II.

Serious shortage of money, as we have seen, and finally the King's death while this preliminary work was in progress, led to its abandonment. The lovely old Tudor buildings survive; the dream of an English Versailles remains unfulfilled.

Wren's disappointment must have been acute. He disliked 'the Gothic rudeness of the old design'. His disappointment was shared by Daniel Defoe, who wrote feelingly in 1724: 'When Hampton Court will find such another favourable juncture as in King William's time, when the remainder of her ashes shall be swept away and her complete fabric, as designed by King William, shall be finished I cannot tell, but if ever that shall be I know of no Palace in Europe, Versailles excepted, which can come up to her either for beauty or magnificence or for extent of building and the ornaments attending it.'

The changes in the gardens went on right up to the time of the King's death. On 19 December 1699, Talman, Comptroller of the Works, informed the Lords of the Treasury, the records state, that the 'works to be done in the gardens' would cost £10,864; but economies had to be made and the figure was cut down to £8,933 11s. Some of this was to pay for work that had already been begun, such as the enlargement of the semicircular parterre and for increasing the number of its satellite fountains to a dozen, and for the provision of Derbyshire marble for the enormous oval fountain at the centre of the parterre; for the making of some little canals, as they were called, though actually each was seven hundred and thirteen feet long and eighteen feet wide; for the extension of the Broad Walk terrace wall right down to the Thames; and so on.

While all this was being done, two men who had come to supervise the work in the gardens were attacked by footpads on their way back to London by road. Their money, watches, snuff-boxes and trinkets were taken; and, for speaking hardly to the thieves, Anthony Row, who had designed the ponds in St James's Park in London, was hit on the head and was lucky to escape with his life.

In the following year 1700, to prevent the passing by the House of Commons of their Address requesting the King to remove all foreigners from his counsels, William prorogued Parliament and left for Hampton Court. After a brief visit to London he returned and spent some weeks at the Palace, irritated and gloomy; he even abandoned his plan to attend the Newmarket spring meeting. Instead, a few days later, a meeting of the Privy Council was held at Hampton Court: it was a meeting charged with drama. The two-party system had by now come into operation. At the head of the Whigs was the King's Chief Minister, the Lord Chancellor Somers. The opposing Tory party saw the King's favourite Lord Albemarle and used him to persuade the King to dismiss Somers, saying 'that all the hard things that had of late been put on him by Parliament were occasioned by the hatred that was borne to his ministers'. The King did not act at once, but eventually it was at Hampton Court that the Earl of Jersey, the intermediary between the Tories and Albemarle, went to the Lord Chancellor's lodgings at the Palace and informed him of his dismissal.

Shortly afterwards William III held a chapter of the Order of the Garter at Hampton Court to elect Albemarle and others Knights of the Garter. Disgusted at this granting to his young favourite so exalted a distinction, several Knights of the Garter stayed away from the ceremony and it was generally said by Matthew Prior, the poet, and others that this was the cause of the King 'losing many friends'.

As he saw the development of what Wren was transforming step by step into a Versailles, William began to invite the ambassadors and emissaries of European sovereigns to see it too. He wanted to entertain them in the growing splendour of Hampton Court, not in London where the Palaces appeared to him to be unimpressive and unworthy of the dignity and importance of the nation over which he ruled. Here in April 1700 he received the ambassador of the Holy Roman Empire and the minister of the King of Portugal. A few weeks later that year he had as his guest the Chevalier Giraldi, the Envoy Extraordinary of the Grand Duke of Tuscany, who was brought to the Palace in one of the King's coaches, with the Royal Master of Ceremonies, Sir Charles Cotterell, in attendance; His Majesty received him in Wren's magnificent new Presence Chamber. One who came for crucial discussions over the Spanish Succession in which both Louis XIV and William were deeply concerned was the French ambassador, the Comte de Tallard. The discussions went on for days. To achieve a balance of power in Europe the two rulers agreed to divide Spain's scattered territories in Europe between the two possible heirs of the childless Spanish King. Some months later, when the Spanish King died, William was shocked to learn that Louis, on finding that the dying King had bequeathed his entire Spanish possessions in the Old World as well as the New to Louis' younger grandson Philip, Duc d' Anjou, had gone back on his treaty. 'I relied much on the engagement with France; but I must confess I did not think they would on this occasion have broken, in the face of the whole world, a solemn treaty. The motives are so shameful.' It led to war.

This and other problems as well as his desire to enjoy the new State rooms at Hampton Court caused William to declare that he would not be going on his annual visit to Holland; but his health had also begun to decline. He became feverish, ate little, took only a dish of chocolate for breakfast. The three doctors quarrelled over the treatment of their patient. One gave him 'ale impregnated with the leaves of ground ivy, fir tops, hart's tongue, wild carrot seed and asses milk'. The other two said the King should eat garlic. A fourth doctor was then called in and, after an affable consultation together, they prescribed '20 drops of the tincture of Salt of Tartar to be taken every day: and the juice of 30 Hog-lice at six o'clock at night'. Surprisingly, the King seemed to be better the next day. 'I should be very well,' His Majesty told Mr Secretary Vernon, 'if they would leave off giving me remedies.'

He soon felt he was well enough to leave England. A meeting of the Grand Council was held at Hampton Court on the day before his departure. The King, who did not like his sister-in-law Princess Anne, but realised that, as his successor, she would have to be accorded both recognition and courtesy, dined with her that day; and very early the next morning left for Holland.

Before going he left instructions for further building operations to be carried out. First the extensive range of old Tudor buildings by the river known as the Water Gallery, in which Queen Mary had spent such happy years while the State apartments were being built, was pulled down: the King said it obstructed the view of the river from his new suite of rooms. The building was of considerable size and Wren was told to rescue after its demolition all the material and use as much of it as he could 'in lieu of new materials'.

Not far from where it stood the King wanted a new building, not of great size, to be erected as a Banqueting House for him and his friends. Of plum-coloured brick and rectangular in shape, it stands at the edge of the old Pond Garden and overlooks the River Thames. It consists of only one main storey, above a basement with groined brick vaulting which incorporates the Tudor work of the Water Gallery. There are two main rooms: the Banqueting Room, thirty-two feet long, and a smaller anteroom, with the Closet or King's private withdrawing-room, only twelve by ten feet.

The Banqueting Room, which is richly decorated, has panelling painted a warm plum-hued grey picked out with gilding; Verrio painted the ceiling with Minerva as the Goddess of Wisdom, surrounded by allegorical figures representing the arts and sciences—Sculpture is seen carrying a bust of King William III. Between the windows are four mirrors, reflecting the light on the water outside, in frames carved by Grinling Gibbons and gilded.

The anteroom has dark oak panelling with paintings of mythological subjects by Pellegrini. Of the closet walls two are panelled, and the other two, originally covered with crimson and gold damask, are now painted.

Here the summer afternoons and evenings were spent by the King with Albemarle, Portland and other male friends.

During the winter, bills kept coming in for the work done at Hampton Court by Wren and the gardeners. The King was informed that the sum of £5,000 was still owing for work completed some years earlier. Masons, carpenters, bricklayers, ironmongers, plumbers and others had not yet been paid—some of them had been asking for their money for ten years. William arranged for £150 to be paid weekly to reduce these debts.

But the work still went on. The Mount, that elaborate structure erected by Henry VIII in 1538 near the old Water Gallery, was dismantled and levelled. The Privy Garden was altered; and part of it was converted into a sunken garden. The cost of all this added a further £1,426 to the total.

Next the Pond Garden, Defoe tells us, was 'laid out into small enclosures surrounded by tall hedges to break the violence of the winds and render them proper for the reception of such exotic plants in summer as were moved out of the conservatories during the season'.

When the King returned from his visit to Holland in the autumn of 1701, he was told that the debt for work on the house was £11,000 and on the garden £4,313 8s. 1d. He now had barely four months to live, yet his ill health, though still persistent, was not what killed him. During the winter he stayed at Hampton Court, receiving deputations from cities, counties, and universities, who had come to express their loyalty because the exiled King James II had died and they had been angered by Louis XIV's recognition of James's son as the rightful King of England.

Both Portland and Albemarle were with him at Hampton Court. While walking in the garden William said to Portland that 'he felt so weak that he did not expect to live another summer'. Yet he went hunting and it was a fall from his horse that caused his death. 'While I endeavoured to make the horse change his walking into a gallop,' he said, 'the horse fell upon his knees. Upon that I meant to raise him with the bridle, but he fell forward on one side, and so I fell with my right shoulder upon the ground. 'Tis a strange thing for it happened upon a smooth level ground.'

The horse had tripped over a molehill and the King died two weeks later on 8 March 1702 at Kensington Palace in London. The followers of the late King James II and of his son James, known as the Old Pretender, for years afterwards drank a toast to the mole—'the little gentleman in black velvet'.

Queen Anne, on succeeding her brother-in-law William, found herself faced with the heavy debts he had incurred for the improvement of Hampton Court. She let Wren complete the actual work in hand, but all thought of constructing a new Versailles was abandoned.

Though she came to Hampton Court fairly frequently during the first years of her reign, she preferred to live in Windsor Castle or in Kensington Palace in London. Alexander Pope summed up her connection with Hampton Court in these memorable lines in *The Rape of the Lock*:

> Close by those meads, for ever crowned with flowers,
> Where Thames with pride surveys his rising towers,
> There stands a structure of majestic frame,
> Which from the neighb'ring Hampton takes its name.
> Here Britain's statesmen oft the fall foredoom
> Of foreign tyrants, and of nymphs at home;
> Here thou, great *Anna*! whom three realms obey,
> Dost sometimes counsel take—and sometimes tea.

Anne was thirty-seven when she came to the throne. A little above medium height, she was not pretty and was thought to be rather simple. Her health was far from good. As a small child she had trouble with her eyes and was sent to France for treatment, staying with her grandmother Henrietta Maria and with her aunt, Minette. Charles II insisted that she and her sister Mary must be brought up as Protestants. Their father, on his accession as James II, offered to make her his successor instead of her elder sister on condition that she become a Roman Catholic. But Anne refused.

At the age of eighteen she married Prince George of Denmark: it proved to be a happy marriage, but, though her pregnancies were numerous, only one child, William, Duke of Gloucester, born at Hampton Court, survived infancy. By the time she was Queen she suffered acutely from dropsy and gout and was often seen with bandages on her legs and arms. Her husband was too fond of his drink and she of her food.

Jonathan Swift, then in his early thirties and long before writing *Gulliver's Travels*, describes in his *Journal to Stella* a levee in Anne's bedchamber at Hampton Court. 'We made our bows and stood, about twenty of us, round the room while the Queen looked at us with her fan in her mouth, and once in a minute said about three words to some that were nearest to her; and then she was told that dinner was ready and went out. . . . I dined at Her Majesty's board of green cloth. It is much the best table in England and costs the Queen £1,000 a month while she is at Windsor or Hampton Court, and is the only mark of magnificence or royal hospitality that I can see in the Royal household.' Swift did not care very much about accepting dinner invitations because of the tips he was expected to give: 'it would cost me a guinea to the servants and twelve shillings coach hire; and he shall be hanged first', he observes on being invited to dine with Lord Halifax.

Anne and her husband were both very retiring and seldom had guests. The Queen's close friend was the former Sarah Jennings, whose distinguished husband was soon to be made Duke of Marlborough. Sarah was made Ranger of Windsor Park so that she could live in the Great Lodge, which was near both the Castle and Hampton Court. While her husband was abroad, leading the armies of England, Holland, and Austria against Louis XIV in the war of the Spanish Succession, which broke out a few weeks after Anne's accession, Sarah spent much of her time with the Queen. But within five years they quarrelled and the Marlboroughs came to Hampton Court no more.

When the Queen and Prince George did entertain at Hampton Court they used the Queen's Drawing Room in the east front, at last completed. The east front's imposing length of façade is divided into twenty-three bays. The entrance gates are in the three central bays on the ground floor, flanked by stone piers supporting the four Corinthian columns crowned by the great pediment, with its bas-relief scene of 'The Triumph of Hercules over Envy', beautifully carved by Caius Gabriel Cibber, father of Colley Cibber the poet and dramatist. This handsome, impressive wing looks out on to the Great Fountain Garden with its large, semicircular parterre, the radiating avenues of lime trees, and its long canal, all of which converge on the middle window of the Drawing Room.

o

Once again Antonio Verrio was brought in to paint the ceiling, although £1,190 was still owing to him for work done many years earlier. His painting depicts Queen Anne as Justice, wearing a purple dress lined with ermine, holding the scales in one hand and a sword in the other. Above her head Britannia and Neptune hold a crown, and around her, floating on clouds, are allegorical figures representing Peace and Plenty. On the walls are large murals of the Queen receiving homage from the four quarters of the world; her husband pointing to the fleet; and Cupid drawn by seahorses over the waves with the British fleet in the background.

Verrio had been pressing for the money and Anne had to give him £600 before he began work on the ceiling. Half-way through he begged for more money as he hadn't enough to buy the colours he needed. Anne gave him a further £200. Wren said it was not enough and insisted that he should be paid £500 when the room was finished. Shortly after he had completed painting the ceiling Verrio's eyesight failed. 'Queen Anne,' wrote Horace Walpole, 'gave him a pension of £200 for life, but he did not enjoy it long, dying at Hampton Court in 1707.'

The bills now began to come in thick and fast. Richard Stacey, master-bricklayer, had £6,481 0s. 11½d. owing to him for work done at Hampton Court—'part of the work was finished in Her present Majesty's reign, although directed by the late King'. He added that the men he had employed for the work, such as bricklayers and lime (mortar) men and others who supplied the materials, were threatening to sue him. But he was informed there was 'no money at present for arrears'. The same answer was given to Matthew Roberts the plumber, who was owed a large sum for work in the gardens; and to Jean Tijou, who had not only received no money for the lovely wrought-iron gates, but not even the iron had been paid for. 'Several persons,' he said, 'are threatening to imprison me.' There were a great many more creditors—Benjamin Jackson, the master-mason, Thomas Highmore, the Queen's sergeant-painter, Tilleman Robart, who had been keeping the gardens in order: the money due to him had been outstanding for nine years. One creditor, Huntingdon Shaw, a skilled artificer, had died without being paid. Another, Rachel Bennett, the widow of the quartermaster of Her Majesty's 1st Regiment of Guards, wrote to say that her husband had brought in men to carry out repairs at the barracks at Hampton Court. She had paid some of the workmen herself and was 'reduced to very mean circumstances and almost to a starving condition'. Queen Anne did not send her a penny. Meanwhile she kept on incurring fresh debts, as Wren's work on the State apartments still went on.

Some rooms were not actually completed and furnished until after Anne's death, and some furnishings have since changed. In the Queen's Audience Chamber, over the fireplace, is a bust of Henry VIII attributed to the sculptor Torrigiano, whose finest work in England is Henry VII's tomb in Westminster Abbey. The pictures on the walls are of James I in his robes; his elder son Henry, Prince of Wales with Robert Devereux, Earl of Essex (they used to play together at Hampton Court); and, most interesting of all, one of Jeffrey Hudson, the famous dwarf, only eighteen inches tall. The portrait, by Daniel Mytens, was a gift to Charles I and Henrietta Maria from the Duchess of Buckingham. The Queen was deeply attached to the dwarf. During one of her pregnancies, while he was on his way to France for a midwife, he was captured by pirates. After his release he was involved in further adventures: for killing a man who had insulted him he had to flee the country, was captured by a Turkish ship and sold as a slave. Some years later when he returned to England he was three feet nine inches tall and attributed his sudden growth to the suffering he had to endure.

On the other side of the State Drawing Room is the Queen's State Bedroom, not completed until after Queen Anne's death. The ceiling, painted by Sir James Thornhill in 1715, shows Aurora, in her chariot rising from the sea. The medallion portraits on the cove are of George I, his son the Prince of Wales (later George II) and his wife, and their son Frederick. The furniture was made for the Prince and Princess of Wales. South of the bedroom is the Queen's Gallery, eighty feet long with a cornice carved by Grinling Gibbons. The handsome chimney-piece of dark grey marble is garnished with a bust of Venus, cupids, and garlands all in white marble. This room was completed for Queen Anne. George I had it hung with tapestries, and it now contains some of William and Mary's fine blue-and-white porcelain.

All these State rooms overlook the Great Fountain Garden. The Queen's private rooms, by Wren, overlook the inner Fountain Court, which is also overlooked by the Queen's Guard Chamber and the Queen's Presence Chamber, designed in the reign of George II. Adjoining the Presence Chamber is a room called the Queen's

Private Chapel, with a wonderful octagonal 'dome' supporting a skylight; this room was used by George II's wife Queen Caroline who listened to the chaplain say prayers while she dressed in the adjoining closet; the door-locks of the domed room bear William and Mary's initials.

To the north of it is the Public Dining Room. It received its name in the reign of George II and is said to have been decorated for him by William Kent the architect, designer of the Horse Guards in Whitehall. On the pediment of the marble chimney-piece are the Royal Hanoverian arms. Beyond this room is the Prince of Wales suite, largely the work of the architect-playwright, John Vanbrugh. It was occupied by George II when his father was King.

Anne got Wren to redecorate the old Tudor Chapel: the ceiling with its large pendants was repainted; the great classical reredos was by Grinling Gibbons; the old Gothic mullioned windows were replaced by Renaissance windows (until Prince Albert restored Gothic ones in the nineteenth century). The floor was paved with black-and-white marble, and new pews, made of fine Norwegian wood, were added. The private royal gallery was renewed for Queen Anne in place of Henry VIII's old pew. A new organ by Christopher Schrider was placed in a little gallery on the south side: Grinling Gibbons' lovely carvings embellish its oak case. The Chapel is a unique mixture.

Anne did not neglect the gardens. In the spring of 1707 she gave instructions for 'the new Turfing and Gravelling of the Great Fountain Garden with some new turfing where the drought of the three last summers has burnt the turf'. This cost £1,141 8s. 3d. She also had fences put up to separate the meadows at the far end of the Home Park from the river and thus keep her stud of horses from getting drowned. An estimate for £686 was sent for this, but Anne halved it and told them to get on with the work at that price.

In the two parks, Queen Anne was chiefly concerned with making improvements for a new form of hunting she had evolved. Crippled by gout and dropsy and unable to ride, she decided to do her stag-hunting in a horse-drawn chaise. For this tracks were made in the parks—all the holes were filled in, mounds were flattened out, ditches and watercourses were dug to drain off stagnant water, and nettles, thorns, and ferns were removed. By going up and down the avenues and round and round the park, she was able to cover twenty miles. Jonathan Swift who saw her at it wrote in his *Journal to Stella*: 'She hunts in a chaise with one horse, which she drives herself, and drives furiously like Jehu and is a mighty hunter like Nimrod.' On one occasion, he saw her hunting until four o'clock in the afternoon. On that occasion she drove her chaise 'no less than forty miles'.

She spent quite a lot of time at Hampton Court during the autumn of 1710. There were a number of meetings of the Privy Council there. The Lord Mayor of London and other City dignitaries came to deliver a loyal address. A Chapter of the Order of the Garter was also held there. After Christmas she left. Often, while staying at Windsor Castle, Anne used to come over to the Palace to attend a meeting of the Privy Council in Wren's lovely King's Gallery.

Coming again in the following autumn in a terrible rainstorm, she entertained some of her ministers and the envoys of the King of France at Hampton Court. Swift would very much have liked to have been present, but, he told Stella, 'they have no lodgings for me there, so I can't go, for the town is small, chargeable and inconvenient'.

The 'town', as he called it, consisted of a small group of houses at the gates of the Palace. There was only one inn, The Toye, which was mostly used as a tavern, though visitors were put up for the night in the few available rooms. When the Court was in residence prices inevitably soared. The inn was almost certainly there in the time of Henry VIII, built possibly by an enterprising taverner to provide ale and other refreshments for those who came up from London to look at the much-talked-of Hampton Court. Certainly by the next century it was used as a 'victualling house', as the Parliamentary Survey records. All through that century there were convivial gatherings at The Toye; and when Queen Anne was at the Palace, a group of gay young men often frequented it. On one occasion, 27 April 1711, a party of eighteen men, including a Member of Parliament, came here: their jests and pleasantries while drinking led to an argument which ended in a scuffle. Sir Cholmley Dering, the M.P., Swift tells us, struck his friend, Mr Richard Thornhill, knocked him down and broke seven of his teeth. The two men were separated. Dering apologised for his behaviour, but Thornhill refused to accept the apology. A challenge to a duel followed. Dering called for Thornhill early on the appointed morning, they drank a glass of beer together and set out in a hackney coach for Tothill Fields (now

Vincent Square, Westminster) because 'Hyde Park will not do at this time of year, being full of company'.

There were no seconds, no distance between the two was paced out. We learn that they rushed at each other—Swift adds that the muzzles of their pistols almost touched. Thornhill fired first and Dering fell dying. Thornhill was tried for murder, but after hearing witnesses declare that he was not of a quarrelsome nature whereas Dering was 'unwarrantably contentious', a verdict of manslaughter was pronounced and the sentence was that he should be 'burned in the hand'. Three months later two men chased Thornhill on horseback from Hampton Court to Turnham Green near Chiswick and stabbed him to death.

Another incident, which occurred that summer apparently in the Palace itself, was the one on which Alexander Pope based *The Rape of the Lock*. A party of friends who included Lord Petre, Sir George Brown, and Miss Arabella Fermor, set out for Hampton Court, not as guests of the Queen but of an official living in one of the lodgings. While they sat drinking coffee after a game of cards, Lord Petre, noticing a lock of hair dangling almost into Miss Fermor's cup as she bent her head, snipped it off. Miss Fermor was angry and upset. Pope, calling her Belinda, makes her say in the poem:

> For ever cursed be this detested day,
> Which snatched my best, my fav'rite curl, away.
> Happy! Ah ten times happy had I been
> If Hampton Court these eyes had never seen!

A furious quarrel flared up at the party. Friendships were broken over this trivial, silly incident. Pope's mock-heroic poem, published soon afterwards, roused so much laughter, that it helped to heal the breach. In it he conveyed a vivid sense of the atmosphere of a palace.

> Hither the heroes and the nymphs resort
> To taste awhile the pleasures of a court;
> In various talk the instructive hours they passed,
> Who gave the ball, or paid the visit last;
> One speaks the glory of the British Queen,
> And one describes a charming Indian screen;
> A third interprets motions, looks and eyes;
> At every word a reputation dies.
> Snuff or the fan supply each pause of chat,
> With singing, laughing, ogling, and all that.

One of the last visitors received at Hampton Court by Queen Anne was the Envoy Extraordinary from the Czar of Moscovy, whose name is entered as 'Monsieur Lieth', possibly an anglicised form for a Russian name that was difficult to spell. He was presented to her by Henry St John, Lord Bolingbroke, her principal Secretary of State.

She died about eighteen months later at Kensington Palace on 1 August 1714. After the sad death of her surviving child, the eleven-year-old Duke of Gloucester, an Act of Settlement had arranged that the succession should pass to the Protestant branch of the family, through Charles I's sister Elizabeth, who had married Frederick, the German Elector Palatine. Had Anne died four months earlier Elizabeth's by then elderly daughter Sophia would have briefly occupied the English throne as Queen Sophia I, but she predeceased Anne and the throne went to her son George. The first Hanoverian king, George I, came over from Germany, knowing hardly a word of English, and put on the Crown the Stuarts had worn for four generations.

George I, Elector of Hanover through his father, was short, very fair-skinned and had large bulbous eyes of a very bright blue. He had divorced his wife twenty years earlier and arrived in England with two ugly German mistresses and two servants, Mohammed and Mustapha, who had been taken prisoner in a war against the Turks. Now fifty-four, he had one son (the future George II) and a daughter Sophia whose son is known to history as Frederick the Great.

Having heard of Hampton Court, King George lost little time in coming to look at it. It appeared to him to be the ideal place to live in —vast, impressive, comfortable, with lovely gardens and parks—a palace beyond the dreams and aspirations of a petty German princeling. What he liked most of all was that by living there he would escape from his new and alien subjects.

The French ambassador, the Comte de Broglie, stated in a letter to the King of France that George had no regard for the English people and never received any of them privately. 'His sacred majesty,' states another, 'spent many hours of the day in the sweet companionship of his ugly fat mistresses, who cut out figures in paper for his royal diversion whilst he, forgetful of the cares of State, lit his pipe and smoked placidly, now and then laughing and clapping his hands when Madam Schulenburg had, in cutting out a figure, hit upon some peculiarity of feature or figure in a courtier or minister.'

This mistress, Madame Schulenburg, being relatively lean and tall, was known at Court as 'The Maypole'; the other, Madame Charlotte Kielmannsegge, enormously fat, was known as 'The Elephant and Castle'. Both were raised to the peerage, the Maypole as Duchess of Kendal, the other as Countess of Darlington. Contempt for them was only too evident. People jeered as they went by in their sedan chairs. Horace Walpole, who met Schulenburg when he was a child, was terrified on seeing 'two fierce black eyes, large and rolling beneath two lofty arched eyebrows; two acres of cheek spread

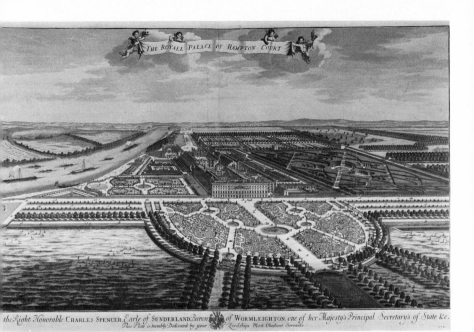

the Right Honorable CHARLES SPENCER Earle of SUNDERLAND Baron of WORMLEIGHTON, one of her Majesty's Principal Secretary's of State &c.
This Plate is humbly Dedicated by your Lordships Most Obedient Servant

The Great Fountain Garden, laid out for Charles II and developed by William III. It was based on a design by Le Nôtre, who helped to make the gardens at Versailles. Three avenues of lime trees and a long canal lead from the semi-circular parterre

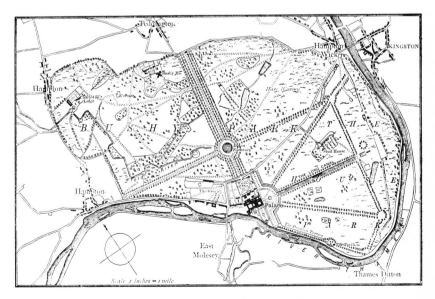

A Victorian view showing the two great parks of Hampton Court – Bushey Park and the Home Park

William III's bedroom has a fine cornice and
Verrio's richly decorated ceiling. Above the
fireplace is Lely's portrait of Anne Hyde, Mary
II's mother

Wood-carving by Grinling Gibbons in the Chapel Royal

The locks made in 1699 by Josiah Key for the State Apartments were so well constructed that their mechanism is still in perfect working order

An attractive fireback in the King's Dressing-room

Wren's Fountain Court

The Dutch Garden and the Banqueting House overlooking the river

One of the magnificent wrought-iron panels designed by Jean Tijou for the Palace gardens

with crimson, an ocean of neck that overflowed and was not distinguished from the lower part of her body, and no part restrained by stays'. He adds that on one occasion as she was being carried through the streets in her sedan chair, she heard a noise and put her head out of the window. 'Good people,' she said, 'why do you abuse us? We come for all your goods.' Someone in the crowd shouted: 'Yes, damn ye! and for our chattels too.'

Heavy in face and figure, the new King lacked both charm and dignity; many considered him dull and boorish, not without justification. His manners were coarse; he ate and drank heavily. He brought with him the rigid etiquette of his own small German court, which was not well received by the English who, though they heartily disliked him, accepted him as King because of their resolve not to have on the throne the Roman Catholic descendants of James II.

His visits to Hampton Court were always made ceremoniously. The royal party set out from London in State barges decorated with coloured hangings. A barge laden with musicians provided music during the entire journey. On arriving at the Palace His Majesty got into the royal sedan chair which was carried by servants dressed in royal livery. Beside it walked the courtiers and attendants; six footmen walked in front, and six Yeomen of the Guard marched behind his chair. Next came two sedan chairs with His Majesty's mistresses, completing the procession from the riverside to the Palace.

A great part of each year was spent by George I at Hanover. During his absence, the Prince of Wales, acting as Regent, adopted the same ceremonial. But, though like his father in many ways, his personality and his attitude to life were, at this stage, a little different. Just turned thirty, he had been married for ten years to Caroline of Anspach in Bavaria, a strikingly attractive young woman, with bright blue eyes, fair hair and an ample bosom. They had at that time four very young children—a son and three daughters. Although they maintained a regal atmosphere, occupying the Queen's State apartments, both the Prince and the Princess were amiable and gay and gathered around them men of intelligence and wit, such as Philip Dormer Stanhope, later famous as the Earl of Chesterfield; the two Lords Hervey, Carr and his younger half-brother John, who inherited the courtesy title on his brother's death; Charles Churchill, the brother of the Duke of Marlborough; and a number of beautiful women, who were also witty and intelligent—the two ladies-in-waiting Miss Mary Bellenden and Miss Mary Lepell; Mrs Henrietta Howard, the Prince of Wales's mistress; and Lady Walpole, the mother of Horace Walpole and wife of the short, fat Sir Robert, who became Prime Minister and held that office for twenty-two years: it is to him that the country owes the Prime Minister's official residence No. 10 Downing Street.

Not content with Mrs Howard, the Prince made repeated efforts, all unsuccessful, to add Mary Bellenden to his list. Of her Horace Walpole said: 'Above all for universal admiration was Miss Bellenden. Her face and person were charming, lively she was almost to *étourderie*, and so agreeable that she was never afterwards mentioned by her contemporaries but as "the most perfect creature they had ever known".' Receiving no response to his advances, Prince George used to pull up his chair beside hers at Hampton Court and begin to count the gold coins in his purse, glancing at her to see if this crude attempt at flirtation was attracting her attention. He did this again and again until Miss Bellenden, unable to take any more of it, sent the coins flying all over the floor and walked out of the room. She eventually married Colonel Campbell, who later became Duke of Argyle.

The diversions at Hampton Court were delightfully varied. In summer all the pretty women and the men set out in boats with the Prince and Princess, talking, jesting, laughing or singing as they were rowed along the Thames. At midday they returned. The Royal couple dined in the Princess's apartments with the entire court, and the ladies-in-waiting served the meals. Then they retired for the afternoon, the Princess usually wrote letters or gossiped with some friends; and in the evenings they walked in the gardens or in the lime groves or went to the bowling green where some played bowls while the others watched. A few went off to flirt in the arbours. In the pavilions built by William III, one at each corner of the bowling green, there were rooms in which some played cards while others drank tea or coffee and one of them played the spinet. The Princess often joined them at cards for long, pleasant hours in the pavilion. On one dark, rainy night, a very stout German lady-in-waiting, the Countess of Buckenburg, tripped and fell on her way back to the main Palace. After that the Princess had her card parties in the Queen's Gallery.

Invitations to supper with the Princess were sent to only a few guests at a time. Those who were not invited arranged parties in their own apartments. Invitations to Mrs Howard's parties on the floor above the Princess's were most sought after; for years afterwards those who attended them wrote to remind her (she was by then the Countess of Suffolk) of various little incidents that still lingered in their memory.

But the fun stopped when George I was in residence. There was a continuous flow of ministers, chief of whom was Sir Robert Walpole, but more important to George I than his ministers was Count Bothmar, a German nobleman, who had come to England even before George became King: he came in fact in 1700 when Queen Anne's heir, the Duke of Gloucester, died and it was clear that the succession would pass to the Hanoverian line. During the sixteen years Bothmar lived in England he took note of all that was going on and sent endless reports home. George I used him now to spy on the Prince of Wales 'to keep all things in order and give an account of everything that was doing'. He was not the only one whose manner was harsh and often off-hand with the Prince. Lord Townshend, on the other hand, whose relationship with the Prince was warm and friendly, slighted the Princess and bestowed his adulation on the Prince's mistress, Mrs Howard, and on Miss Bellenden. Lord Sunderland, another of the King's ministers, was equally lacking in tact and deference to the Princess. A heated argument developed between them at Hampton Court. The Princess asked him not to speak so loudly as the windows were open and he could be overheard in the garden. 'Let them hear,' he retorted rudely. At which the Princess suggested that they should go right up to the windows, 'for, in the humour we both are, one of us must certainly jump out of the window and I'm resolved it shan't be me.'

When the King was in residence at Hampton Court at the same time as the Prince and Princess of Wales, the change in atmosphere was quite marked. Cheerfulness vanished. Dullness reigned supreme. Alexander Pope, unfortunate to be at the Palace on one of these occasions, wrote: 'I can easily believe that no lone house in Wales, with a mountain and a rookery, is more contemplative than this Court; and as proof of it I need only tell you Miss Lepell walked with me three or four hours by moonlight and we met no creature of any quality but the King, who gave audience to the Vice-Chamberlain, all alone, under the garden walk. In short, I heard of no ball, assembly, basset table, or any place where two or three were gathered together except Madame Kielmannsegge's, to which I had the honour to be invited and the grace to stay away.'

There had always been antagonism between the King and his heir. His Majesty rarely referred to his daughter-in-law except as *cette diablesse la Princesse*. Some months later, when the Princess gave birth to a son at St James's Palace in London, a Gentleman of the Bedchamber came to Hampton Court to inform the King. No response was made by His Majesty, but shortly afterwards a notice appeared in the *Gazette* stating that the King would not receive anyone who had been in contact with the Prince of Wales.

To show that he could provide better diversions than his son, the King had a stage erected in Henry VIII's Great Hall and engaged the King's Company of Actors to put on two plays a week during the summer. A delay in the completion of the arrangements led to the summer being more than half over by the time the first play was presented on 23 September 1718. It was *Hamlet*: how much, if any, of it was understood by the King we are not told. But the second play by Shakespeare, was however the King's own choice, *Henry VIII*: he felt it was appropriate to have Henry and Wolsey impersonated in the setting that was once theirs. What the King particularly enjoyed (it was possibly explained to him beforehand) was Wolsey's whisper to his servant Thomas Cromwell that he was really responsible for a pardon granted by the King:

A word with you;
Let there be letters writ to every shire
Of the King's grace and pardon. The grieved commons
Hardly conceive of me; let it be noised
That, through *our* intercession, this revokement
And pardon comes.

Colley Cibber, who played Wolsey, walked right up to the King's box to deliver these lines and rejoiced on seeing the reaction on the King's face, for His Majesty, it was well known, often accused his ministers of taking the credit for what he had ordered them to do. Cibber records in his *Apology for My Life* that, when asked by a nobleman how the King liked the play, he replied: 'So terribly well, my Lord, that I was afraid I should have lost all my actors; for I was not sure the King would not keep them in the posts at Court that he saw them so fit for in the play.'

The players were given a day's pay as well as their travelling expenses, which worked out at £50 for each play. Wax lights, music, and a *chaise-marine* for their wardrobes were provided by the Lord Chamberlain. But the King was so delighted that, when the series of plays were over, 'His Majesty was graciously pleased to give the managers £200 more' as a bonus. The stage was not dismantled and it was hoped that there would be another season of plays at Hampton Court in the following year. But the players were not invited there again.

In that same year, 1718, Sir Christopher Wren, the distinguished architect and Surveyor-General of the Works for forty-nine years, who had been appointed by King Charles II and had served five sovereigns, was suddenly dismissed. Though in his eighty-sixth year he was in full possession of all his faculties: for his dismissal some of the German favourites of the King, who wanted to see a friend of theirs in that high office, were said to be responsible.

Wren retired without complaining to a house on the Green at Hampton Court which he had leased from the Crown ten years earlier. An old house of wood and plaster, it had been the official residence of the Surveyor-General but was in a sad state of decay. Wren rebuilt it completely of brick, developed the charming garden and added a terrace on the river. There he lived for the five years that remained to him of life, facing the Palace he had expanded and embellished and had hoped to convert into a Versailles on the Thames. Once a year he went up to London and spent the day at St Paul's, which he had rebuilt after the Great Fire. During his last visit, in his ninety-first year, he caught a chill. He died peacefully in his sleep in his London home in St James's Street one day after dinner in February 1723. A year after his dismissal his successor was discharged from the office of Surveyor-General.

On St George's Day 1720, King George I had a public reconciliation with his son. They embraced and kissed. Neither the King nor the Prince of Wales visited Hampton Court during the remaining seven years of that reign.

During those seven years the Palace was by no means empty, for quite apart from the guards, the domestic staff, the gardeners and park keepers, a great many of the lodgings and rooms were occupied by people of whom the King had no knowledge whatsoever. They had apparently been allowed to move in by some friendly official or by one who was corrupt and was receiving rent from them. This had been going on ever since the time of Henry VIII, who had tried to drive them out and abolish any recurrence of this practice, but despite Henry's stern orders, some months after they were turned out the squatters returned. And it was not only at Hampton Court that this was going on.

George I also tried to put an end to it. He wrote to the Lord Chamberlain: 'Whereas we are informed that, contrary to the Standing Rules and Order made for the better care and government of our Houses, several persons are lodged in our Palaces of Hampton Court, Windsor and Kensington, who have no places or offices about our person to entitle them to lodgings. These are, therefore, to require you not to permit any person to have lodgings in our Palaces of Hampton Court, etc., who are not by their offices entitled thereto, and that you give orders to the Keepers of our said Houses not to admit any of our servants who have lodgings appointed them for their attendance in our service there, to make use of their lodgings, without leave first had from you, or the Chamberlain of our Household for the time being, as they shall answer the contrary at their peril.' It had no effect. The practice of unauthorised squatting in palaces continued.

Not until a year after his father's death did George II go to stay at Hampton Court. He went there on 2 July 1728 and stayed for several months; and returned every summer for two or more months during the ten following years.

But the atmosphere was no longer as gay as in his Prince of Wales days: indeed it was markedly dull. Possibly he was a little too conscious of his new dignity. An indication of what it was like is given by his mistress Mrs Howard in a letter to the lovely Miss Lepell, who was by now married to Lord Hervey: 'Hampton Court is very different from the place you knew. . . . *Frizelation, flirtation,* and *dangleation* are now no more and nothing less than a Lepell can restore them to life; but to tell you my opinion fully, the people you now converse with in books are much more alive than any of your old acquaintance.'

Mrs Howard possibly expected her position to be improved by George II's accession to the throne. But it wasn't. Queen Caroline, for whom the King still had a lusty passion which she reciprocated to the full, imposed a number of menial duties on his mistress; not through any feeling of jealousy, for Caroline had none, and listened with delight to the details revealed by her husband of his various amours; but she felt that, as she was now Queen, Mrs Howard, as Lady of her Bedchamber, should kneel on handing her the cup of chocolate or setting down the basin and ewer for her to wash her hands. Though rebellious, Mrs Howard put up with it until her brother-in-law's death made her husband Earl of Suffolk and raised her to a more exalted position in the Queen's household. She was moved to a more beautiful suite of rooms at Hampton Court, on the ground floor instead of in the half-storey above the Queen's. The King, always a very precise and punctual man, used to visit her regularly at nine o'clock each evening and waited outside her door with his watch in his hand and knocked only at the right time.

The other ladies-in-waiting, less modest and more daring than Mrs Howard, tried to break the monotony of life at Hampton Court by indulging in their own private frolics. At night they used to creep into the gardens and go round tapping at various windows. Possibly, on hearing of these pranks, George II decided to provide the ladies with an evening of diversion. The stage his father had erected in the Great Hall was still there: it had not been used for more than a dozen years. So he invited the Actors Company to give a performance on 18 October 1731 and paid them £100 for it, not only to divert the ladies, but he happened to have the Duke of Lorraine staying at Hampton Court at the time. It was, however, for just that one evening.

His Majesty much preferred stag-hunting and coursing, all summer long. 'We hunt,' Mrs Howard said, 'with great noise and violence and have every day a very tolerable chance to have a neck broke.' She wasn't far wrong. A few days later a newspaper reported:

'The royal family were a hunting, and in the chase of a stag started upon the Princess Amelia's horse, which, being frightened, threw her. The Hon'ble Mr. Fitzwilliam, page of honour to His Majesty, fell with his horse among the coney-burrows, as also a servant to the Queen's coachmaker.' All three on the same day.

Surprisingly a strong objection to fox-hunting was constantly voiced by the King. He told the Duke of Grafton, a descendant of King Charles II through Lady Castlemaine (the Duke's familiarity as a relative was strongly disliked by the King) : 'A pretty occupation for a man of quality, and at his age, to be spending all his time tormenting a poor fox that was generally a much better beast than any of those that pursued him.' The Duke said he did it for his health, at which His Majesty asked why he did not walk. 'With your corpse of twenty stone,' the King added, 'no horse, I am sure, can carry you within hearing, much less within sight, of the hounds.' This was said in the presence of Lord Hervey, the Vice-Chamberlain, who recorded it in his *Memoirs*.

After spending the morning coursing or hunting, the King and Queen (she followed in a chaise with Lord Hervey riding beside her) generally dined with the entire Court in the Public Dining Room, at the north end of Wren's State suite, redecorated with white marble doorways, a massive white marble chimney-piece bearing the arms of George II, painted panelling with distempered walls above it and a heavy cornice. The Queen's Presence Chamber and the Guard Chamber appear to have been altered at this time too, the ceiling being raised to take in the half-storey of round windows. William Kent, a favourite architect of the King as well as of Sir Robert Walpole, is said to have been responsible for these changes, although the rooms in the north-east angle of Wren's new structure, which had not been completed, seem to have been dealt with by Vanbrugh. Kent also rebuilt part of the old Tudor structure overlooking Clock Court, above its east gateway. As a result we have a mock Gothic doorway, a pointed window, a vaulted ceiling of stucco and two new turrets which he put up in place of the beautiful old bay windows, all this replacing several old rooms on the first floor, near Wolsey's Closet and full of memories of Tudor and Stuart times, with the so-called Cumberland Suite. The decoration apparently by Kent has recently been splendidly refurbished.

Alterations in the gardens were made by Queen Caroline. She had the elaborate scrollwork and lace patterns of the flower-beds in the semicircular Great Fountain Garden removed and replaced by large lawns. All the fountains except the enormous central fountain were also removed. Pope wrote a couplet about it:

Tired of the scene the parterres and fountains yield,
He finds at last he better likes a field.

A line of yews trimmed into the shape of obelisks were planted at the base of the parterre on the Broad Walk, which Pope dismissed as 'the mournful family of yews—pyramids of dark green, continually repeated, not unlike a funeral procession'.

Queen Caroline did not do much more at Hampton Court, although she loved gardens and was responsible for linking the small scattered lakes in Hyde Park to form the Serpentine. Time was running out for her. A silly but shattering domestic upheaval involved the King and Queen in their most dramatic quarrel with their son Frederick Prince of Wales—a small, slightly built, conceited, self-opinionated young man, whose attitude towards both his father and mother was off-hand and often contemptuous. Born in 1707 he did not come to reside in England until he was twenty, the year his father succeeded to the throne. Nine years later, after two betrothals, he married Augusta, the daughter of the Duke of Saxe-Gotha. His parents were delighted. The King arranged to give him an allowance of £50,000 a year, but in defiance of his father, he asked Parliament to increase it. Parliament's refusal made the relationship between father and son far more critical.

At first the hostility between them was not unlike the quarrel George I had with George II. But it grew steadily worse. His mother loathed him just as much and wished 'a hundred times a day that he might drop down dead', a sentiment heartily shared by most of his sisters. This hatred was generated by his ceaseless ridicule of his parents which attained wide publicity in a book, inspired by him, entitled *Histoire du Prince Titi*. He stirred up his father's political opponents and caused endless trouble, which eventually came to a head in 1737 at Hampton Court.

The Prince and Princess came to spend the summer at the Palace with the King and Queen and the entire Court. There were rumours that the young Princess was pregnant, but the Queen could detect no sign of it: her enquiries were brushed aside, the Prince had instructed his wife to give the unvarying answer 'I don't know'. After a time the Queen came to the conclusion that no child was really expected and that the Princess was possibly unable to have one. She wondered if the Prince, who was capable of any deception, was planning a mock confinement, perhaps in London away from the royal family, and would pass of as his offspring a baby acquired from other parents. Inquiries as to date and the place chosen for the confinement revealed nothing and only confirmed her suspicions of her son's diabolical plot to interfere with the succession to the throne.

The King ordered the Prime Minister, Sir Robert Walpole, who was staying at the Palace, to tell the Prince that His Majesty desired that the birth of the child should be at Hampton Court. Sir Robert, who had been given the impression by the Prince or Princess that the child was not expected until October, felt there was plenty of time and delayed in delivering the message.

A few days later, on Sunday 31 July, after dining with the King and Queen in public, the Princess of Wales returned to her own room near the Public Dining Room. There waiting for her was the Prince, who had not spoken to his parents since Parliament refused to increase his allowance. The King withdrew to play a new game of cards called 'commerce' with Lady Deloraine, his current mistress: the Queen and the Princesses played various other card games, such as quadrille and cribbage, with Lord Hervey in another room upstairs.

Meanwhile in the Prince of Wales's suite the Princess began to have acute labour pains. Resolved that the child should not be born at Hampton Court, the Prince ordered that a coach should be brought as quietly as possible to a nearby door to take the Princess to London. The Princess, groaning and begging to be left alone, was lifted from her bed by an equerry and the dancing master and carried down the Prince's private back stairs with the Prince behind them, followed by his mistress Lady Archibald Hamilton.

Begging him 'for God's sake' to abandon his foolish plan, the Princess was urged to endure her suffering by the Prince's futile solace of 'Courage! Courage!'

The stairs led down almost to the cloisters of Fountain Court; the coach, to be near enough, would have waited at a side door in Tennis Court Lane. Five people, including the Princess, the Prince and his mistress, got into the coach. Two others, one of whom was the Prince's valet and claimed to be also a surgeon and a male midwife, sat by the coachman, and two more stood behind. Thus they set off at a gallop all the way to St James's Palace in London. A midwife was sent for, napkins and a warming-pan were brought from various nearby houses. There were no sheets on the bed and the Princess had to lie down between two table-cloths.

At a quarter to eleven that night, which implies that they must have left Hampton Court at about half-past eight, the Princess was delivered of, as Lord Hervey put it, 'a little rat of a girl, about the bigness of a good large toothpick case'. Christened Augusta, she grew up to be a fine healthy woman and married the Duke of Brunswick. There are two pictures of her at Hampton Court, one as a girl of fourteen in Knapton's group of the Prince's family, the other by Angelica Kaufmann as a woman of thirty-three.

A courier was despatched at once by the Prince to inform the King and Queen of the child's birth. On his arrival at half-past one in the morning, one of the women of the bedchamber hurried up to the Queen's room with the news. Startled from her deep sleep, her Majesty asked in an alarmed voice: 'What is the matter? Is the Palace on fire?' On being told of the child's birth, the Queen said: 'Are you mad? Or are you dreaming?' The King, when told, flew into an angry passion. 'You see now how they have outwitted you,' he told his wife. 'This is all your fault!'

The Queen got dressed quickly and set out by coach for St James's Palace with her two eldest daughters, the Duke of Grafton, Lord Hervey, and Lord Essex. The Prince greeted her affectionately and said that he would be coming in the morning to see the King and ask him to arrange the christening.

'You had better not come today,' she said. 'The King is not well pleased; and should you come today nobody can answer what your reception will be.'

The Queen was herself worked up. To the Duke of Grafton and Lord Hervey, and later to Sir Robert Walpole, she said: 'Do you think there ever was so insolent as well as silly a behaviour? My God! There is really no human patience can bear such treatment; nor indeed ought one to bear it, for they will pull one by the nose in a little time if some stop is not put to their impertinence.'

On her return to Hampton Court she found the King in a state of extreme rage. He sent Lord Essex back to tell the Prince that he looked upon his action as 'a deliberate indignity' and 'resented it to the highest degree'. To this he added a verbal message stating that His Majesty would *not* see the Prince.

Letters from the Prince with excuses that were neither true nor convincing kept arriving in quick succession: humbly he craved leave to come to Hampton Court and lay his grief at the feet of His Majesty. But the King would have none of it.

Nine days later Queen Caroline and her two eldest daughters went again to St James's Palace. The Prince ignored them completely, saying not a word to his mother or his sisters. But when they were leaving, on seeing a crowd by their coach, the Prince knelt in the dirty street and kissed his mother's hand.

On 10 September His Majesty, after a consultation with his Ministers, ordered his son to leave St James's Palace forthwith and take his family with him. At the same time he wrote to all foreign ambassadors, privy councillors, peers and peeresses to warn them that 'whoever went to the Prince's Court would not be admitted into the King's presence'. As a further sign of his displeasure the Prince's normal military guard was taken away.

Soon those who hated the King and his chief minister Walpole began to join the Prince's large party of friends, not only because they felt that His Majesty had treated his son badly, but chiefly with the intention of building a powerful opposition to wrest the government from Walpole. It took five years for them to achieve it.

Tobias Smollett, the novelist, too young at the time to know the Prince well, described him as being a tender husband and a magnificent patron of the arts. Horace Walpole, though not much older, was close enough to the King and the Prince to make a more accurate estimate of his personality. He dismissed the Prince's interest in the arts; and added that his chief passion was women; his other interest was gambling, 'and in all his money transactions his conduct was not regulated by ordinary considerations of honour'.

A few weeks after the prolonged and unnecessary quarrel brought on by the folly of the Prince, the Queen fell ill. Although she knew she was dying, she refused to see her son. The King, always devoted to her despite his occasional, uncontrollable outbursts, wept by her bedside. Tenderly she took his hand and begged him to marry again. Through his sobs he said: 'Non—j'aurai—des—maîtresses', to which the Queen said: 'Ah! Mon Dieu! cela n'empêche pas'— marriage had never before prevented him from having mistresses. She died on 20 November 1737.

George II hardly ever came to Hampton Court after that: when he did it was usually just to walk in the gardens on a bright summer afternoon with his friends, including a new mistress, Lady Yarmouth.

Coaches drawn by six horses brought them with a troop of Horse Guards in front raising the dust.

After a heavy meal they strolled for an hour or so along the Broad Walk admiring the Great Fountain Garden, then walked down to the river or perhaps tried to pick their way through the Maze. Before darkness fell they got back into their coaches and returned to London. Only occasionally did he stay for a day or two.

The Prince of Wales died in 1751, fourteen years after his mother, leaving a thirteen-year-old boy, the eldest of his five sons, to be groomed as the next King George by his grandfather. The irritability and tempestuous outbursts of the old King, now sixty-eight, became increasingly frequent with his advancing years. Often he gave vent to his feelings by kicking his hat and wig about the room. Once he vented it on his grandson while they were at Hampton Court. It occurred in the State apartments. What angered the King is not known, but the young heir was so startled when his grandfather's hand struck him across the ears that he never forgot it.

George II was the last British sovereign to live in Hampton Court. On succeeding to the throne in 1760, George III made it only too plain that he had no intention of making it his residence; this was attributed by his son, the Duke of Sussex, to his lingering memory of the humiliation suffered when his ears were boxed in that house by his grandfather.

Thus after two and a half centuries, Hampton Court ceased to be a royal residence. The new King was twenty-two and proud of being English, for, unlike the earlier Georges and even his father, he had been born in England and had since his infancy spoken the English language. He had been a difficult pupil, partly because of his inherited obstinacy but also because of his inability to concentrate. Tall, dignified, and more civilised in behaviour than his predecessors, he married rather rashly in the following year Princess Charlotte of Mecklenburg-Strelitz, on the very day he met her: she was ugly and said to be stupid, but she was a good, resigned wife and provided him with fifteen children.

Caretakers looked after Hampton Court—there was a housekeeper, a custodian to keep an eye on the costly pictures, a foreman to attend to the repairs and various officials and workmen, in all a staff of about forty. The gardens were already under the care of Lancelot Brown; a brilliant landscape gardener, he became in time very distinguished and is known to this day as Capability Brown from his quickness to point out what a landscape was capable of becoming at his hands. Appointed by George II, he was given lodgings at Hampton Court and granted leave by the King to attend also to the gardens of some of his friends. Brown spent much of his leisure talking to George III, dining with the Duke of Northumberland at his nearby residence, Syon House, and even getting to know the great Lord Chatham, with whom he corresponded for some years. At Hampton Court he made hardly any changes. The story has often been told that George III specifically suggested that he should sweep away the formal Great Fountain Garden facing the east front, including the magnificent parterre, but Brown refused.

The great vine was planted by him in 1769 and is still flourishing. It was taken as a cutting from Valentine House near Ilford in Essex and now has a girth of more than six feet; its main branch is over one hundred feet long and would have been even longer but for the confining size of the greenhouse.

Bit by bit in succeeding years most of the furniture and many of the pictures were removed to one of the other Royal Palaces. Even the kitchen utensils were taken away. The State apartments, where the Royal family had lived and entertained distinguished visitors, were left bare. But the rest of the Palace was not. Aware that squatters had been living in some of the rooms since the sixteenth century and that even the most rigorous efforts had failed to keep them out, George III gave orders that nobody should be allowed to occupy any lodgings or even single rooms without a written authority from the Lord Chamberlain. This authority, indicating the exact location of the lodgings or room, had to be delivered to the housekeeper, who escorted the persons mentioned to the quarters assigned them, and a register was kept stating clearly who was staying where.

It was on this basis that the 'Grace and Favour' residents came to live at Hampton Court. Begun in the year of George III's accession, the privilege is still in operation more than two centuries later.

Among the earliest 'Grace and Favour' residents were peers, a Duke of Devonshire, a Duke of Marlborough, a Duke of Portland, and an Earl of Hertford. Surprise that such exalted members of the nobility should seek lodgings here caused Hannah More, the author and reformer, who often stayed with the actor Garrick in his villa near Hampton Court and moved into the Palace herself for a few days to see what it was like, to write to Horace Walpole: 'The private apartments are almost all full; they are occupied by people of fashion, mostly of quality; and it is astonishing to me that people of large fortune will solicit for them. Mr. Lowndes has apartments next to these, notwithstanding he has an estate of £4,000 a year. In the opposite one lives Lady Augusta Fitzroy. You know she is the mother of the Duke of Grafton.'

Of course, not all people of quality had ample means; often, when the head of a noble family died and his son took over the estate, his widow moved into the small dower house. It was the King's purpose to provide lodgings at Hampton Court for those who had rendered some service to the country or for their families—this rule still operates. But, in any case, even in these early years not all the people who were given rooms in the Palace were either rich or noble. One was Mr William Hamilton, a former secretary to the Earl of Halifax; another was Mrs Brudenell, who had been a great beauty; a third Mr Richard Stonehewer, a friend of Horace Walpole's. It is, of course, obvious that influence was required to get in.

The famous Dr Samuel Johnson applied to the Lord Chamberlain, the Earl of Hertford, in 1776 for accommodation there. He wrote:

My Lord—Being wholly unknown to your lordship, I have only this apology to make for presuming to trouble you with a request—that a stranger's petition, if it cannot be easily granted, can be easily refused. Some of the apartments at Hampton Court are now vacant, in which I am encouraged to hope that, by application to your lordship, I may obtain a residence. Such a grant would be considered by me a great favour; and I hope, to a man who has had the honour of vindicating His Majesty's government, a retreat in one of his houses may not improperly or unworthily be allowed. I therefore request that your lordship will be pleased to grant such rooms in Hampton Court as shall seem proper—My Lord, your lordship's most obedient and humble servant. Sam. Johnson.

The request was refused. Dr Johnson was then twenty-seven years old and very hard up.

Many members of the Walpole family were given accommodation —one was Sir Edward Walpole's beautiful illegitimate daughter Maria, who had married Earl Waldegrave but was now the wife of George III's brother. Living there with her were her three pretty daughters whose portrait by Sir Joshua Reynolds is so much admired. Another resident was Margaret, the daughter of Clive of India: she was the widow of Colonel Walpole. For more than a hundred years members of the Walpole family, most of them descendants of Sir Robert Walpole, had rooms in the Palace.

Horace Walpole lived within four miles of Hampton Court and often came to visit his relatives and friends. A nasty fall there bruised him badly. He describes it in one of his letters: 'It was dusk; there was a very low step at the door, I did not see it; it tripped me up. I fell headlong on the stones, and against the frame of a table at the door, and battered myself so much that my whole hip is as black as my shoe, besides bruising one hand, both knees, and my left elbow, into which it brought the gout next day.' A friend of his living at Hampton Court had a tragic end there. Richard Tickell, a brother-in-law of the playwright Sheridan and a Commissioner of the Stamp Office, threw himself from one of the uppermost windows of the Palace—it was sixty feet high. 'Some attribute his despair to debts; some to a breach with his political friends.'

Some years later, pretty Julia Storer, daughter of a maid of honour and niece of Lord Carysfort, lived in a 'Grace and Favour' apartment, with her mother, brother, and sister. Beau Brummell, very young at the time, fell in love with her, but she was not very responsive. She was already in love with Colonel Cotton, an officer in the 10th Dragoons, who lived in another apartment with his wife and nine children.

Julia had been educated partly in France. One evening at a dance at Hampton Court, she became madly infatuated with the Colonel when he partnered her. Nine months or so later, showing no hint of her condition, Julia, 'while in the act of paying her respects to Her Majesty'—Queen Victoria—was 'seized with the pangs of labour', Harriette Wilson records in her *Memoirs*.

On her return to Hampton Court Mrs Cotton shouted vile abuse at her. Nobody sent for a midwife and 'in about five hours, unassisted, she became the mother of a fine boy'. Her brother challenged the Colonel to a duel and wounded him; but Julia continued her meetings with Colonel Cotton and in time added five children to the nine he already had.

She told Harriette Wilson that the Colonel first made love to her 'on a stone staircase. I can scarcely describe to you the difficulty which existed in the Palace of securing a tête-à-tête: with all our hopes of happiness depending on it, we did not accomplish more than three private interviews a month.' Later Cotton induced her to let him come into her bedroom. Her sister, who shared her mother's bedroom, used to change in Julia's room while the Colonel hid under the bed until she left. The Colonel, she said, was 'a very gallant and handsome man', who was treated in a repulsive manner by his bad-tempered wife.

Surprisingly a 'Grace and Favour' lodging was given to Prince William of Orange, the son of George II's daughter Anne. He fled from Holland in 1795 when the French Revolutionary troops invaded the country. George III did all he could to make him and his family comfortable and allowed them to use the Queen's Guard and Presence Chambers in the Wren suite as their reception rooms.

Occasionally, King George, while staying at Kew, which was on the Surrey side of the river, rode to Hampton Court to see the Prince and used the wooden bridge across the Thames which had been erected at Hampton about 1751—until then the crossing was made by ferry. A man named Feltham, who had rented the bridge for £400 a year, demanded a toll of one guinea from every horseman and vehicle using it. During a hunt in which King George took part the hunted stag swam across the river and the hounds crossed the bridge in pursuit. As the riders followed somebody raised the cry of 'The King!' The party was allowed to go through without charge. Feltham had no sooner shut the gate after them when a second group of riders came up and once more the cry of 'The King!' was heard. Feltham refused to open the gate for them. 'I've let King George through, God bless him,' he said. 'I know of no other King. If you have brought the King of France, hang me if I let him through.' At that moment King George rode up and was angry that the sport had been interrupted; but later he sent a donation to Feltham.

The great Duke of Wellington's mother, the Countess of Mornington, also occupied a 'Grace and Favour' apartment at the Palace. Her stay at Hampton Court, which began when Prince William of Orange moved in, lasted for about thirty years. She occupied rooms under the Prince of Wales suite. The small enclosed garden adjoining it where she loved to sit is still known as Lady Mornington's Garden. Both Wellington and his elder brother the Marquess Wellesley, who had been Governor-General of India, came often to see her. Her daughter, Lady Anne Fitzroy, occupied another apartment and a younger son, the Rev. Gerald Wellesley, was Resident Chaplain and also had an apartment there.

Another Viceregal link was provided by Lord Dufferin and Ava, who was there as a child with his mother. He said later: 'I cannot tell you what an affection I have for that place—what tender memories it brings back to my recollection.'

Some 'Grace and Favour' residents, it was discovered, were letting out their apartments to friends—sometimes for months at a time and for a considerable rent. This was eventually stopped. Apartments not occupied by the persons to whom they had been assigned were immediately allotted to others.

For centuries visitors have been allowed to come and look at the Palace and wander in the Parks and gardens. It is not known precisely when this concession was granted. It is unlikely that Wolsey, Henry VIII, or Queen Elizabeth would have let visitors drift in and look round, though certain nobles are known to have come out of curiosity to see the Palace when the sovereign was not in residence: this was possibly arranged with the Lord Chamberlain or one of the officials. In James I's and Charles I's time the public were admitted on certain days to the Public Dining Room to watch from a barrier while His Majesty ate his meals. William III hated it, and so did George I, though occasionally and most reluctantly both consented to exhibit themselves in this zoological manner. George II cooperated wholeheartedly.

After the death of Queen Caroline, George II allowed the public to see the Palace. Soon it became a show place. Excursions were organised by enterprising coach and boat owners and people kept arriving by road and river from towns and villages within a radius of thirty miles or so and in quite large numbers from London. They were taken round in small groups to see the Great Hall, the old Tudor Galleries and rooms, and Wren's State apartments. Their guide was the Deputy Housekeeper, who charged a fee, the bulk of which found its way into the pocket of the Housekeeper.

Before long a regimental band was provided to play to the visitors on Thursdays and Sundays; and the visitors, increasing in numbers through the years, danced while the band played.

Among the visitors were such notable people as Sir Walter Scott, the novelist, who came three or four times for he was greatly 'struck' by what he saw. On one of these visits he was accompanied by the poets Samuel Rogers, Thomas Moore, and Wordsworth, who brought his wife and daughter. Moore noted in his journal that the public 'were all *eyes* after Scott, the other scribblers not coming in for a glance'. Earlier Fanny Burney, the novelist, had come with Mrs David Garrick and other friends to stroll in the gardens.

Another visitor was Theodore Hook, the dramatist and wit, who, feeling weary after a long ramble through Bushey Park, decided that if he staggered and fell some sympathetic sightseers might carry him. A group of Cockneys, finding him stretched out on the ground in the middle of Chestnut Avenue, rushed up to help: a door was brought from the gatekeeper's lodge and on it the grateful Hook was carried towards the Palace. More conventional sightseers included Miss Mary Mitford, author of *Our Village*, Sir Thomas Lawrence, the celebrated painter, Sir Francis Chantrey, the sculptor, even Mr John Murray, the publisher, possibly with his famous Guides in mind.

Throughout the two centuries and more since Hampton Court has ceased to be a Royal residence, the most careful attention has been given to its structure and endless repairs have had to be carried out. Early in George III's reign the Great Gatehouse, the principal entrance to the Palace, was found to be in a state of decay. But it was decided that instead of repairing it, a part of the Gateway should be dismantled, reducing the elegant structure to its present height. This dwarfing deprived it of much of its impressive beauty. The lead cupolas on the four turrets with their gilded weather vanes were removed in 1771, leaving just bare, truncated stumps; and a hundred years later the lovely dark red, almost purple bricks went too and were replaced by bright Victorian bricks.

There has always been a Royal Stud at Hampton Court; some of the paddocks were in the Home Park and others in Bushey Park just across the Kingston Road. William III increased the number of horses in the Stud and Queen Anne had walls built to prevent the horses from roving too far. She entered her horses for various races; her husband's interest was in breeding. The Stud was maintained by the first three Georges.

George IV, as Prince of Wales, visited the Royal Paddocks regularly and spent 'many gay hours at the Stud-house'. When he became Regent, he set up an additional stud here to breed only grey horses of pure blood; eight years later, on succeeding to the throne, he sold all the horses, and the Stud was taken over by his brother, the Duke of York, who bred racehorses, one of which, Moses, won the Derby two years later in 1822. When the Duke died George IV took over the Royal Stud again and bred racehorses. The stabling and the paddocks were extended and improved. He had as many as thirty-three brood mares; of the stallions Waterloo, Tranby, and The Colonel are best remembered.

His brother William IV kept the Stud going, though he was not particularly interested in horses. To the horses left him by George IV he added four Arabs, presented by the King of Oude and the Imam of Muscat, and some famous English stallions, including Actaeon, which was later sold for a thousand guineas. In June 1830 his trainer asked which of his horses should be entered at Goodwood. The Sailor King replied: 'Take the whole fleet; some of them will win I suppose'—in fact the King's horses took the first three places for the Goodwood Cup: Fleur-de-Lys, 1; Zinganeee, 2; and The Colonel, 3.

When William died the entire Stud was sold for 15,692 guineas. The paddocks were let to Charles Greville and Colonel Peel, but fourteen years later, in 1851, Queen Victoria, on the advice of the Prince Consort, started a Royal Stud once again. Sainfoin, the Derby winner in 1890, and Memoir, winner of the Oaks, were both bred in the Hampton Court Stud, but had been sold earlier. Other purchases of yearlings from the Stud went to Lord Randolph Churchill (Winston Churchill's father), the Duke of Westminster, and Baron Hirsch. Most of the horses used for Queen Victoria's State carriages and for her household were kept at the Stud and it was there that the Queen's cream-coloured horses were bred, many of them being descendants of horses brought over by George I from Hanover.

The cost of keeping the Palace in repair and paying for lighting, cleaning, draining, wages and salaries was over £5,000 a year in the reign of George IV; the gardens cost £2,880 a year.

Though William IV never lived at Hampton Court, he lived at Bushey House, the residence of the Ranger (honorary royal park keeper), for more than thirty years. Originally the house had been occupied by the Earl of Halifax, who founded the Bank of England and was the organiser of the National Debt; sixty years later the Rangership was given by George III to Lord North, who as Prime Minister and Chancellor of the Exchequer was responsible for the Boston Tea Party and the eventual loss of the American colonies. Lord North's physical likeness to George III was so striking that many believed he was the King's illegitimate half-brother—both had large protuberant eyes, a wide mouth, thick lips and a bloated face. So that he should not have to surrender his seat as a Member of Parliament, by holding an office of profit under the Crown, the Rangership was entered in his wife's name. On the death of Lady North, it passed to William IV, at that time the Duke of Clarence. He was a jovial, easy-going man who joined heartily in all the local diversions—races, cricket matches, dances, and dinners; and was President of the Toye Club which met in the tavern at the gates of Hampton Court, drinking, singing seafaring songs, and contributing to the amusing stories told by the members.

His interest in Hampton Court was intense. On becoming King in 1830 at the age of sixty-five, he did everything possible to restore its former glory. The dilapidated state of the King's Great Staircase distressed him and he gave orders for its repair and repainting. From Windsor Castle, Kensington Palace, St James's Palace, Carlton House (which had recently been demolished) and from Buckingham House while it was rebuilt Buckingham Palace, paintings were brought for display in the State rooms at Hampton Court. His purpose was to draw still more visitors to the Palace. After paying a shilling a head, the guests gathered at the foot of the King's Staircase and were taken up to the State apartments by the Deputy Housekeeper or by one of the housemaids: the Housekeeper, generally a member of a noble family (Lady Anne Cecil, Lady Elizabeth Seymour, and Lady Emily Montagu in turn held that office), never acted as a guide. As visitors gaped, each painting and piece of furniture was indicated with a long stick and a bellowing feminine voice supplied brief details about the artists, their subjects, and a sprinkling of dates.

The astronomical clock put up by Henry VIII in the Clock Tower had needed attention through the centuries. William, finding that its wheels were no longer able to perform their functions accurately, had the clock removed in 1835 and replaced it by one from St James's Palace. Some years later, in 1879, the original Henry VIII clock was rescued, equipped with new mechanism, and replaced; it performs all its former functions with reasonable accuracy, rarely gaining or losing more than half a minute in a month.

Above the clock is a wooden cupola, built in the reign of Charles II, which contains the clock's three bells. One of these bells belonged to the Knights Hospitallers and was made more than thirty years before Wolsey rented the old manor-house. The oldest thing at Hampton Court, it can still be heard striking the hours.

The Banqueting House on the river, built for William III, was found to be in a shabby state and by the King's order it was repaired and fully restored. The beauty of the carved panelling and the painted ceiling was revived and the house was used by a friend of the King's, Sir James Reynett, as a private residence.

William IV often went to visit his friends at Hampton Court, generally joining them at dinner. On some of them he conferred Hanoverian knighthoods. Among the recipients were three members of the Toye Club. One of them, Sir Horace Seymour, a tall, handsome man who had fought under Wellington at Waterloo, lived in an apartment at Hampton Court and attracted the attention of a great many of the women who knew he was a widower. On a hot Sunday morning in the summer of 1831, during a service in the Chapel, a young woman fainted. Sir Horace instantly rose and went to help her. He 'raised the prostrate fair one in his arms, carried her to his apartments, deposited her on a sofa, left her to the charge of his housekeeper, and straightaway returned to his seat'.

On the following Sunday another young lady fainted in the Chapel and was carried out by the handsome Sir Horace. By the next Sunday many wondered as they walked to the Chapel whether there would be still another fainting. There was—and once again it was a young lady who was carried out by Sir Horace Seymour.

But this was too much for Sir Horace's aunt. When the service ended she had a word with the Chaplain and this bold notice was put up on the Chapel door:

Notice

Whereas a tendency to faint is becoming a prevalent infirmity among young ladies frequenting this Chapel, notice is hereby given that for the future ladies so affected will no longer be carried out by Sir Horace Seymour, but by Branscombe the dustman.

Which ended the epidemic.

On William IV's death Queen Adelaide returned to Bushey House where she and her husband had lived for so long. She later gave a morning party for the young Queen Victoria in a summer house there: among her guests were the Queen's husband Prince Albert, the King and Queen of the Belgians, and the King of Holland.

Soon after Victoria came to the throne in 1837, she made a decision about Hampton Court. In future the Palace, she said, would be open to the public on certain days without any charge whatsoever. The death of the last of the noble Housekeepers, Lady Emily Montagu, made this possible: no Housekeeper was appointed to succeed her. The State apartments were closed for a time to be cleaned and redecorated, and so that the pictures and furniture could be more attractively displayed. Then the public proceeded to come in ever-increasing numbers to enjoy its architectural magnificence, inspect its treasures, and wander through its parks and gardens. They came in coaches, in dog-carts, in cabs and brakes, buses and delivery vans, and later in crowded railway trains to the station on the Surrey side of the bridge. Many came up the river from London's spreading suburbs in rowing boats, sailing boats gay with coloured sails, houseboats adorned with bright curtains and flowers, and later in steam-launches. Many brought picnic hampers and sat down in the parks for their meal.

There were forebodings of the damage that would be done by shoals of 'working-class' hooligans tearing down priceless tapestries, destroying the costly furniture, and stealing paintings by Tintoretto and Titian. But nothing like that happened. The visitors were well behaved and took a keen and delighted interest in what they saw.

For many years before Queen Victoria's accession the Palace had been open to the public on Sundays. While visitors were comparatively few, little was known about it and hardly anything was said about the desecration of the Sabbath. The practice was begun by the early Housekeepers who found that many more people came on a Sunday than on all the rest of the days of the week added together and of course it brought them personally a considerable income. But now the number of visitors rose to thousands.

Hampton Court was the only place of 'entertainment' in or near London which was open to the public on Sunday, and Sabbatarians began vehemently to protest, Personal letters were sent to the Queen. Clergymen denounced it from the pulpit: one went so far as to say that Hampton Court was 'a hell upon earth' on the Sabbath; it emerged later that he had never been there. Dr Selle, organist at the Chapel for seven years, stated in a letter to *The Times* that 'the conduct of the masses is orderly, quiet and respectable, nor do I ever remember seeing a drunken character'; and those who complained that many went to Hampton Court instead of going to church were reminded that, as the public were not admitted before two o'clock, they had time enough to attend morning service.

For many years the care of the Palace as well as the parks and gardens was under the supervision of Mr Edward Jesse. Not only were the repairs carried out with skill and thoroughness, but important restorations were attended to as well. At various times sash-windows had been let into the old Tudor buildings. He regarded them, rightly, as a disfigurement and had them replaced by appropriate Gothic mullioned openings with latticed casements. The old ornamental stone carvings were restored. Chimney-shafts of finely moulded red brick replaced the yellow bricks used during the Georgian repairs.

The roof of Henry VIII's lovely Great Hall was redecorated and stained glass was put into the east and west windows. The walls, bare for many years, were once again hung with old tapestries. The roof of the Chapel was also restored. Raphael's Cartoons, which during George III's reign had hung at Buckingham House and then at Windsor until the Prince Regent had them returned to Hampton Court in 1809, remained there in Wren's gallery until the Queen— inspired by her late husband's love of Raphael—decided in 1865 that a more studious public should see them at the South Kensington Museum, now the Victoria and Albert, where they have been ever since. Tapestries made from the cartoons now hang in Wren's gallery instead.

A cousin of Queen Victoria, Princess Frederica of Hanover, moved into one of the lodgings in Hampton Court in 1880 with her husband Baron von Pawel Rammingen. Some months later their daughter Victoria was born in the Palace, but died three weeks later. The Princess was so deeply affected by the tragedy that she decided to start a convalescent home for poor married women who had recently become mothers and needed medical care, fresh air, and good food. There was no institution of the kind in the country at the time. To raise funds she was allowed by the Queen the use of the Great Hall for a musical and theatrical entertainment. The last time the hall had been used for the production of a play was a hundred and fifty years earlier for George II on a stage erected for George I, for just one night. Seventy years later that stage was removed on the orders of George III so, after a further eighty years, a new stage had to be put up. The programme included two short plays, *Yellow Roses* and *Tears*, in which Sir Charles Young and Lady Monckton played the leading roles, followed by a musical selection played in the Minstrel Gallery by the band of the Military School of Music. More than five hundred people attended and the money raised helped to start 'Princess Frederica's Convalescent Home'.

From time to time since then the Great Hall has been used for various diversions. Shakespeare's *Twelfth Night* was performed there for three and a half weeks in July 1964, and on 7 November 1967 a ballet performance in the Great Hall diverted the President of Turkey and numerous distinguished guests.

Queen Victoria never stayed at Hampton Court, but she occasionally visited Princess Frederica and others who resided there. Her father, the Duke of Kent, lived from 1807 to 1820 in one of the pavilions built near the bowling green by Wren for William III. It was the only surviving one of the four.

Lady Roberts, the mother of Field-Marshal Lord Roberts (known affectionately in the Army as 'Bobs Bahadur' because of his brilliant campaigns in India), was given apartments at Hampton Court and so was Lady MacGregor, the wife of Sir Charles MacGregor, Lord Roberts' Chief of Staff. Earlier, Professor Michael Faraday, son of a London blacksmith, who became one of Britain's greatest scientists and made important discoveries in the uses of electricity, was given a house on the Green, two doors from Christopher Wren's: the house is still known as Faraday House. After his death the daughter of Admiral Hardy, Nelson's Flag Captain at Trafalgar, made her home there.

In the course of its long history there has been only one murder at Hampton Court. It occurred in June 1838. A trooper of the 12th Lancers, John Rickey, returned drunk from a race meeting in the nearby town of Hampton. His arrest was ordered. Seizing a pair of pistols, he tried to flee, but was chased by a sergeant and some other members of the regiment. As they approached him in a passage, he fired. The bullet hit Sergeant Hamilton who died a few days later.

Tried at the Old Bailey, Rickey was found guilty of murder, but he was later reprieved.

During the sixties it was rumoured that Irish Fenians were planning to blow up Hampton Court on Christmas Eve. The guard was increased, most of the gardeners were enrolled and placed on duty at the principal approaches to the Palace. Throughout the night and right into Christmas Day the watch continued. But nothing happened and the residents were able to attend the Christmas service in the Chapel, to which a thanksgiving was most gratefully added.

There were two outbreaks of fire. The first, which broke out on the morning of 14 December 1882 in a bedroom above the Queen's apartments in Wren's east front, was caused by a stove on which a housemaid was preparing tea for her mistress. It was put out by the Palace Fire Brigade, but the servant unfortunately was suffocated by the smoke and died shortly afterwards. About six rooms were damaged by fire and smoke; their restoration cost £4,000.

The second fire occurred four years later, again in the morning. It began in a housemaid's closet in what was at one time Edward VI's Nursery in the north-east corner of the old Tudor Palace, between Chapel Court and Henry VIII's covered Tennis Court. The Nursery had been largely rebuilt by the Georges. As the closet was small and dark the housemaid had lighted a candle which quickly ignited the flimsy, inflammable woodwork.

The flames spread rapidly. It was a long and strenuous battle in which the Palace Fire Brigade was assisted by men of the 10th Hussars and by a dozen fire brigades from nearby towns. About forty rooms were destroyed or damaged by the fire. One 'Grace and Favour' lady, Miss Louisa Somerset, daughter of Lord Edward Somerset, who was elderly and had been living in the apartment for more than forty years, was rescued by the warder of the Garden Gate, Mr Thorne, who carried her across the roof to safety. He was awarded the Royal Humane Society medal for this brave act.

The restoration of this section of the old Palace, which cost over £8,000, greatly improved its appearance. The stout outer walls, which were Tudor, survived the fire, but the whole of the interior had to be rebuilt. The sash-windows and shapeless chimneys put in during the Georgian years were replaced by stone mullioned windows and moulded chimney-shafts; deep crimson bricks of Tudor type were used for the structure, as a result of which much of its earlier appearance was restored.

The 'Grace and Favour' apartments, as we have seen, are not confined to the Palace: some are in houses in the parks and gardens, or on the Green just outside the Palace gates. Before the new occupants move in the lodgings are put into excellent repair; but further decorations and repairs have to be carried out by the residents, who also contribute a suitable proportion to the rates. The tenants bring in their own furniture.

Until recently more than fifty 'Grace and favour' apartments were assigned at the discretion of the sovereign. Although some had large and luxurious rooms on the top floor of the Wren building there were no lifts and the climb to the top floor for elderly residents was tiring: later some lifts were put in, but even so the residents had to lower baskets for their milk and bread and groceries and haul them up by rope. Most of these lofty lodgings are now left untenanted.

Almost all the residents are women—widows, mothers, and daughters of men who have distinguished themselves in the services or in science and the arts. About twenty-six lodgings in the Palace are occupied now. Some are in the north and south wings of Wolsey's first court, known as Base Court; others overlook Tennis Court Lane or are in Edward VI's Nursery section rebuilt after the fire. In that area there are a number of most attractive small courts, some with archaic names which visitors normally miss seeing—Fish Court, Lord Chamberlain's Court, Master Carpenter's Court, the very attractive Back Court near the Fish Kitchen, Great Hall Court, Chapel Court and, not far away, Round Kitchen Court and Chocolate Court. In and near them are some fascinating centuries-old lamp-posts and rain-water pipe heads, known as hopper-heads, going back to the time of Wolsey, Henry VIII, and Queen Elizabeth.

The residents have evolved a delightfully diverse social life of their own. They invite each other in for drinks, give dinner parties, arrange dances and organise amateur dramatic performances. And they can play 'real tennis' on Henry VIII's old Tennis Court (by joining the Tennis Club), play golf in the Home Park, or row, sail, and fish on the river.

But above all else they have around them, by night and by day, the glorious setting, with its many historical associations—Cardinal Wolsey being paid a surprise visit by Henry VIII and his courtiers, all masked and laughing as he tries to guess which is the King; the conversion of the Palace into a fortress in the reign of the boy King, Edward VI, by his uncle the Protector, and their departure by night for the greater safety of Windsor Castle; Queen Elizabeth with her lover the Earl of Leicester, later offering him to Mary Queen of Scots for a bridegroom, and the furious insulting letter in reply; Charles I's quarrel with his Queen Henrietta Maria breaking the windows with her tiny fists until dragged away with bleeding arms by her husband; Charles I's imprisonment in Hampton Court. . . . The associations are numerous, some sad, others happy and gay and filled with music, whirling couples in ruffs and embroidered dresses. . . . Shakespeare's plays with Shakespeare himself in the company of players. . . . The ghosts of Catherine Howard, running along the gallery to the Chapel, and Mistress Sibell Penn, Edward VI's nurse and foster-mother, muttering as she works the spinning-wheel in a room of the old Palace. The great building is still very much alive.

To this setting a million people come each year from all over the world to admire the architecture, walk along the mile-long avenues, look at the famous paintings assembled through the centuries, breathe in the delightful scent of the flowers, and take away memories of what has happened here in the course of four and a half centuries.

Arkrigg, G. P. V., *Jacobean Pageant*. Hamish Hamilton, 1962.

Ashley, Maurice, *The Greatness of Oliver Cromwell*. Hodder & Stoughton, 1957.

Baxter, Stephen B., *William III*. Longmans, 1966.

Bohun, Edmund, *Life and Character of Queen Elizabeth*. 1693.

Bryant, Sir Arthur, *Charles II*. Longmans, 1932.

Cartwright, Julie, *Madame*. 1894.

Chapman, Hester W., *Queen Anne's Son*. André Deutsch, 1955.

Defoe, Daniel, *A Tour through England & Wales*. 2 vols. Dent, 1928.

Dunlop, Ian, *Palaces and Progresses of Elizabeth I*. Cape, 1962.

Dutton, Ralph, *English Court Life—Henry VII to George II*. Batsford, 1963.

Evelyn, John, *Diary*. Edited by E. S. de Beer. Oxford University Press, 1959.

Firebrace, Capt. C. W., *Honest Harry*, being the biography of Sir Henry Firebrace. Murray, 1932.

Fletcher, Major Benton, *Royal Homes near London*. Bodley Head, 1930.

Froude, J. A., *The Reign of Edward VI*. Dent, 1909.

Grammont, Count de, *Memoirs*. Edited by Anthony Hamilton, 1902.

Green, David, *Grinling Gibbons*. Country Life, 1964.

Green, David, *Queen Anne*. Collins, 1970.

Hartman, Cyril Hughes, *Charles II & Madame*. Heinemann, 1934.

Hervey, John, Baron, *Memoirs of the Reign of George II*. Edited by the Rev. R. Sedgwick, 2 vols. Eyre & Spottiswoode, 1931.

Hume, Martin A., *The Wives of Henry VIII*. Grayson, 1905.

Hutton, William Holden, *Hampton Court*. Nimmo, 1897.

Jordan, W. K., *The Chronicle & Political Papers of Edward VI*. Allen & Unwin, 1966.

Laver, James, *The Ladies of Hampton Court*. Collins, 1942.

Law, Ernest, *The History of Hampton Court*. 3 vols. George Bell, 1885–91.

Law, Ernest, *Cardinal Wolsey at Hampton Court*. George Bell, 1923.

Lindsay, Philip, *Hampton Court*. Meridian, 1948.

Marillier, Henry Currie, *Tapestries at Hampton Court*. Medici, 1931.

Marples, Morris, *Poor Fred & the Butcher*. Michael Joseph, 1970.

Ministry of Public Building and Works, *Hampton Court Palace*, guidebook, current ed.

Nichols, John Gough, F.S.A., *The Literary Remains of King Edward VI*. Edited from his autograph manuscript. 2 vols., 1857.

Oman, Carola, *Henrietta Maria*. Hodder & Stoughton, 1951.

Pepys, Samuel, *Diary*. G. Bell, 1928.

Petrie, Sir Charles, Bt., *The Stuarts*. Eyre & Spottiswoode, 1937.

Pollard, A. F., *Henry VIII*. Longmans, 1905.

Pope-Hennessy, [Sir] John, *The Raphael Cartoons*. HMSO, 1966.

Royal Commission on Historical Monuments, *Middlesex*. HMSO, 1937.

Salzman, L. F., *England in Tudor Times*. Batsford, 1926.

Sands, Mollie, *The Gardens of Hampton Court*. Evans, 1950.

Strickland, Agnes, *Lives of the Queens of England*. 6 vols. G. Bell, 1895.

Taylor, Francis Henry, *The Taste of Angels, A History of Art Collecting*. Hamish Hamilton, 1948.

Wedgwood, C. V., *Oliver Cromwell*. Duckworth, 1939.

Wren Society, The, Vol. 4: *Hampton Court Palace*. Oxford University Press, 1935.

Yates, Edward, F.S.A., *Hampton Court*. Duckworth, 1935.